LAW, LIBERTY
AND LOVE

A STUDY IN CHRISTIAN OBEDIENCE

LAW, LIBERTY
AND LOVE

A STUDY IN CHRISTIAN OBEDIENCE

FOUNDATION OF
EUROPEAN CIVILIZATION

Columba Cary-Elwes

MONK OF AMPLEFORTH

With a Preface by
PROFESSOR ARNOLD J. TOYNBEE

1951

THE DEVIN-ADAIR COMPANY
NEW YORK

PERMISSU SUPERIORUM
CONGREGATIONIS ANGLIAE
ORDINIS SANCTI BENEDICTI

. . .

NIHIL OBSTAT:
JOANNIS P. ARENDZEN, D.D., PH.D., M.A.
CENSUS DEPUTATUS

IMPRIMATUR:
E. MORROGH BERNARD
VICARIUS GENERALIS
WESTMONASTERII
DIE 14° Octobris, 1949

PRINTED AND BOUND IN GREAT BRITAIN
FOR THE DEVIN-ADAIR CO., NEW YORK,
BY HAZELL, WATSON AND VINEY, LTD.,
AYLESBURY AND LONDON

I OFFER THIS BOOK
TO ALL THOSE WHO
SEEK PEACE AND PURSUE IT
AND
TO MY BRETHREN OF AMPLEFORTH
WHO HAVE FOUND IT

'THE very first step towards wisdom is the desire for discipline, and how should a man care for discipline without loving it, or love it without heeding its laws, or heed its laws without winning immortality, or win immortality without drawing near to God?'

(*Book of Wisdom*, vi. 17–18.)

PREFACE

THE subject of this book is both the present crisis in the history
of the Western world and the eternal problem of man's relation to God. In probing a wound on the social surface of life,
the writer lays bare the spiritual quick; and, in grappling with
this abiding religious issue that underlies the political and
economic struggles of our day, he does not deal with it in
abstract terms, but studies it in action in Western history since
the birth of Western Christendom. This 'stereoscopic' unity of
vision is the distinctive feature of the book; and it is no accident
that the author is a monk of the oldest of all Western Orders.
Founded at a moment when, in the West, the Roman way of
life was in its death agonies, the Benedictine Order nursed a
new civilization into existence, saw the medieval Western
Christian Commonwealth reach and pass its zenith, and is now
seeing a modern secular Western Civilization likewise falling
out of prosperity into adversity. For a Benedictine observer it
is natural to look at history in terms of religion, and at religion
in terms of history; but in the Western world to-day this unity
of vision is rare, and Father Cary-Elwes' book will therefore be
illuminating for readers of all religious and political persuasions
—particularly for non-Catholics, because for them it will be a
less familiar approach than it will be for their Catholic contemporaries to problems which concern us all alike.

Till a short time ago, many non-Catholics would have been
quite impervious to Catholic ideas about the way the Western
world had gone and might be going, but there have been two
recent changes in the general psychological and intellectual
climate of our Western Society. The peoples of the West have
awoken to the fact that their civilization is in danger of coming
to grief, and at the same time they have become historical-

minded. They are therefore now concerned to find out what has gone wrong with our modern Western Civilization, and they are inclined to look for an answer to their question in the Sibylline Books of history. The greater the crisis, the older its origins in all probability; and our consciousness of the greatness of our present crisis counsels us to cast far back into the past for a clue to the cause of our present malady which may give us a key to the remedy. But, the farther one travels back into our Western past, the more Catholic does the soil and spiritual landscape become; for our modern secular Western Civilization is the child of a medieval Christian Western Civilization in which the master institution was an œcumenical Church presided over by the Papacy. For this reason, non-Catholics as well as Catholics to-day should have a lively interest in a diagnosis of Western history by a member of a monastic order which has been living its life, without a break, since the sixth century of our era. The Benedictine Order is the continuity of Western history incarnate; and light on Western history from this source is bound to be illuminating for any living Westerner who is seriously concerned with our present troubles and their causes. Non-Catholic readers of the book may differ, and this perhaps even in vital points, from the writer's analysis and conclusions, but this will not prevent them from profiting by his exposition of our modern secular civilization's religious historical background. They will find it hard not to take his thesis to heart, and impossible not to appreciate the sincerity with which he expounds Catholic beliefs and the frankness with which he grasps Protestant nettles.

The prickliest of these nettles is the principle of Obedience. This is indisputably one of the cardinal principles of medieval Western Christian Society; it was indisputably thrown over when our secular modern Western Society broke out of its religious chrysalis; and indisputably this modern society is now in grave difficulties. Is the repudiation of the principle of

Obedience one of the causes of our present plight? Was an abuse of the principle of Obedience one of the causes of medieval Western Christendom's breakdown? No principle could well be more controversial, yet few controversies take us nearer to the heart of the riddle of our Western history.

On this account, Father Columba's readers of all persuasions will no doubt take particular note of his discussion—which runs through all the book—of the relation between Obedience and Love; for, while Obedience is a matter of controversy between Christians, Love is not. In a passage quoted on p. 157, Saint Thomas Aquinas declares that love for God is the end towards which obedience to a religious superior is the means. In this spiritual perspective the Christian controversy over Obedience is swallowed up in the Christian agreement over Love, and this brings within view the possibility of a common spiritual effort to save our Western Civilization by replacing it on its Christian foundations.

> *Our wills are ours, we know not how;*
> *Our wills are ours to make them Thine.*

Willing God's will is man's only way of overcoming a disharmony in human nature which is at the root of every crisis in human society. But man cannot will God's will without loving God as man is loved by him. Love is the master key; and Father Cary-Elwes' book is one more testimony to a truth that is never stale.

Arnold Toynbee

FOREWORD

THE learned will find nothing new here; this is not a learned book, but a reconsideration of the Christian basis upon which our society has rested. Men only take note of their body when they are ill. Men only take note of the principles by which instinctively they live when their way of life is called into question. Ours is being called into question to-day. We must know where we stand. Therefore I write this for those with less time to think than I have or who have not had the opportunity to see the history of our civilization in its Christian and true perspective.

This little series of essays is therefore offered to those who would learn something of the spiritual basis of Christendom. Each of us has only a few brief years of life, and if we were to wait until we knew all, or until we had leisure to say all we knew, we should end by saying nothing. Let each contribute the little that he has reaped from his reading and his meditation, so that between us we may be the more prepared, fighting shoulder to shoulder, to withstand the forces of destruction which compass us about on every side.

For quotations from the Old Testament I have used the Douai Version and, for the New, the translation recently made by Monsignor Ronald Knox. I have chosen this partly because I personally like it, partly because it is scholarly and up-to-date, and partly because it is fresh, waking the mind up, instead of sending it to sleep owing to much familiarity, as perhaps do those versions which we know so very well.

It remains for me to thank those who by their kindness have helped me in this book, and firstly my friend Professor Arnold J. Toynbee who not only consented to write a preface, but also discussed the whole conception with me many times. It would

be unfair to him that the readers were left with the impression
that he agrees with every word here written; in the first place,
he is not a Catholic in union with the Church of Rome, but,
in the second place, as this has been written not for the 'converted' but for those outside the 'sheep-fold', and as he is as
anxious as I for the reintegration of Christendom, he has consented to associate his name with this little work done in charity
to all men.

I am also grateful to Fr. Columba Ryan, of the Order of
Preachers, for reading through the chapter on St. Thomas
Aquinas and making valuable suggestions; to Fr. Francis
Devas, of the Society of Jesus, for giving valuable assistance
in the section on Saint Ignatius; to Mr. Philip Smiley, for his
most helpful comments on the chapter concerned with the
Greco-Roman world; and to Monsignor Knox for the quotation from the Book of Wisdom. I wish also to express my
thanks to my Brethren at Ampleforth for their assistance on
many small points, to one who wishes to remain anonymous
for helping in the translation of the Papal Bull which is quoted
in the chapter on Cluny, but specially to Dom Kentigern
Devlin for his help with the index. As is customary, I wish to
make it quite clear that any errors of fact or of judgement are
entirely my own.

I also wish to acknowledge with thanks the permission
granted to me by His Eminence the Cardinal, Archbishop of
Westminster, to use Monsignor Knox's version of the New
Testament, and to the Early English Text Society for permission to use a passage from Harpsfield's *Life of Thomas More.*

St. Wilfrid's Day, 1949

CONTENTS

CHAPTER I

INTRODUCTORY

IF only chronicles are history, then this book is no history; but if the study of an idea which has moulded a civilization is history, then perhaps this book may in some measure claim to be so, for the ideas here considered lie at the root of the great tree we call Western Christendom. Law and liberty, as we have known them for nearly two thousand years, are basic to our way of life; they themselves, we shall attempt to show, developed out of the Christian love of God in a synthesis we call 'loving obedience'.

These ideas of law, liberty and love in the story of Western Europe derive in large measure from the Gospels, and only slowly their significance became apparent. It is this development both in thought and in act with which the following chapters are concerned. Thus the reader will find, not only exposition of theories upon these ideas, but also chapters upon how these ideas influenced events, indeed made Europe. The aim, therefore, is not merely to prove a truth historically or philosophically, but to show it in operation. Love, the heart of the Christian way of life, expressed itself in obedience, and obedience expressed itself in action. It was thus that Western Christendom was made and unmade. Love, like a light in a lamp, having been snuffed out, our feet stumble in the darkness.

History, thus examined, is not merely a straight line, but a study in depth, strata under strata appearing beneath our gaze. On top are the actions which may or may not have significance, and below the layers of law and liberty, and below that again the love for God and for men which underlies all the construction of the mighty edifice which we see now toppling to ruin. At the centre is the pure love of God for men and of men for God. This fundamental principle of life is safe-guarded by true obedience, first to God's own voice in the conscience, then to an authority which God himself set up on earth.

We are agreed upon love and upon obeying conscience; liberal Christians, Protestants of an established Church and Catholics all agree that we must love God in himself and must follow conscience; it is with the third, authority, or obedience to a human superior, that we are not in accord; this is the crux. It is therefore with this last that the book is primarily con-cerned. There are many and wonderful books on the love of God in himself, from the simple Gospel story of the Crucifixion to the austere splendours of St. John of the Cross. But on the relationship of law to love there are few.

Though the love of God in himself is left somewhat in the background in the following pages, let it not be thought that we under-estimate its pre-eminence. Our Christian life is made up of action and contemplation, the love of God's will and the love of God's Person; the former is the study of these pages, the latter would be a study upon prayer. But it will be seen all the way through, that act depends upon prayer, active love depends upon contemplative love. Love in act, the carrying out of God's will, is no substitute for the love in contemplation; it is its complement.

It is evident, therefore, that the aim is to make obedience to an ecclesiastical authority less repellent to the modern Western mind, brought up upon the dogma of private judgement and the sanctity of the human conscience. Among other things we are prepared to show that conscience remains supreme for all men and that therefore the primacy ever remains with the intellect, with Truth.

Here in the twentieth century we are divided into those who

are convinced that there is no hereafter and, on the other hand, Christians who, for the most part, believe that the aim of life is to love God and to love their neighbours for his sake. But of these there are many shades, from the Catholic in communion with the Pope of Rome to the individualist who accepts what he can of the message of Christ in his own heart and is unwilling to submit to any authority outside his conscience of the moment.

At one time this was not so in Western Europe; in the Ages of Faith the mass of the people, peasant and burgher, scholar and priest, all were subject to ecclesiastical authority. The break with Rome came violently at the Reformation. Now only are the full effects of that division apparent, Christendom is in a state of collapse, not merely an economic and military, political and physical one—a falling birth-rate—but a spiritual one. Western man is at a loss to know his destiny.

At the root of this Schism in the Soul, to use the phrase used by Professor Toynbee, lies a misconception about law and liberty, as though these two were contraries; but deeper still is the problem of obedience, which again is considered as something almost abhorrent; while underlying them all is the true notion of love, the love of God.

It is the aim of this book to pick up these broken pieces and to mend them in the mind. The author can think of no better way than to retrace the steps of our progress from life towards decline through the history of the Western Christian world.

No man may surrender his conscience except to truth, whether he be Catholic, Protestant, Theist, Hindu or Moslem. That is the inexorable law of our nature; and he who does surrender his will to anything else is a slave who deserves our pity. For conscience is the power of the practical judgement to discern what it is right to do in given circumstances, and what it is right to do can only be discovered by our intellect; it is a form of truth. To surrender our judgement, or conscience, to force or to some imagined danger, to passion, is to surrender the soul, its reason and its will, to something unworthy of it.

The Theist thinks he can find his chartered course in life only from his own reasoning. The Christian believes that Christ added to that information some more, not only by telling him things he could have found out by a long process of reason and with difficulty—thus making doubly sure—but also other matters which reasoning alone could not discover, such as the raising of men to a sonship with God by grace, the fact of the Redemption. Here is more material than the mind unaided could provide for guidance in action.

Catholics go farther and say that Christ not only taught truths but instituted a body of men to preserve them intact through the ages, so that any man or child in any epoch could say: what did Christ teach? and be told for certain. Then he could get on with the job of living. Search Scripture, they say, and you will find evidence of the founding of this institution.

Here, then, are further data on which to ground one's judgement for action; here is more truth, or more accurately, the same truth guaranteed, for the Church does not claim to add to the truths revealed, but only to preserve them intact, unsullied, clear, certain.

No non-Catholic should submit to the authority of the Church until his conscience tells him it is reasonable to do so. Faith is not blind, and the Church maintains that the evidence for her claims is enough for certitude, given an unbiased mind. Even a Catholic should not remain a Catholic if his conscience tells him that he should not. But here the Church, as she claims that the evidence is sufficient for certitude, maintains that a Catholic who was properly instructed could not in fact arrive at such a conclusion without fault. The fault might be in trusting too much to his own reasoning and not relying upon grace for support; more often it would be in the moral sphere, due to the difficulty of living according to the Church's exacting laws. But the fact remains that conscience must stand supreme all the time for Catholics quite as much as for any other human soul. (Cf. *The Spirit of Catholicism*, by Karl Adam, translated by Dom Justin McCann. Sheed & Ward, revised edition, pp. 224–9.)

Catholics, like Protestants and Theists, have to decide their action on the evidence. The Theists have their reason; the Protestants have their reason and Christ's word as recorded in the New Testament; Catholics have their reason, Christ's word and the Church's sure interpretation of it. Theists and Protestants are bound to surrender their judgement to truth as they see it, and it is also certain that a Catholic must do the same. The former two may be in greater doubt as to what truth is. But surely that is no advantage, nay rather a disadvantage?

All men have the support of God's guidance in their souls no matter what their religion, and any man who humbly asks for help may be assured that he will be granted it provided he takes all the ordinary means for finding out God's will in his regard. That was the reason why God implanted intelligence within us. But the snare of this method of direct guidance alone is that our desires get entangled in the answer. The wish is father to the thought, and never more so than in those moral questions which beset the soul like a storm. Few men are good judges in their own cause.

It is the writer's plea that history should be primarily concerned with the most important element in man, his spirit, and this is chiefly manifest in religion; he is convinced also that the Christian Way of Life, taught by Jesus Christ, did in fact make the world of the West, and that we are unmaking it in proportion as we withdraw our spirits from that life-giving source.

The chapters on the Reformers and the 'iconoclasts' of the preceding and later centuries may seem crude in the extreme and unfair. True, a facet here and there has been selected and an over-simplified picture may result. Therefore, it is honestly admitted here at the beginning that much good was enshrined in the teaching of those who broke away. There was a call for a return to Christ, a return to simplicity, a revulsion from legalism, a plea for personal responsibility. These and other elements of Christ's teaching the author readily admits were stressed by many of the Reformers. His aim, however, is to show how they deviated from the traditional view and to examine whether these deviations were perhaps part cause of the present deep unrest and sense of frustration in the souls of Western men.

There have been influences at work upon our civilization other than the Christian influence : to name the chief, the Greek, the Mohammedan; but at least it cannot be denied that in its formative years after the breakdown of the Roman peace the Church's influence was paramount. Therefore the writer has felt impelled to make his contribution to the restoration of the good life in Europe, to the peaceful and ordered life for which we all so long, by examining without any spirit of antagonism or controversy the principles of law, liberty and love, as they emerge in the Gospels and the remainder of the New Testament, in the early Church, in the Benedictine centuries and after. The writer is convinced that the chief ill of our day is a failure of spirit, a failure to grasp and to hold these basic ideas, more especially in relation to God, and also in the relations between men. Liberty and law are often treated as contraries, love and law likewise.

The fact that unity of mind and heart in our civilization has been lost is not by any means due primarily to the reformers of the sixteenth century, who certainly of course actually broke the unity. The fault lies with those Catholics of the later Middle Ages who were careless of their heritage and squandered their wealth of sound principles. If a Luther and a Rousseau seem to us prodigal of the treasures of the civilization to which they were heirs, this sin cannot be laid entirely to their charge; they inherited also the distortions and misuses of these treasured truths. Unless we can appreciate that, we cannot begin to help in the restoration of the broken thing, Christendom.

This salutary thought brings in its train another. We are upon the frontiers of a new age; we are feeling in the night between two civilizations. It may be that we shall come out into an age of barbarism; we may emerge upon an ordered plain in which the rule of Christ holds sway. Which it will be depends primarily upon our thoughts; for it is precisely in thought that the uncertainties of our day consist.

Men have long since abandoned truly Christian ideas, on authority, on morality, on justice, on economics. They have invented other ways, the rationalist way, the romantic way, the liberal way, the scientific way, and lastly the dictator's way. And only too often these ways have been shown to lead to a hell upon earth for someone : for the poor or for a minority, or indeed for a majority.

The Christian answer is never out-of-date; it remains as true as when Christ first propounded it. But each age needs a new application of these same truths. The problems are different and therefore require new answers, even though by the application of the same principles. But modern man has forgotten those first principles upon which his civilization has been based. The real nature of liberty is blurred, and consequently so is the real nature of law, while love, owing to the wild imaginings of the Romantics, has become equated with passion, and its connection with law effaced. Thus, before applying the principles, we must rediscover them. Men cannot get on with the job until they have been given the tools.

Yet, for all the breakdown in our fundamental ideas, three principles have become paramount in the West during this first half of our century. The first is that the centre of religion is love; the second that personal liberty is the last citadel of human rights; but thirdly, that spiritual obedience is wrong.

The writer is convinced that the first two principles are true and fundamental, the third, he is convinced, is a misunderstanding, believing that obedience, far from being alien to love and to liberty, is in fact their safeguard, if properly understood; and finally that this true interpretation of obedience can be found in the records which are the very basis of our Way of Life.

We must not underestimate the achievement of the Greeks. When we consider the fact that it was done with the help of unaided reason; when we realize that in this sphere even Saint Thomas added little to the findings of Aristotle; when we appreciate sufficiently the huge weight of traditional barbarism which lay upon the Greeks, as it lay on all other races; when we consider how imperfect the Christian achievement has been in practical application of Christian principles, we shall pause before criticizing that greatest of pagan civilizations —with the possible exception of the Confucian.

Therefore, if in the following slight introductory remarks upon Greek thought we seem to minimize its greatness, this is only so in regard to absolute truth and not in comparison with previous or later civilizations, not excluding the Christian; for the latter had all the advantages of a divine revelation backing its certitudes. Comparisons are odious and unprofitable; for who can judge of the difficulties a people may have had in making effective the vision they saw? Yet, in regard to absolute truth, it may remain a fact that the Greeks were far from it for all their high thinking; but this should not blind us to the greatness of their achievement.

A very summary examination, therefore, of Greek and Roman thought and behaviour in these matters is necessary before proceeding to the main subject of this book.

(i) *Liberty*

Great minds in ancient Greece certainly grasped the majesty of freedom. It is true that Solon, in the words of Lord Acton, 'By making every citizen the guardian of his own interest . . . admitted the element of Democracy into the State' (*The History of Freedom in Antiquity*, p. 7, 1907 ed.). Yet, as Lord Acton goes on to point out, that was not sufficient to create true democracy or liberty. A collection of laws was needed over and above the citizen, a kind of framework, which all would accept as immovable, and which would therefore guarantee to each his rights. It must not be within the power of any, not even of a majority, to change this code of fundamental principles. For otherwise a majority could tyrannize over a minority as easily as could a single man. This in fact occurred with the first Athenian great experiment in democracy. Lord Acton sums up the situation in the well-known axiom, 'It is bad to be oppressed by a minority, but it is worse to be oppressed by a majority' (*ibid.*, p. 11).

The Athenians were aware of the gap in their constitution, but 'the repentance of the Athenians came too late to save the Republic' (*ibid.*, p. 13). All that remained was the memory that institutions were necessary to 'uphold the permanent reign of law against arbitrary revolutions of opinion' (*ibid.*). But how find this absoluteness in law or institution in the Ancient World? That was a problem which the successively more sceptical generations could not solve.

Though the Greeks certainly caught sight of the goal, it remained for the Christian civilization to attempt to put it into practice.

By liberty we mean, subjectively, the right of all men to live by what they think right without let or hindrance. Objectively it is the power to follow the dictates of right reason and divine revelation. We do not mean the right to do anything one likes—that we call licence—but what is or what we think is reasonable to be done. According to this analysis the discipline of law or of reason is above liberty; it is the field within which liberty has play.

In ancient times a chosen few had this right, so it would seem, and no others. The remainder were slaves, and, where slavery is, there is no true liberty. In Greece there was slavery; while even the most enlightened of the Athenians had so little respect for the persons of women that he maintained they were, like the slaves, without souls. Aristotle indeed divided mankind into 'freemen by nature' and 'slaves by nature'.

If the form that slavery took in Greece was gentle, that of Rome was the reverse. In early Christian times Rome was a city of slaves, a proletariat harvested from the plains of Europe and Asia and Africa by the swords of the imperial armies. Yet, for all that, the idea of the equality of all men was not unknown. Alexander is credited with it; while the Stoics, with their principle of universal law, developed the idea very fully. Zeno of Citium (335–263 B.C.), a founder of the Stoic school of philosophers, indeed maintained that we could only make one true division among men, according to whether they were good or bad. Cicero explicitly writes, 'Omnes homines natura sunt pares'.

But theory is not practice. The Rome of the Empire was a slave state in which lip service was paid to the idea of equality, but where facts told a different story. Lord Acton wrote, 'But in all that I have been able to cite from classical literature, three things are wanting—representative government, the emancipation of the slaves, and liberty of conscience' (*ibid.*, pp. 25–6).

It might be recalled that the Emperor Caracalla in the third century granted political and legal equality to all free citizens of the Empire. But we must remember that already his predecessor, Septimius Severus, had subjected the various municipal bodies of the Empire to a curator nominated by himself;

he had superimposed a commission of ten on the local bodies which were supposed to decide taxation. Even earlier, Marcus Aurelius had abolished the election of magistrates. All Caracalla's edict did was to subject all citizens directly to the central government's plans for taxation (cf. Jacques Pirenne, *Les grands courants de l'histoire universelle,* vol. I, p. 353, and Christopher Dawson, *Enquiries,* p. 203).

After the anarchy of A.D. 235–68, the authority of the central government was greatly shaken, in spite of the courageous efforts of Aurelian; but when the Empire officially recognized the Church, it soon began to recognize what was already probably a *fait accompli,* namely, the grouping of the notables of each city round the bishop of the place. From the time of Constantine, the bishops were recognized as representative of their cities. Anastasius I (491–518) decreed that the city buyer of corn and the 'defender' of each city should be elected by the bishop and notables. Justinian decreed that the curator, who had been the nominee of the emperors and the instrument of absolutism, should now be elected by the bishop and the notables. Indeed, the very governors of the provinces themselves were to be chosen by the same means.

We may conclude this too rapid survey of imperial liberties by pointing out that the Empire was forced into absolutism by fiscal problems of immense magnitude; that this solution was no solution—indeed, that the bureaucracy created buried the Empire under its weight; that even political liberty in a minor way returned to the men of Europe through those elected representatives of the people and the clergy, the bishops, who in charity had taken the burden of administration upon their shoulders.

(ii) *Law*

Law, in the Roman Empire, from the time of Christ, had become, for all its nobility, the will of the sovereign, and was no longer, except by legal fiction, from the people. Some emperors were good and others bad; and the law therefore suffered from that sickness of absolutism which is to be at the mercy of the ruler's whim. Yet the early Christians did not deny authority to the emperor of the day; it is astonishing how loyal they were considering the persecutions they suffered at the hands of their rulers. The saying of Pope Gelasius I is well known : 'There are two things by which the world is governed —the authority of the pope and the rule of the emperor.' The submissiveness of the Christians came from their belief that all just authority came from God.

When the Empire had become Christian, the Church, as can be seen from the action of such outstanding popes as Leo the Great, supported the Empire even in its death agony, indeed, until the authority ceased to act. The Church did not support the ghost of the Empire; for, when it showed itself incapable of controlling the barbarians, then the Christians went over to the barbarians, and sometimes physically, as when the Christian slaves poured out of Rome to meet the barbarian horde, not in order to fight it, but to join it.

While the Church had supported the Empire so long as it lasted, its recollections of its laws did not encourage it to maintain them. Rather, the early medieval Europe made new laws out of the precepts of the Gospel, and only in the time of Charlemagne did the idea of the Roman Law return to Europe, and then in a Christian dress. Medieval Europe created out of its inheritance a new law which was based upon the rights and duties of Christian free men. It is true that the Emperor Justinian with great care and great success reformed and codified the ancient Roman law, at about the same time as for instance St. Benedict was creating a new law out of the Gospels for the new conquerors of Europe. But Justinian's work, in the words of Professor Toynbee, was 'a Herculean task which was virtually labour lost'; and in the note to that page he adds : 'Justinian was codifying a law which was not merely old, but was on the verge of becoming an anachronism owing to the disappearance of the social conditions which the Roman law had been designed to meet. For fully three centuries after the Justinian codification was completed, this code was altogether inapplicable to the new social conditions that supervened upon the final bankruptcy of the Hellenic culture' (*A Study of History,* vol. III, p. 266).

Yet it would be an unfair picture of the Ancient world to give only that side of it which the early Christians themselves experienced at the hands of the Roman Empire. Though the Greek genius had been unable, as Lord Acton points out, to put into practice the thoughts that it had evolved, yet those same thoughts later became for Christian thinkers the basis of a whole Christian philosophy of law. This we shall see when we glance at St. Thomas's writings on the subject.

The deep thinking that went to the making of the syntheses of Aristotle and of Plato cannot be ignored; the broad Stoical view of the cosmos and of the world's own law had deep influence, notably on the Christian Platonists among the early Greek Fathers, and on St. Augustine. The story of the death of Socrates alone is a lesson for all time; and it certainly must have been, for the early Christians brought up in the schools of Athens and elsewhere, a symbol of the respect due to the laws of one's country.

As Socrates was awaiting death, and his friends were standing round him, they were persuading him to make good his escape before it was too late. His answer is memorable, and to quote part may serve here as a mark of the respect every Christian should have to the wise men of the Hellenic world from whom they learnt so much. He replied, 'Perhaps the Laws will say to me, "Are you not then breaking your compacts and agreements with us, though you were not led into them by compulsion or fraud, and were not forced to make up your mind in a short time, but had seventy years in which you could have gone away? . . . And now you will not abide by your agreement? . . .

"Ah, Socrates, be guided by us who tended your infancy. Care neither for your children nor for life nor anything else more than for right, that when you come to the home of the dead, you may have all these things to say in your own defence" ' (*Crito,* pp. 185, 189, Loeb series, Plato I).

It is a noble speech, in which Socrates is prepared to submit to a law, though he thinks it unjust, because he has agreed in principle to submit to the laws. He follows the principle of 'government by consent'. But it must be noted that this is not the highest form of law; that would be a law which was of its nature just, and obeyed for that very reason. However, as we have already noted, seeing that the Athenians of this age had only their intelligence to work from, it was well-nigh impossible for them to set up a law, or a criterion for law, which was either considered as truly just or in fact was so. This could only come with the intrusion of a divine revelation—should such a revelation ever be made—which would both be, and be accepted to be, true and just. (Cf. 'Liberté et civilisation chez les Grecs,' par. A.-J. Festugière, O.P., ed., *Revue des jeunes,* 1947, Paris, which gives a very favourable view of the Ancient Greek thought on liberty, stressing the idea that, for the Greeks, law was reasonable and consented to, and consequently freedom.)

(iii) *Love*

What did the ancients know of love? Passions they knew, true personal self-sacrificing love of friends they also knew— though Aristotle reduced this to self-love. They knew also patriotism. But no one can surely deny that with Christ, first, an all-embracing love entered the world, and secondly, that this became, not a theory but a fact, so that men even loved their enemies, those who persecuted and murdered them.

An Asoka, an Alexander, a Confucius may have seen afar off the truth of the brotherhood of all men, and even stated it, the principle of reciprocity and the like; yet they had neither done this thing themselves to its extreme limits nor could they persuade others to do so either.

While love of some neighbours was practised in the ancient world, love of God was practically unknown outside the Jews. For God, that supreme Being, Creator of the universe, was buried under a jungle growth of other gods—nature gods, mother gods, a swamp of demons and malignant spirits, of practices of magic inspired by fear and preserved by the same. Why worry, they said, about a good God, if he is likely to do one no harm? It was the evil ones who needed to be appeased. God, the perfect Being, Goodness itself, was forgotten and therefore could not be loved.

Yet both Confucius, who taught the fatherhood of God, and certain Hindu books, notably the Bhagavadgita, deserve our deep admiration. But if one is to judge by the fruits of these systems, neither the Hindu ethos which covers the slavery of the caste system with the decorum of religion, nor that of Confucianism, which countenanced abandoning children, was strong enough to resist the selfishness of men and lead them to that unselfishness which even Gandhi found only in the words of Jesus. It is true that Confucius himself did not defend abandoning children, and a case may be made for the caste system, as has been done by the late Dr. Coomeraswamy.

The Western world was ignorant of both the Hindu and Confucian systems in its own formative years and did not learn the love of God from either.

Consequently we are left with a Greece that saw liberty from afar, and the Rome of the Emperors, which once may have possessed it, but discarded it for the more 'efficient' dictatorship, and the Christians who had a book, the Gospels and Epistles, and a tradition which gave them both liberty and love.

As for the People of the Jews, of whom the Christians are also the heirs, to discuss their teaching and their practice of these things would demand another volume. Let it suffice to say here that Law for them was the voice of God, that Love was keeping his Law, as anyone acquainted with that marvellous psalm the 118th will know. Liberty, abstractly, had not been analysed; but it would be found that, apart from the concentration of authority in a theocratic government, the Jewish ideal of liberty is much the same as the Christian. When Christ admitted the right of Cæsar to rule, he broke with the Jewish tradition. Further, though the prophets often showed that God intended salvation for all men, and that therefore all men were equal in the sight of God, yet the Jews as a race, at the time of Christ and after, tended to divide the world into those of the Promise, themselves, and those outside, the Gentiles. Here again the universalism of the Christian outlook was a seed which bore with it the fruit of liberty for ALL men, not only for the chosen few.

It is, then, to the Christian tradition that we now turn.

Before we consider the Christian interpretation of these subjects, it is not out of place, in view of the strong current of doubt in modern minds, to treat shortly the question : have the Christians after all made any better use of their knowledge than the Greeks made of theirs? Or in different forms : is modern Europe a better place to live in than ancient Greece? has Christianity failed? or more strongly : why has Christianity failed?

All these questions are continually being asked, more especially to-day, as there is a strong attempt in these disillusioned times to restore the Christian tradition.

The first answer often given, and a poor one in our view, is that the Christian religion is not concerned with this world, but with the next. This is the 'other-world' answer. It is an alibi; but is it justified? Although some extreme Protestants hold this view, on the principle that all is sin and shame, it is not the Catholic attitude and never has been. The Catholic spirit has always been to grapple with this world in order to improve it, to apply the Gospel precepts to ordinary life in order to transform it. The answer which claims that the Church should not meddle in these things is soothing to the conscience, but it is not true to Christ.

The cry that the Church should not interfere in politics, or economics, or education, or international affairs, or in family life, is part of that retreat from the world which may be Protestant—though all Protestants would not hold with it—but certainly is not Catholic.

Therefore the Church accepts, in a sense, part responsibility for the failures in a Christian society.

Another reply is that the Church, since the Reformation, has not been able to influence affairs even if it would; that the collapse of the West is precisely due to the fact that those who govern it have repudiated the Christian ethic in human affairs. There is some truth in this. An extreme example will bring the point out. The horrors of Belsen and other Nazi atrocities, people say, were due primarily to this, that Hitler and his henchmen had thrown over a belief in such fundamental truths of the Christian religion as the universal brotherhood of men, the supreme rights of the individual person over against the community. These atrocities were committed, not by Christians, but precisely by men who had repudiated Christ.

Similarly, the appalling economic and social injustices of the nineteenth century were most prevalent in an England where it was the fashion to maintain that economics did not have to submit to any laws outside its own. The *laissez-faire* school of thought was essentially unchristian.

In international affairs the most striking symbol of the unchristian atmosphere was that the Pope was kept out, by secret treaty between Great Britain and Italy, from participating in the Peace Settlement after the 1914–18 War. No one would dare to hold the thesis that international relations (for the last four hundred years) have been governed by the spirit of Christ.

From this reply, that the Western world is not governed by the laws of Christ, we may at least draw this conclusion, that the failure is not due to attempting to solve our problems by the teaching of Christ and finding that the teaching did not work, but rather is it due to the fact that men have failed to live by Christianity.

The argument is then narrowed. Was Christianity a success before the collapse of the unity of the Church at the Reformation?

Did men cease to live by Christian principles because they were unworkable? To take the second first. It is perfectly clear that the not following of Christ has itself proved unworkable. We have suffered from unchristian behaviour all this century. So we know to-day that abandoning Christ at least has not improved things.

Has Christianity ever been tried? By this we supposedly mean, has the government of a country or group of countries ever been actuated by Christian principles for any length of time? And if so, has it worked well? The answer is difficult to make, because one would have to bear in mind all the antecedent circumstances which might make just government exceedingly difficult. Thus Europe, as it emerged from the first barbarian invasions, scarcely had time to recover before it was flooded by another and even worse invasion, and this in its turn by a third. The first five hundred years of Christian rule were a period of struggle against fearful odds. The twelfth century was the beginning of internal peace, and one might perhaps judge a Christian society on that age.

It would be an interesting study to compare it with our own,

or with the Ancient Greek society. The comparison would have
to be on the following lines :

1. The degree of justice granted to all, in law, in social
   justice, in personal liberty.
2. The degree of intellectual attainment for all—how can
   we assess this, for each age valued the same truth
   differently?
3. The degree of happiness.
4. The degree of neighbourly love.
5. The standard or level of moral goodness.

Many other lines of comparison occur to the mind, but these
might do. It becomes immediately apparent that the standards
of the three ages are different; the moderns value the material
higher than the spiritual, the medieval men valued the spiritual
above all; therefore it is particularly hard to compare them as
better or worse. Indeed, it is a hopeless task. All we can hope
to do is to see whether the High Middle Ages practised what
they preached.

The answer to this gives the clue to the whole problem. No
age, not even the High Middle Age, has lived or will live by
what it preaches. The reason, according to Christian teaching,
is that truth is always opposed by concupiscence : grace is at
war with original sin. Thus in a sense Christianity will always
fail because Christians are not Christs but sinners. Should we
expect it to succeed? In general we might answer that grace
will be victorious but not completely; there will only be a
partial success. This is true of the picture we can make of the
Middle Ages. Compared with the horror and the fear and the
despair of to-day, the thirteenth century seems almost a paradise. The town dweller plying his trade within the framework
of a guild looking to his spiritual and his material welfare; the
clergy and the monks fulfilling their office; the nobles acting
as local authorities within the framework of medieval law; the
villein working for his lord, it is true, but with rights of his

own, his own plot; the yeoman farmer, independent yet bound by duties. All men in that age were bound by status, and in that sense they were less free than men of the nineteenth century and perhaps those of the twentieth century who are still so in theory. There was work for all, and it seems generally agreed that the poorest were not starving, though their living conditions were bad. Plumbing has undoubtedly improved.

The causes of the failure to fulfil the promise of that great awakening in the twelfth to thirteenth centuries would take us too far afield at this point; but essentially the cause was a moral one : popes and bishops, emperors and kings, guilds men and farmers, all for various reasons failed to live up to their principles and so corrupted the good.

It might be argued that, though the Reformation cut Europe in two, the southern half of Europe did survive as Catholic and did go through a reformation from within. Why, then, it may be asked, did not this half keep up its Christian principles and prove a success?

Italy was exhausted by wars and by cynicism; France and Spain, while remaining Catholic, were infected with the same spiritual disease as the rest of Europe. They had become absolute monarchies, they were grappling with national economies which had burst the bonds of city units; the governments, while paying lip service to Christ, managed their affairs much on the lines of Machiavelli's book, *The Prince*. Besides, the divided Europe was at war with itself, had exhausted itself and had ruined its economic foundations.

Perhaps we dare make this generalization, that during the Middle Ages more men and women acted upon higher principles than at any time in history; that the institutions, upon which life was governed, were based on higher principles and were more often acted upon than at any other time in history. This is all that can be expected of men, for the fight between original sin and grace will only be resolved at the world's end.

In the ancient world a few men worked out the principles of justice and a very few lived by them. It is not surprising that no more did, considering that human reason was their only guide. But it also seems true that these ideas, elaborated by the rare philosophers, did not become the bases of social life for any length of time anywhere or over any large area.

HISTORICAL OUTLINE

From the point of view of these studies the history of the West may be conveniently divided thus:

1. THE FIRST THREE HUNDRED YEARS, during which the Church was a persecuted minority.
2. PEACEFUL INTERLUDE, for a hundred years, A.D. *c.* 311–400, during which she was protected by the Empire.
3. THE COLLAPSE OF THE EMPIRE and THE SAVING OF EUROPE BY THE CHURCH, which lasted from the time of *St. Benedict* to the rise of *Cluny*, that is, from *c.* 500–1000.
4. THE HIGH MIDDLE AGES, of which St. Thomas and St. Francis are fair examples.
5. THE PROCESS OF BREAKDOWN:
    (*a*) The beginnings, Marsilio of Padua.
    (*b*) The rising tide, Machiavelli, Luther, Rabelais, Rousseau.
6. ATTEMPTED RECOVERY:
    (*a*) The Jesuits.
    (*b*) Leo XIII.

CHAPTER II

THE NEW TESTAMENT

The Gospels

CHRIST APPEARS AS A REVOLUTIONARY.—He is claimed as such by Communist Russia. This view of Christ has in it an element of truth. He was unconventional to a marked degree: an itinerant preacher, almost an outcast, sleeping in the open, fleeing for his life, now from the Jewish authorities, now from Herod. As a child, he was carried over the frontiers to Egypt, at the end he was abandoned to be crucified by his own people, unwilling to receive him. The soldiers of the Roman empire did the deed.

His teaching had a challenge in it. He condemned the pharisaic spirit, he encouraged men to cast off the bonds of society, of riches, and to follow him; he whipped the buyers and sellers out of the Temple, he prophesied the doom of the little Jewish world in which he lived.

The acts of Christ might also lead us to think of him as against the rule of law. When he and his disciples walked through ripe corn on a sabbath day, he let them pick the corn and rub it and eat it, a thing contrary to the teaching of the official interpreters of the law; and in defence of his attitude he laid down the principle that men were not made for the sabbath but the sabbath for men. This was not the only time he ignored, indeed flouted, the law of keeping holy the sabbath day. He cured men and women on that day.

To the leaders of the nation he undoubtedly appeared to be a revolutionary. 'I come to bring not peace, but a sword.' He was come to cast fire upon the earth. His teaching has divided ever since, not only the Jews, but all men. We must be either for or against him. He came, 'to make all things new'.

Christ did not believe that the new wine could be put into old bottles, for danger of their bursting.

Though, truly, Jesus was breaking away from existing conditions in many respects, yet, on the other hand, we must admit that he frequently described himself as the restorer of the original and true and more perfect order. He was revolting, not against law and order as such, but against a false interpretation of these things. When about to be baptized at his own wish, he said, 'It is well that we should thus fulfil all due observance' (Matt. iii. 15).

It is easy, also, to sentimentalize the 'message' of Jesus and to speak as though he substituted love for law. Jesus had said of the sinful Magdalen, 'She has never ceased to kiss my feet since I entered. . . . If great sins have been forgiven her, she has also greatly loved' (Luke vii. 45, 47). The sign of discipleship, we are told, is to love the brotherhood. Taken out of its context such a phrase as, 'I have a new commandment to give you, that you are to love one another' (John xiii. 34), might seem to confirm this view. But such ideas are soon corrected by examining them more closely; for instance, the last quotation is immediately followed by 'your love for one another is to be like the love I have borne you'. That was no soft love.

Christ submitted to the law. His first submission, which is symbolic of the rest, was his being taken, at the command of a Roman Governor, to Bethlehem to be born; then he submitted to be circumcised. For thirty years he was subject to his parents, and at twelve he went with Mary and Joseph to be offered in the Temple according to the Jewish law. Even during the busy two or three years, the years of the Message and of the establishment of the Church, he went up to Jerusalem for the ritual feasts.

'Believe me, heaven and earth must disappear sooner than

one jot, one flourish disappear from the law; it must all be
accomplished' (Matt. v. 18). The point of this saying of
Jesus was the exact reverse of abandonment of the law; he
meant to perfect the law, by an internal assent rather than by
a mere outward conformity. 'But you are to be perfect, as your
heavenly Father is perfect' (Matt. v. 48).

What, then, did Jesus detest in the spirit of the Pharisees?
After all, they were fulfilling the law perfectly. 'If your justice
does not give fuller measure than the justice of the Scribes and
Pharisees, you shall not enter into the kingdom of heaven'
(Matt. v. 20). It could not be that Jesus disapproved of their
fulfilling of the law. Jesus approved of the law. But the Phari-
sees added laws of their own making, and not ordained by
God.

'The Scribes and Pharisees,' he said, 'have established themselves in the place from which Moses used to teach . . . they
fasten up packs too heavy to be borne, and lay them on men's
shoulders' (Matt. xxiii. 2, 4).

'Woe upon you, Scribes and Pharisees, you hypocrites that
will award to God his tithe, though it be of mint or dill or
cummin, and have forgotten the weightier commandments of
the law' (Matt. xxiii. 23).

'Their worship of me is vain, for the doctrines they teach
are the commandments of men' (Matt. xv. 9).

So the first part of the indictment is not only that they add
to God's law, but that while they may keep their own man-
made law, they do not keep God's.

But the attack goes even deeper. 'You hypocrites, it was a
true prophecy Isaiah made of you, when he said, this people
does me honour with its lips, but its heart is far from me' (Matt.
xv. 7–8); 'They act, always, so as to be a mark for men's eyes'
(Matt. xxiii. 5); 'You hypocrities that are like whitened
sepulchres, fair in outward show, when they are full of dead
men's bones and all manner of corruption within' (Matt. xxiii.

27). Their keeping of the law, therefore, was exterior but not interior, and so worthless.

Secondly—and this is fundamental to the understanding of the Redemption—Jesus condemned them for supposing that by keeping the law they had merited a title-deed to inherit heaven. All men will only be saved by the mercy of God. This of course becomes the burden of St. Paul's message, and he was a converted Pharisee. It is a difficult doctrine to express concisely without omitting an essential element. Thus it would be unchristian to omit the use of good works, and their essential contribution to salvation. Nevertheless, the teaching of Christ is clear. He came, not to the just, but to bring sinners to repentance. On the other hand, not those who cry : Lord, Lord, will enter into Christ's kingdom, but those who perform the will of the Father.

St. Luke has a compelling sentence (xvii. 10) : 'You, in the same way, when you have done all that was commanded of you, are to say : we are servants and worthless; it was our duty to do what we have done.' Writing of the Pharisee who went into the Temple to pray, he says, 'There were some who had confidence in themselves, thinking they had won acceptance with God' (Luke xviii. 9). The publican went away higher in the favour of God because 'everyone who exalts himself will be humbled, and the man who humbles himself will be exalted' (Luke xviii. 14).

To take any other view makes nonsense of Christ's life. He saw the law as God's law, God's will, his Father's will, and that he thirsted to do.

To treat of Christ's submissiveness to the law and to other men without treating of his submissiveness to his Father would be like attempting a painting of someone without the sitter. Obedience to the law does not make sense, unless it is seen to proceed from a desire to obey God, whose law it is. Men and their laws had an authority over Christ as man precisely

because they received their authority from God. Thus Jesus
obeyed his Father in obeying them. He does not say *Moses*
said, 'Honour thy father and mother', but '*God* has said'
(Matt. xv. 3). He saw beyond the instrument to the source.

It has been maintained that Jesus only became aware of his
mission when being baptized by St. John in Jordan. But such
a view ignores the fact that in all the MSS. of St. Luke's Gospel
the Presentation in the Temple is included. Already at twelve
he was about his Father's business (Luke ii. 49).

The motif of the Father's will became not less prominent
with the years but more insistent. When his family circle including his mother came to save him from the press of the
crowds, he replied to their entreaties, 'My mother and my
brethren are those who hear the word of God and keep it'
(Luke viii. 21).

On another occasion the Jews had objected to his doing a
cure on the sabbath for the crippled man at the Sheep Gate
pool. Jesus replied by claiming to know the Father's will, God's
will; and on this occasion he revealed something of the union
of love between them.

'Believe me when I tell you this, the Son cannot do anything at his own pleasure, he can only do what he sees his
Father doing; what the Father does is what the Son does in
his own turn. The Father loves the Son, and discloses to him all
that he himself does' (John v. 19–20).

In those short sentences we have perhaps the supreme statement of Christian love : a union of mind and will, not by force
but freely, in a harmony which knows no limit.

The central driving force of Christ's life was the will of his
Father in heaven. As the crucifixion approached, the human
side of Christ shrank from the things to come. But that shrink-
ing of the flesh from pain did not in any way make him shrink
from the duty. 'Jesus began to make it known to his disciples
that he *must* go up to Jerusalem . . . *must* be put to death . . .'

(Matt. xvi. 21). St. Peter objected, and Christ showed a vehemence uncommon in his dealings with his friends : 'Back, Satan,' he said, 'these thoughts of thine are man's, not God's' (Mark viii. 33).

Three times Jesus prepared the minds of the apostles in this manner. On one further occasion he spoke his secret thoughts freely. He is contemplating his future death. He is laying down his life freely, yet being obedient too. He and his Father have agreed that he should accept all the consequences of sin, including dying at the hands of sinners.

'This my Father loves in me, that I am laying down my life, to take it up again afterwards. Nobody can rob me of it; I lay it down of my own accord. I am free to lay it down, free to take it up again; that is the charge which my Father has given me' (John x. 17–18). (Cf. the like ideas in Phil. ii. 4 ff.)

Once, at the beginning of the Passion, Jesus prayed in that mode : 'My Father, if it is possible, let this chalice pass me by; only as thy will is, not as mine is' (Matt. xxvi. 39). And once, at the very end, 'Consummatum est' (John xix. 30).

It is therefore an error to think that Christians have a servile delight in obeying creatures. They have a liberating delight in obeying God. The example of Christ on this point is conclusive. He saw and taught and acted upon the principle that God is our Father, whose will governs all life with a loving care. Naturally we want his will to be achieved. The whole of a Christian's obedience is an obedience to God the Father. Therefore it follows that, far from putting authority above all restraint, the Christian teaching keeps all authority within bounds—the bounds of the moral law.

That a man should be responsible to other men may be a useful check upon the tyrannical tendencies of those in power; but it is no infallible check, as we have seen to our cost over and over again this century, when the best of democracies have been overwhelmed by guile and subterfuges of all kinds. Even democracy cannot stand alone against the wiles and will of men with a craving for power. Conscience, or submission to God, in the long run is the only check upon the urge to tyranny.

Absolute power corrupts absolutely; that saying of Acton is true enough. But if it is applied to the government of the Catholic Church it is a misunderstanding of the nature of ecclesiastical government in the Church. The Pope, for example, is not an absolute ruler. The words 'Vicar of Christ' which have so incensed some are in fact a proof that the Pope does not claim any authority except delegated authority, such as all rulers have, and that consequently he will be responsible to God for the stewardship.

All is related to its source; law is not man-made, but God-made; and this is the principle of Christian polity. A law therefore ceases to be arbitrary: it is either just and from God or unjust and against his will. It is in this sense that Christ could say, 'Give back to Cæsar what is Cæsar's' (Matt. xxii. 21).

As we study to-day the world of politics and note how far governments are from professing obedience to Christ, it does not amaze us that law has been prostituted to serve force, ambition and pride; that law, which before was regarded as queen and as the merciful safeguard of the poor and helpless, should now be looked at with suspicion, contempt, hostility and indeed terror. For what now masquerades as law through many countries of the earth is not God's law, nor professing to be, but starkly the will of evil men, intent only upon power. Their laws are the measure of their closeness to or estrangement from Christ.

There is the third element in this study now to be considered —love. Law is the expression of someone's will; and to obey law is to submit to another's will. The doing of another's will is obedience. But it also may be the expression of love. Here we have the three : law, love, obedience.

Liberty seems absent. Jesus Christ, it must be admitted,

spoke little on the subject, but much about love, which is free giving, the supreme freedom.

Confusion is common between what is truly love and what is often called love but is really desire or hope. The latter is self-regarding, trying to make the world ours. The former is self-forgetting and trying to get into the world of another. For Jesus, loving his heavenly Father, included obeying him. 'My meat is to do the will of him who sent me and to accomplish the task he gave me' (John iv. 34); 'While daylight lasts I must work in the service of him who sent me; the night is coming, when there is no more working' (John ix. 4). This was not an obedience of servitude, but one freely given. As we have already pointed out, he freely lays down his life and as freely would take it up again.

The nature of Christ's prayer or love for God as a man escapes us, for though we know that he prayed and often, we do not know how he prayed, save once. Before beginning the active life of sacrifice for men, he withdrew into the desert for forty days and forty nights; but strangely enough he only left on record the temptations which he there underwent, and not the union of being and will that he must have had with his heavenly Father. On other occasions too he left his disciples, choosing the night in order to pray. The Garden where he was to experience his agony appears to have been a regular place for him to withdraw to in order to pray at night; for Judas expected to find him there.

The one occasion when we do know his prayer, it consisted of the simplest words, Not my will, but thine be done. This he repeated three times. Christ at that moment manifests that the prayer in the final crisis of his life was one of giving and acceptance. He was to do it in fact two days later upon the Cross; but that had to be preceded by the mind and will readily accepting and positively offering beforehand what was to be accomplished afterwards. In that simple prayer is enclosed the whole

secret of Christian love : the essential immediate union of man
with God by a process of giving, and the inevitable product
thereof, the sign and the proof, the act, the outward performance of God's Will. The second utterly depends upon the first
as a fruit depends upon its stem. The act is the evidence of the
state, the state is the essential love, the outward act the life of
love. Thus the death of Jesus was not an accident with no
intrinsic significance to his teaching : it was the seal upon his
love for his Father.

Jesus and our Obedience

Jesus taught men four things about obedience : the first that
men must obey the commandments of God; the second that
they must obey Christ himself; the third that they must want
to be servants of all, and the fourth that he has set men over
his Church to govern it. These obediences are not really distinct obediences, but in the words of Jesus himself are reducible
to submission to God.

The first is everywhere in the New Testament, as in the Old,
and needs little proving. 'If any man does the will of God, he
is my brother and sister and mother' (Mark iii. 35). Or, 'The
man who belongs to God, listens to God's words' (John viii. 47).

The second, obedience to Christ himself. It is here that he
goes beyond the Old Testament, for he wants obedience to his
own word to be on the same footing as obedience to that of
God to Moses : his New Law above the Old (Matthew v.
27 ff). 'And they were amazed by his teaching, such was the
authority with which he spoke' (Luke iv. 32). This was not a
misunderstanding of Christ's person. He really did speak in
his own name. 'You have one teacher, Christ' (Matt. xxiii. 10).
Take the final instruction. 'All authority in heaven and on
earth has been given to me' (Matt. xxviii. 18). Mary, his
mother, once expressed it thus : 'Do whatever he tells you'
(John ii. 5).

The third kind of obedience was that which we should give to all men. In the words of Jesus, 'A disciple is no better than his master' (Matt. x. 24); and in this matter his example was to be the servant of all, of the maimed, the blind, the sorrowful, the sinful, the unbeliever, the proud. He submitted to their importunities, to their crimes, to their contempt, violence. Humble submission to men in all save sin was a sign of being his disciple. 'Whoever would be a great man among you, must be your servant, and whoever has a mind to be first among you, must be your *slave*. So it is that the Son of Man did not come to have service done him; he came to serve others' (Matt. xx. 26–28). The greatest in the kingdom of God are the least upon this earth. The liberty that Christ gives us is gained by an abandonment of self to others and to the will of God. 'If any man has a mind to come my way, let him renounce self, take up his cross and follow me' (Mark viii. 34). (Cf. Luke ix. 23; Mark x. 44.)

Even while still among men himself, he sent other men to teach their fellows. Thus, even in his day many had to accept revelation, not from his lips, but from those of ordinary creatures like themselves. 'He who listens to you', he said to the seventy-two disciples, 'listens to me; he who despises you, despises me; and he who despises me, despises him that sent me' (Luke x. 16).

St. John, the apostle of love, also records Christ's words: 'Believe me when I tell you this: the man who welcomes one whom I send, welcomes me; and the man who welcomes me, welcomes him who sent me' (John xiii. 20).

Lastly, Christ did in fact set up an institution which he intended to be the instrument of spreading his message throughout the whole world and for all time. That he should have done so seems almost natural, for how otherwise could the message be spread or preserved intact and safe?

Speaking to the apostles at the end he said, 'You therefore

must go out, making disciples of all nations, and baptizing them in the name of the Father, and of the Son, and of the Holy Ghost, teaching them to observe all the commandments which I have given you' (Matt. xxviii. 19 ff.); and, 'Behold I am with you all through the days that are coming, until the consummation of the world' (Matt. xxviii. 20).

This command was no bolt from the blue; from out the vast crowd who had followed him, Jesus had solemnly chosen twelve, to be called apostles, or 'sent'. Out of these twelve he had picked Peter to be the chief. He gave him a special name, Rock or Stone, when by nature he was far from having the solidity of stone. But he had later explained why. 'Thou art Peter, and it is upon this Rock that I will build my church . . . and I will give to thee the keys of the kingdom of heaven; and whatever thou shalt bind on earth shall be bound in heaven, and whatever thou shalt loose on earth shall be loosed in heaven' (Matt. xvi. 18 ff.).

Jesus knows Peter's weakness, he prophesies his denial. But it is to Peter that he says, 'Simon, Simon, behold, Satan has claimed power *over you all*, so that he can sift you as wheat; but I have prayed for *thee*, that *thy* faith may not fail, when, after awhile, thou hast come back to me, it is for thee to be the support of thy brethren' (Luke xxii. 31 ff.). At the end, also, after the Resurrection Jesus singles Peter out, and says, 'Feed my lambs . . . tend my shearlings . . . feed my sheep' (John xxi. 16 ff.).

We are not here trying to prove the primacy of Peter or of the Papacy. Yet it remains an historical fact that when the moment came for the Church to 'take over' from the Empire, it was the Papacy that took the lead, and upon such texts as these. One only has to read the account of the early Councils to see that. The Rock upon which at least Western Christendom was founded was in fact the Papacy, with its unshakable belief. Led by the Popes, a St. Leo or a St. Gregory, the men of that transitional age went forward with the conviction that Christ was God, and that what he had taught was true beyond a a doubt. They also believed that Christ spoke in the Church, of which he was, and is, the life. The Church is the Incarnation continued. When Leo spoke it was not he but Christ. Now, it is not we who live but Christ who lives in us. No metaphor but plain Truth. That gave certitude.

The moment that the Papacy faltered—though it never failed—then the rock-like certainties faltered also. The Great Schism, the Avignon captivity, the moral degradation of individual popes, were so many splintering explosions in the very foundations of society. Men should have distinguished between the person and the institution; but they were human and frail themselves, not infrequently proud or impatient, and they did not.

Faith became opinion, and opinion was divided; divided opinion led to wars, wars about religion; and after that exhaustion and indifference. The ancient basic certainties had vanished, leaving men of Western Europe with no way of life, only a house swept and garnished into which would enter seven devils worse than those which the advent of Christ had driven out at the beginning of the story.

Among these seven devils, who have entered into the inheritance of Christ and who stand there unashamed, are the worship of Self, which recognizes no law outside itself, the idolatry of Force or Power, ruthless and unrepentant, terrifying to-day in all its fearful might, the cult of Wealth, the lusts of the flesh, crude and perverted, destructive of civilization. And now the old pagan idolatries, but on a vast and cruel scale, the idolatry of Blood, the idolatry of the State, the supremacy of Class, have returned to destroy us unless we turn at this last hour from them, and humbly, with repentant hearts, give due worship to that supreme God whom alone men should worship and obey.

The difference between divine faith and human opinion for history is that the former can give a certitude strong enough for men to build order out of chaos, while the second is so fluid that it produces chaos out of order. As Pascal saw, once man is reduced to searching for right with the pale flickering light of human reason alone, he is reduced to accepting might as the only safeguard of order. 'Might is the sovereign of the world, and not opinion' (*Pensée No.* 303, Brunschvicg ed.).

The Acts and The Epistles

'Here they are, the men who are turning the state upside down' (Acts xvii. 6). That must have been the first thought of the outside world, particularly the governmental world, to this new, unaccountable, unpredictable thing, the Church. The reason was that the leaders of the Church threw a challenge. 'Peter and the other apostles answered, God has more right to be obeyed than men' (Acts v. 29).

It is not surprising that the Jews, who were finding more and more following the one they had crucified, should press their point. 'All these folk defy the edicts of Cæsar; they say there is another king, one Jesus' (Acts xvii. 7). That was the unpalatable truth : Cæsar was not supreme, but rather one Jesus.

The hierarchy of values in the ancient world had been overthrown. The emperors, as we know, took up the challenge, as every dictator must; and persecution followed persecution.

Yet the Church did not deny the authority of the state. The Christians of the first century were not political anarchists. The very man, Paul, who was being accused of this anarchy by the Jews cried out before Festus, the governor, 'I appeal to Cæsar' (Acts xxv. 11). St. Paul proves by the rest of his writings that this appeal was no mere act of expediency when finding himself in a tight corner. In the epistle to the Romans he wrote, 'Every soul must be submissive to its lawful superiors; authority comes from God only, and all authorities that hold sway are of his ordinance . . . the magistrate is God's minister' (Rom. xiii. 1–3). In a letter to Titus he stressed the importance of preaching this obedience. 'Remind them that they have a duty of submissive loyalty to governments and to those in authority' (Titus iii. 1).

St. Peter, as we would expect, teaches the same doctrine, but adds the element of love, even in this mundane setting. 'For love of the Lord, then, bow to every kind of human authority; to the king, who enjoys the chief power, and to the magistrates who hold his commission to punish criminals and encourage honest men' (1 Pet. ii. 13).

This submissiveness is so extreme as to be almost at the opposite pole from anarchy. Are Christians perhaps, as J. J. Rousseau fondly thought, fit subjects for tyranny? A Christian, then as now, believes that all authority derives from God, that therefore rulers must be obeyed in so far as they are agents of God. On the other hand a Christian obeys a ruler and his law only in so far as they are in conformity with the law of God. So we conclude that the early Christians were neither anarchists nor slaves, but men who obeyed rulers in so far as the law of God would allow.

The problem of slavery was a very present one to the early Church. It was one thing obeying the state, another obeying a master who bought you in the market-place. In the new dispensation all men were equal before God. 'Here is no more Gentile and Jew, no more circumcised and uncircumcised; no one is barbarian or Scythian, no one is slave or free man; there is nothing but Christ in any of us' (Col. iii. 11). Some Christian slaves might be tempted to shake themselves free of their chains.

But the New Testament does not bear out such an interpretation of St. Paul's words to the Colossians. 'Hast thou been called a slave? Do not let it trouble thee' (1 Cor. vii. 21), wrote St. Paul; while St. Peter, 'You who are slaves must be sub-

missive to your masters' (1 Pet. ii. 18). It is all summed up in
the epistle to the Ephesians, 'You who are slaves give your
human masters the obedience you owe to Christ, in anxious
fear, simple-mindedly, not with that show of service which
tries to win human favour, but in the character of Christ's
slaves, who do what is God's will with all their heart. *Yours
must be a slavery of love,* not to men but to the Lord'
(Eph. vi. 5–7).

Slavery is no longer slavery if done out of love; for slavery
essentially is an unwilling service, love is willingness.

St. Paul gives advice also to the master. 'And you who are
master give your slaves just and equitable treatment; you know
well enough that you, too, have a Master in heaven' (Col. iv. 1).

That saying contains the death sentence to the system of
real slavery as the ancients knew it and practised it. Social justice was born. Not that the relationship, master, servant, was
done away with, but that of master and chattel. 'Do not think
of him any longer as a slave; he is something more than a slave,
a well-beloved brother' (Philemon, verse 16).

The problem of slavery is only one facet of the whole Christian attitude to human laws, and to law in general. St. Paul
wrestled with the problem many times. To avoid confusion we
must remember that he uses the word in five different senses:

   (i) There is the law of Moses.
  (ii) There is the law of conscience. Sometimes this coincides
       with the law of Moses; so that at times we hear him say
       that the law of the Old Testament is finished, at others
       that it still holds sway.
 (iii) The law of nations.
  (iv) The law of the flesh.
   (v) The law of liberty, or of Christ.

Are Christians bound by the law? The story of the Gentiles
and the Jewish law is too well known to require more than a
summary treatment here. Were the Gentiles bound by the

Mosaic law, specifically in regard to circumcision? The answer given at the first council of the Church, that of Jerusalem, was that they were not. But the old law included much of the natural law which did still bind, and also revealed truths which could not be abrogated. Therefore it could not be said that the old law in its entirety was abolished.

Yet, if the law was not, in part, of permanent worth, what power had it now or ever to save? It was in this setting that St. Paul wrestled with the problem of the relationship between the law and salvation. The Reformers differed from the Catholic Church as to St. Paul's answer; they differed among themselves. It will be on the lines of the answer given by the Church that we shall treat the subject here. Thus : 'It is those who obey the law who will be justified' (Rom. ii. 13). But later, 'And justification comes to us as a free gift from his grace' (Rom. iii. 24), or, 'A man is justified by faith apart from the observance of the law' (Rom. iii. 28).

In general, the Church's understanding of these passages is as follows. St. Paul has often denied the power of the law of the Old Testament to save—all, Protestants and Catholics, are agreed on that—therefore the law, which if kept would justify, must be the law of God engraved on the tablets of the heart of every man. Yet justification is a free gift, a gift by which we are enabled to keep his law. St. Paul was too much a Pharisee not to know that observance of the law was not able to save; it was the thing he had escaped from when he was given the free gift of faith on the road to Damascus.

The slavery of the law had been broken by the liberating action of the Cross. 'Where the Lord's spirit is, there is freedom' (2 Cor. iii. 18). But the Christian freedom was not intended to be one divorced from law. Liberty and law are not opposites in the Christian dispensation; liberty was not conceived as a liberation from the law, but as the power to obey the true law, that of Christ. 'Yes, brethren, freedom claimed you when you were called. Only, do not let this freedom give a foothold to corrupt nature' (Gal. v. 13). Or, 'I am free to do what I will; yes, but not everything can be done without harm. I am free to do what I will, but I must not abdicate my own liberty' (1 Cor. vi. 12), by which St. Paul means that he must not allow his will, which should be supreme, to be subjected to something lower than itself. (Cf. 1 Cor. ix. 21.)

Christian liberty is a subjection to Christ. St. Paul encouraged the Romans to be 'slaves of obedience, marked out for justification', and reminded them that they had 'become God's slaves'. He loves to play on these two ideas of slavery and freedom, 'If a slave is called to enter Christ's service, he is Christ's freedman; just as the free man, when he is called, becomes the slave of Christ' (1 Cor. vii. 22). (Cf. Gal. i. 10, 'The slave of Christ.')

Yet in 2 Cor. iii. he wrote, 'And where the Lord's spirit is, there is freedom'. It was freedom from sin and a free subjection to Jesus Christ. 'It is by letting the spirit lead you that you free yourselves from the yoke of the law' (Gal. v. 18), so that these terms now almost have no meaning. 'No one is slave or free man; there is nothing but Christ in any of us' (Col. iii. 11).

The objective reasonableness of a thing does not necessarily make it subjectively free; for, subjectively, a man may still be pinned down by his evil desires. Freedom is not only in the intellect, it must be in the will. A man must want to do a thing before that thing becomes freely done. To want is to love. We now approach the third point.

'Yours must be a slavery of love,' writes St. Paul, 'not to men but to the Lord' (Eph. vi. 7), and that means people 'who do what is God's will with all their heart' (previous verse). In that sentence is summed up the nature of obedience and one element of love : love includes the doing of God's will. This was how the life of Christ struck St. Paul. 'He dispossessed himself, and took the nature of a slave, fashioned in the likeness of men

. . . accepted an obedience which brought him to death, death on a cross' (Phil. ii. 7). In the epistle to the Hebrews these words are put on Christ's lips : 'See, then, I said, I am coming to fulfil what is written of me, where the book lies unrolled : to do thy will, O my God' (Heb. x. 7).

St. Peter carries this teaching a stage farther. 'For the love of God, then, bow to every kind of human authority' (1 Pet. ii. 13), while for St. John, the mystic, love is proved by obedience. 'My little children, let us show our love by the true test of action : not by taking phrases on our lips' (1 John iii. 18), and, 'Loving God means keeping his commandments' (1 John. v. 3). In the second epistle he writes, 'Love means keeping his commandments; *love is itself the commandment*' (2 John i. 6). This gives the lie to the theory that the mystic must not be fettered by obedience, his spirit must not be enchained by laws. This is false. Never has a saint so persistently repeated that love requires the keeping of God's law. The reason is that God's commandment is God's mind expressed, his will; while to love is to be united in will with the person loved. Therefore to keep God's commandment is to love him truly.

Law, God's will, done willingly, is our supreme freedom and a way of love. Here they all meet in peace.

LIBERTY AND THE MIND OF CHRIST

Men of great sincerity outside the Catholic Church are restrained from advancing towards her because they fear that by so doing they would lose their freedom. Liberty is a possession they cherish above all things, more especially liberty of thought. To these we reply that submission to an ascertained truth is being more free than to refuse—for to refuse is to be unreasonable. The difficulty has arisen chiefly through the false idea current among Protestants that faith is blind, that reason cannot bring a man to the brink. Reason can show, as the Vatican Council (1870) maintained, that God is, that he has spoken through Jesus Christ. If that is true, then what Jesus Christ has taught is true.

There is a difference between the truths of the Church and those of any other body, for it claims that its truths are necessary. Among the philosophers we may pick and choose which we are prepared to accept. If we accept that Christ is God, then we cannot pick and choose what we like out of his message. He said, 'I am the way, the truth and the life'.

St. Paul understood it so. He was 'a servant of Jesus Christ' (Rom. i. 1). 'I came to you and preached Christ's message to you' (1 Cor. ii. 1), not to preach his own. 'I had no thought of bringing you any other knowledge than that of Jesus Christ' (1 Cor. ii. 2). 'After all, it is not ourselves we proclaim; we proclaim Jesus Christ as Lord' (2 Cor. iv. 5).

St. Peter writes in the same strain. 'But the word of the Lord lasts for ever' (1 Pet. i. 24). St. John as ever sums up : 'Our message concerns that Word who is life; what he was from the first, what we have heard about him; what our own eyes have seen of him; what it was that met our gaze; and the touch of our hands' (1 John i. 1).

They all believed that Christ was the Truth, that by submitting to him they were submitting to the truth. They placed truth above liberty; indeed they would have thought a man mad who wanted to be free of truth. The followers of Jesus wanted to be free of sin. By love the law lost its chains, for if the law that they followed was God's wisdom, the law became liberty.

The Catholic view of the Church is, then, that it is the continued life of Christ on earth, and this will explain how we Catholics can and must accept unswervingly its teaching; we hold that it is Christ continuing to teach us, and not merely an opinion, among many conflicting ones, upon what he taught. Thus we hold that the obedience required of us by the Church is in real truth obedience to God himself, whose instrument and mouthpiece it is and through which he speaks.

CHAPTER III

EASTERN MONACHISM

THE Gospels, Acts and Epistles, as we have seen, give us a complete picture of the ascetic and mystical way, a way which includes mortification, law, liberty and love, a way in which obedience is central.

It now remains to examine the use the early Christians made of this wealth of teaching; and in order not to include too wide a landscape, we shall take the first experiments in monasticism, to show how very gradually obedience emerged as the vital instrument in the spiritual life; and in so doing we shall have a better idea of the background to St. Benedict's creation in the West.

The ground has been well worked and excavated by experts. It is the interpretation of the facts which is relevant here. We gratefully accept the fruits of the labour of the scholars.

THE FACTS.—Probably the first ascetic practice was that recorded in the Acts when the disciples of Jesus agreed to have all in common, not out of an obligation but from zeal. Reading between the lines, we may guess that the experiment failed and proved a considerable liability to the whole Church. Voluntary poverty, then, proved difficult.

On the other hand, the counsel of virginity, taught by our Lord, was certainly practised in the various churches, as is proved by the epistles of St. Paul (1 Cor. vii.).

'I am not imposing a rule on you. I wish you were all in the same state as myself; but each of us has his own endowment from God, one to live in this way, another in that' (vii. 6–7).

'To those others, I give my own instructions, not the Lord's' (vii. 12). He himself practised virginity. He goes on in praise of it:

'About virgins, I have no command from the Lord; but I give you my opinion, as one who is, under the Lord's mercy, a true counsellor. This, then, I hold to be the best counsel in such times of stress, that this is the best condition for man to be in' (vii. 25–26).

Jesus had said, 'There are some eunuchs, who were so born from their mother's womb, some were made so by men, and some have made themselves so for the love of the kingdom of heaven: take this in, you whose hearts are large enough for it' (Matt. xix. 12).

It was through those two counsels of poverty and virginity that the early Church ventured along the unmapped road of the Cross. The emergence of obedience as the third of the three was very gradual. In those first centuries the cry that was repeated over and over again was, 'One thing is lacking to you . . . sell all and come follow me'. Obedience came with the rise of monachism.

At first those who determined to follow Christ more closely, whether by practising voluntary poverty or by virginity, did so in the bosom of their family, rather as St. Catherine did for many years in Siena in the fourteenth century, or St. Gemma Galgani did in the nineteenth. This is clear from the writings of the early Fathers such as St. Hippolytus, St. Cyprian, in the West, Clement of Alexandria, Origen and St. Methodius in the East—the evidence for which may be read in the article by Dom Leclercq, 'Monachisme', in the *D.A.C.L.*[1]

The name which stands out above all others in the first period of monastic life is that of St. Antony of Egypt, the father both of hermits and of monks. He was born during the age of persecution, about the year 250, in the Roman province of

[1] *Dictionnaire d'archéologie chrétienne et de liturgie.*

Egypt. Like his predecessors in the ways of Christian asceticism, he began by following Christ more closely in his own native place. Only after fifteen years of such a life, a kind of anchoritism within the home circle, did he withdraw to Mount Pispir near the Nile (modern Der el Memun, in the Fayum). After a period of twenty years, he came out of his retreat to instruct others in the 'way'; but once again he withdrew, and this time to an inaccessible part of the desert by the Red Sea. He lived to be over a hundred; and he, who had wished to be forgotten by all, was sought after by all, not excluding the emperors of the day. The most authentic facts about him are to be found in the life written of him by his friend, St. Athanasius, a work now generally accepted as genuine.

Up to the fourth century, indeed, up to the moment when St. Antony emerged from his empty tomb at the entreaties of his imitators, there had been no cenobitical life, as we understand it : the Catholic world had, in its more zealous moments, so far only produced hermits. But in A.D. 305, the date when St. Antony was persuaded to come forth from his retreat to help the many solitaries who had withdrawn into the desert following his example, we have the creation of something new : the beginning of the life of the counsels in common. The beginnings were very slight, almost imperceptible, but the age of the hermit was over. It is true that no set way of life was created there and then; there was no rule, no abbot; this was but the first stage in a very gradual process of unfolding; hermits were clubbing together, but trying to remain hermits. Nevertheless, it truly was an admission that absolute solitude in the main was unpractical and dangerous, that advice from a more experienced ascetic was a good thing.

The second stage came with the rise of the Pachomian monasteries. Here a rule existed : the monks lived in common —the Antonian monks mostly lived alone—the number of psalms to be recited every day was settled, the times of meals were fixed. The rule was very precise. The following should be borne in mind when we come to compare it with St. Benedict's.

Firstly, the whole tone was extremely strict. But instead of being the norm, it remained only the minimum, and every monk was expected to go far beyond. For example, a monk was not bound to attend meals if his ascetic enthusiasm encouraged him to abstain.

Secondly, though it was recognized that, once a man was a monk, he remained so, yet there seemed to be no obligation upon him to remain in any particular monastery or under any particular rule.

Thirdly, an underlying aim was competition in asceticism. Not for nothing does Cassian call these monks athletes of Christ.

Fourthly, with the numbers in one monastery mounting to a thousand, it was impossible for the monks to live under one roof or consider themselves as a family.

It would be a travesty of the facts to paint the picture as one of thousands of monks, like so many ascetic individualists, vying with each other in extremes of mortification. A cursory glance at Cassian is sufficient to dispel that mirage, though it might not be an unfair description of the pre-Pachomian monks. (Cf. Leclercq, loc. cit., col. 1808.)

Cassian is a very suitable sample to take of the pre-Benedictine monastic ethos, and this for two main reasons : he was widely travelled among the monasteries of the Near East, and yet he was a monk of the West, becoming abbot of a monastery he had founded near Marseilles. His earliest biographer would have us believe that he was a Scythian. It is probable, as he had had a liberal education, and he certainly spoke Greek. A native of Roman Scythia would be bilingual. By 382 he was a monk in Bethlehem, and he had been born in 360 only twenty-two years before. He and a friend were given permission by their abbot to visit the monasteries of Egypt. Although the abbot had put a time limit on their absence, they spent nearly ten years journeying, and this in spite of repeated letters from the abbot telling them to report home immediately. Cassian was a good man, and this behaviour did not appear to him wrong; it therefore gives one a glimpse of how monks of that period treated obedience. It is perhaps even more remarkable that after their return to Palestine they were once again allowed to visit Egypt. Then, finally, instead of returning home, they went to Constantinople (*c.* A.D. 400), and took sides with St. John Chrysostom. Cassian was now ordained deacon and moved to Rome, as the representative of the Church of Constantinople, to put St. John's case before the Pope. This again is symptomatic of the attitude of those monks towards stability: they felt no obligation either to obey a particular abbot or to remain in one place.

In Rome, Cassian was ordained priest. At this point he went to Gaul, where, in the virgin forest near Marseilles, he established a monastery, later to be famous as that of St. Victor. He based the life on the principles he had learned in those beloved monasteries he had visited in the delta of the Nile and loved to speak about. It was at this time that he wrote the two books which have made him famous and which St. Benedict told his monks to read—the *Institutes* and the *Conferences*; they both described the life of the ascetics and cenobites of Egypt. Cassian died in A.D. 435.

It is in these two books of Cassian that we get a fair picture of the spirit of the early monks by the Nile. We will find that obedience, strangely enough, is at the root of their spirituality; but we shall have occasion to point out the limited understanding they had of this virtue compared to that which St. Benedict had, as has already been observed in the very actions of the author.

Thus in the fourth book of the *Institutes* we read (chap. 10): 'Next, the rule is kept with such strict obedience that, without the knowledge and permission of the superior, the juniors not only do not dare to leave their cell, but on their own authority do not venture to satisfy their common and natural needs. And so they are quick to fulfil without discussion all things that are ordered by him, as if they were commanded by God from heaven.' Nor was this obedience servile, for Cassian writes elsewhere (Book 2, chap. 3): 'Nor can anyone obey an Elder but one who has been filled with the love of God.' In chapter 12 of the fourth book Cassian goes even farther. He writes that when the monks hear the knock summoning them to pray, 'everyone eagerly dashes out from his cell', leaves unfinished whatever he was doing, 'without even waiting to finish the letter he had begun', and 'hastens with the utmost earnestness and zeal to attain the virtue of obedience, which they put not merely before manual labour and reading and silence and quietness, but even before all virtues'. (He is here describing the Pachomian monastery in the Thebaid desert.)

There follow various stories of Abbot John, which show his exceeding obedience. A notable one describes how a senior tried his spirit—before he was abbot—by ordering him to plant a dry and mouldy stick in the ground and to water it. This he did daily for a year, even though his water supply was two miles distant.[1] This activity proved his obedience, but somewhat as sin proves a man's free will. The watering of the dead twig was not a particularly rational form of obedience. The Fathers of the desert could tell many a story of such a kind, more full of zeal than of sense, meritorious for the subject, perhaps unwise for the superior; but one and all are to our purpose, for they prove that obedience was venerated as a queenly virtue in the Thebaid.

The element of exaggeration was not infrequently present in the spirit of these athletes of Christ. They were competing with one another; they were blazing a trail, and for that purpose it was inevitable that they should stretch to the limits, reach to

[1] Book 2, chap. 24.

the boundaries of the new land of asceticism. St. Benedict was to profit by their discoveries and their mistakes, and at no point so deeply as in the province of obedience.

In spite of the quotations of Cassian above, discipline rather than loving obedience is the key-note among Egyptian monks; that is to say, obedience was looked upon rather as an ascetic practice, like fasting or keeping vigil, or any other austerity they might invent. Yet it must be admitted that Cassian shows in more than one place that these monks were groping to a more profound understanding of the virtue. He has noted its close connection with the love of God. But among the first generation of hermits turned monks, obedience had an almost practical use. Cassian, in one of his *Conferences*, lets Abbot John describe why he abandoned the anchorite life to join a monastery. The reason he gave was that the wilderness had become so crowded that the early peace had melted away. 'A large number of the brethren began to seek a dwelling in that desert, and by cramping the freedom of the vast wilderness, not only caused that fire of divine contemplation to grow cold, but also entangled the mind in many ways in the chains of carnal matters' (Book 19, chap. 5). In the same chapter Abbot John consoles himself by saying that if he had lost the ecstatic joy, at least he was imitating Christ. 'Finally, even if there is any diminution of my purity of heart while I am living in the cœnobium, I shall be satisfied by keeping in exchange that one precept of the Gospels . . . I mean that I should take no thought of the morrow, and submitting myself completely to the abbot, seem in some degree to emulate him of whom it is said : "He humbled himself, and became obedient unto death"; and so be able humbly to make use of his words : "For I came not to do my own will, but the will of the Father who sent me." ' (Cf. Phil. ii. 8; St. John vi. 38). He thus ends chapter six.

The aim of these Eastern monks was, as we find over and over again in the works of Cassian, purity of heart, by which is meant the condition of mind, free from all impurities, making it capable of contemplating God. They were aiming at the contemplation of the God-head. For them the instruments were mortification and vigils and also specially obedience. At times they rise to the idea that obedience is something more than the supreme ascetic practice and see in it an effect of the loving imitation of Christ. But they are far from seeing in it love itself. This seems to arise from the nature of their quest, which is wholly contemplative; activity appeared to them to have no intrinsic use in itself. The Benedictines, while not repudiating the aim, contemplation, and the means, purity of heart, give to the practical reason, to activity, a real spiritual richness; and this they derive from their deeper understanding of the very nature of the act of obedience, which does not only arise out of love, but is in itself an act of love—love in act.

Of the two elements in love here briefly stated, the contemplative and the active, the more fundamental is undoubtedly the contemplative; loving God in himself cannot cease being so. Love is love. But obedience, while being done from love in the Benedictine school of spirituality, in itself might always degenerate into legalism, as unfortunately it did towards the end of the Middle Ages. Obedience at best can only be one side of love, an expression of love and deriving from the central fire of the soul searching for God in himself.

The centre of the third experiment and advance in depth into monastic spirituality was not Egypt but Asia Minor, not far from Neo-Cæsarea; and the leader into the unknown was St. Basil the Great, whom St. Benedict recognized as his chief master.

St. Basil came of a family of bishops and saints. St. Gregory of Nyssa was his brother, Macrina (a pious lady), his sister, Peter, a younger brother, was bishop of Sebaste. He himself was born about A.D. 330 at Cæsarea in Cappadocia. While studying in Athens he became eager for the ascetic life, and in order to study the matter he travelled extensively in Egypt, Syria and Arabia; for by this time hermits, anchorites and cenobites were flourishing in all these parts. He returned to Pontus, where his family had emigrated while he was still a child, and there by Neo-Cæsarea he founded a monastery. Among his innovations were a lessening of austerity and a greater stress on manual labour; his monks of course practised chastity and poverty and obedience. He died in 379, bishop of Cæsarea in Pontus. (Cf. *Encyclopædia Britannica,* 11th ed., art. 'Basil, St.'.)

St. Basil set great store by obedience. He seems to have been acutely conscious of discord within the Church. The significant thing is that he is more drawn to discipline of the will than to that of the body.

'Continence and all bodily hardship have a certain value; but if a man does what is pleasing to himself, following his own impulses, and does not obey the counsels of the Superior, the sin will outweigh the good act' (*St. Basil's Ascetic Works,* translated by W. K. L. Clarke, p. 142).

Neither St. Basil nor Abbot Pachomius before him really made obedience more than of ascetic value in the religious life, as St. Benedict was to do. Obedience was still only a means, if the chief, to perfection. As Cassian pointed out in the *First Conference of Abbot Moses,* chapter 4 : 'The end of my profession . . . is the Kingdom of God . . . but the immediate aim or goal is purity of heart.'

St. Basil diminishes the austerities of the monks and increases their obedience; he stands midway between the early experiments and the Rule of St. Benedict. But the paradox is that St. Basil wrote no rule for monks as we would understand it, though two works from his pen go by that name, the Shorter and the Longer Rules. This is more significant than may at first appear, for these so-called rules are only a series of questions and answers, all naturally on spiritual matters, but scarcely a complete statement of how to live the daily round of the monastic life, nor are they a scheme of ascetic practice.

Consequently, it still remained true that the rule was the will of the superior and not some written document which he had to interpret and to which the superior was subject as much as the subjects. Now, no matter how holy most superiors might be, this fact introduced an arbitrary and disturbing element in community life. In the case where the superior proves to be unreasonable, the monk can follow one of two courses; he may either disobey or follow a blind obedience. The former is understandable if to be regretted, the latter will be meritorious but not conducive to the ideal kind of submissiveness which included that intelligent obedience so much to be desired.

One of the differences, as will be seen, between the Rule of St. Benedict and those of St. Basil and those of all his predecessors is in this, that St. Benedict's does lay down the law, clearly, concisely, comprehensively. And, while St. Benedict allows for modifications here and there for practical reasons—e.g. modifications in dress owing to climatic conditions—he submits the abbot to the rule as much as he does his monks. Here he reintroduced very strongly that old Roman element of law above ruler, an element somewhat obscured in the declining years of an autocratic imperium.

To sum up: the monastic experiment began as an attempt to be free from the world in order to follow Christ. Men fled from money, power, the flesh, from communing with men. But they not only often encountered the devil, as St. Antony did, they also encountered themselves. They would therefore conquer themselves. They began by attacking the body, they would be free from their own flesh. They slept little, ate less, imposed pains upon their bodies. But even with this they were not free of themselves. There remained the unconquered citadel of the will. It was this, the last fortress, the keep, that the hermits-turned-monks, under such leaders as St. Pachomius, now determined to overwhelm, and so be free to follow Christ.

Even in this last assault there were stages. The first was the acceptance of a guide; the second that of a rule, the third stability. The first was the work of St. Antony, the second the work of St. Pachomius and St. Basil, the third will be that of St. Benedict. We shall find that St. Benedict's synthesis is new in other respects also.

The men of those days had found a leader, Christ, whose law they were willing, nay eager, to follow. Obedience now was a delight. The common man of the new Europe, following the example of these pioneers, also was ready to submit his will to this new yoke, not the bondage of Rome, but the yoke of Christ; doing so with delight, he did so freely, of his own volition and without constraint.

CHAPTER IV

ST. AUGUSTINE

THE weighty significance of St. Augustine in history can scarcely be exaggerated. Here was a man whose mind was set upon the highest things, whose whole being was one, emotions, imagination, tongue, mind, will, whose every gift was equal to its task. Who was more sublime a thinker among mortal men, who more vivid a writer, more penetrating in his analysis, more moving in his appeals than St. Augustine of Hippo? Besides, his life was such as to move the imagination of men in all centuries: he stood at the summit of the intellectual world of his day, he had tasted of all its knowledge, that of Greece, and also that of the East; citizen of a mighty empire, born in its most flourishing province, flower himself of its traditional education, he stood for all the greatness of the past. But he was born at the turn of history. The barbarians were bursting the barriers of the northern frontiers; the magnificent and proud structure of the Roman Empire was not sure of itself, within its bounds were millions who owed allegiance to another king than Cæsar, who looked to another city, the one not built by hands. They were the heirs of the promise. Was Augustine with the old or with the new world? In the event he proved to be the bridge.

In the thought of St. Augustine we shall discuss three things; firstly, his response to law, and especially that of submission to a spiritual authority; secondly, his cherished belief in the liberty of men, which he does not consider destroyed by obedience, and finally, his teaching on love, which for him was a search for God, his truth and his law, and by which he was finally set free.

Even on such a limited subject as this, St. Augustine's thought is too vast to be encompassed within the bounds of a chapter. We can therefore here only give pointers to an understanding of his position. This may seem scarcely worth doing; yet, to leave out St. Augustine would be to omit one of the strongest strands in the rope which is tradition.

St. Augustine was born in A.D. 354 and died in A.D. 430. He was an African, from Tagaste, educated in the Roman traditions of his day; he became a professor, first at Carthage and afterwards in Rome. It was by meeting St. Ambrose that he came to see that the Catholic Church might have more to give than childish nonsense.

His conversion was not, however, purely intellectual; it was at root a submission to authority. So at the foundation of his Christian and Catholic thought we have the idea of LAW; for what is submission to authority but submission to the rule of another?

Law

He submitted to the authority of revelation, that is, to the sacred scriptures, because he submitted to tradition; but he only submitted to the tradition because it was preserved by the Catholic Church. We quote the famous lines:

'Ego vero evangelio non crederem, nisi me catholicæ Ecclesiæ commoveret auctoritas.' [1]

And yet he was, of all the Fathers, the one most ready to exercise his reason upon the things of faith. This was possible because he was convinced that all truth sprang from that same divine source which could not contradict itself. Thus he saw the whole history of the world as one great unfolding of truth, and submission to the Law of Revelation as reasonable. He had no fear that, by submitting his mind to the Church, he was

---

[1] *Contra, epist. Mani,* c.v. 6, *M.P.* 42, *St. Aug.,* VII, col. 176: "I would not indeed believe in the Gospel, unless the authority of the Church persuaded me." *M.L.* The Abbé Migne's edition of the Latin Fathers in 221 volumes.

thereby cutting himself off from all other sources of truth, or
that he might find one day that he would have to deny his
reason because it had discovered something which contradicted
the truths taught by the Church. He knew that the fount of
truth was God, and that water in the stream which flowed
through the channels of the Church was from the same source
as was that which flowed through the human mind. Thus he
was ready to accept any truth wherever it was discovered, because truth was one. He compared the acceptance by the
Church of all truth to the despoiling of the Egyptians by the
Jews at the moment of the Exodus. The Christian tradition
was, for St. Augustine, the heir of all things, as the Master of
the Christian was said to be by St. Paul in the first chapter of
his epistle to the Hebrews.

Liberty remained within that submission to the Church,
because St. Augustine did not require any liberty outside
truth.[1] He was convinced, after years of searching, that God
had spoken through Holy Scripture, that therefore this was one
strand of truth; he was sure that the human mind could by its
own resources also reach some truths. His own mind had
utterly convinced him that God was truth; he had reached that
point even in his pagan days, as a neo-Platonist. He describes
in the *Confessions* how the Platonists had seen that the Logos
was God; they had, however, failed to know—how could they?
—that the Logos had been made flesh. This he could only
know through the gospels which were guaranteed for him by
the Church, and therefore it is true to say he knew it through
the teaching Church. Thus these two aspects of truth were not
contradictory but complementary.

St. Augustine was prepared always to submit his mind to
the law of truth; he would have none of that liberty which
went beyond the bounds of truth : *'Quæ est enim pejor mors*

---

[1] But to have remained outside the Church would have been to have
excluded himself from a part of truth.

animæ, quam libertas erroris' (Ep. cv., cap. 11, sect. 10, col. 400, *M.L.*, vol. XXXIII).

St. Augustine may have had a high idea of the law of the universe, but he had a poor idea of laws as in fact existing.

The contrast between St. Augustine's admiration for the philosophers of the civilization into which he was born and his contempt for that civilization itself is truly remarkable. The whole point of his great work, the *City of God*, is to contrast it with that other city built by another love, namely, the love of this world.

His view comes as a shock to the modern student who has been brought up to think of the Roman Empire as the finest symbol or example of a state based upon law. How was it that St. Augustine could see so little in it to praise? It is simple enough. He who lived in it did not confuse theory with fact, as it is so easy for later historians to do, who do not live in the Roman Empire but can only read about it; in theory there was much great thinking on the lines of the natural law, but in fact St. Augustine saw mostly corruption and theft on a grand scale.

There is another reason for St. Augustine's apparently extreme view, and which may make us feel that he was exaggerating. In A.D. 410 Rome was sacked, and the pagans said this was all due to the citizens becoming Christian, and so having no fight in them. St. Augustine was determined to show that, although it was true that the world was becoming Christian, this was not the cause of the collapse of the Roman Empire; this was the occasion of his great work, the *City of God*.

His main contention is that in the first place the Roman Empire was not built upon law or justice. 'Set justice aside, then, and what are kingdoms but great robbery?' (*City of God*, iv, 4). In the same chapter he tells the story of a pirate's answer to Alexander when the latter asked him how he dared to molest the high seas. His reply was, 'Because I do it with a little ship only, I am called a thief; you do it with a great navy and are called an emperor'.

Even though great men like Cicero could proclaim the good life, they could not save their empire from the decay of morals. 'Behold now this commonwealth of Rome, which I am not the first to assert but repeat the words of their own writers, how it declined from good by degrees, and from an honest and honourable condition to have fallen into the greatest dishonesty and dishonour possible' (loc. cit., ii, 19). In the next famous chapter he goes on to describe the state to which the empire has sunk. The pagan citizen has no regard for justice, he regards only his own ease. 'No, they say, let it but be rich and victorious; or let it (and that is best of all)—let it but enjoy security and peace, and what care we? Let the poor obey the rich for their own belly's sakes, so that they may live at ease under their protection. Let not the king's care be how good, but how subject his people be. Let there be a good store of common harlots. Let a man drink, eat, game and revel day and night, where he may or will; let luxurious and bloody delights fill the theatre, with dishonest words, and shows, freely and uncontrolled' (loc. cit., chap. 20).

It is established that St. Augustine, the man on the spot, saw little good in the *de facto* empire of his day. He did not believe that it was grounded on true justice but on desire. Indeed, his whole treatment of 'the Two Cities' is that two loves have built two cities, the one self-love and the other the love of God.

In his discussion of the nature of these two cities, St. Augustine is led to consider the very nature of law itself. This he does at some length in the nineteenth book; and the analysis he there makes is the *locus classicus* for the medieval men. He is speaking in Roman terms but with a Christian spirit.

In the first place he points out that sin brought government into the world and so law. In the beginning it was not so, and, taking his stand upon Genesis—that wonderful picture of the early ages of mankind and its slow progress towards civilized life—he maintains that the earliest men were not rulers and ruled, masters and slaves, but 'rather shepherds than kings. . . . In all Sacred Scripture, we never read the word servant until such time as that just man Noah laid it as a curse upon his offending son. So it was guilt and not nature that gave a beginning to that word' (xix, chap. 15). And a little later : 'Sin therefore is the mother of servitude, and first cause of man's subjection to man.'

He recognized that many wars were won by unjust aggressors and many states ruled by unjust rulers, many Christian slaves in servitude to unjust masters; yet St. Augustine does not advise revolt, he suggests rather subjection. But he does clearly state, as St. Thomas Aquinas will do after him, that an unjust law is no law. For instance, when discussing whether Rome ever had a true commonwealth he remarks that if *'Respublica est res populi'*, then 'Rome never had any, for it never had an estate of the people, which is Scipio's definition of the commonwealth; for he defines the people to be a multitude, united in one consent of law and profit . . . where true justice is wanting, there can be no law. For what law does, justice does, and what is done unjustly, is done unlawfully. For we may not imagine men's unjust decrees to be laws : all men defining law to arise out of the foundation of justice' (xix, chap. 21).

In spite of that condemnation of unjust laws St. Augustine does not say 'Rebel'. He distinguishes; in the first place a Christian must not obey those laws which are positively against the Christian religion, 'never respecting the temporal laws that are made against so good and religious a practice' (xix. chap. 17); and secondly, 'not breaking, but observing, their diversity in divers nations, all which tend to the preservation of earthly peace, if they oppose not the adoration of the one only God' (*ibid.*).

As for servants and slaves, the most manifest miscarriage of justice in the ancient world, St. Augustine suggests the highest form of obedience. Those who would seem to be condemned to living in spiritual chains will find, he says, in the teaching of St. Paul and of Jesus, their Master, the sublime answer of loving obedience, thus putting his finger on the essential point: that it is the will that counts.

'Therefore the apostle advises servants to obey their masters and to serve them with cheerfulness and good will; so that if they cannot be made free by their masters, they make their servitude a freedom to themselves, by serving them, not in deceitful fear, but in faithful love, until iniquity be overpassed, and all men's power and principality disannulled, and God only be all in all' (xix, chap. 15).

This fundamental idea of true obedience, of course, reappears in the famous letter which has become the foundation for the rules, not only of many nuns and medieval canons, but also of the Dominican Order. He there writes: 'May the Lord grant you to observe all these things with love as lovers of spiritual beauty and fragrant with the goodly scent of Christ in your good behaviour, not then as slaves but as free women in grace' (Letter 201, Loeb ed., last paragraph).

Law, then, for St. Augustine is a matter of justice and reason. He is not impressed by the law as shown forth in the city of this world and as exemplified in the Roman Empire. But neither is he in favour of refusing obedience; rather, where possible, he would have Christians obey from a higher motive, that of the love of God, from whom all authority derives.

As this world's city is not built upon the foundation of justice, he can see little liberty within its walls. For God gives rule to the godly and also to the ungodly alike (*City of God*, v, chap. 21). Therefore we cannot expect freedom from this source. There is only one way to freedom, according to St. Augustine, and that is through the religion of Christ: 'This is the religion which contains the universal way of the soul's freedom' (x, chap. 32), and later, in the most extreme form, he writes, speaking of the religion of Christ: 'This is the way . . .

besides this way ... no man has ever had freedom, or ever has or ever shall have' (x, chap. 32). We now pass on to St. Augustine's views on liberty.

Liberty

What is freedom for St. Augustine? All we can attempt is to show his approach to the problem.

If, since the thirteenth century, Catholics have in the main grounded their philosophic thinking on the work of St. Thomas, between the fifth and thirteenth centuries it is even more true to say that St. Augustine was the Master of Masters in the West, especially in Philosophy. Thus in the matters of the Will and Liberty and Love his teaching may be said to be standard for the pre-scholastic period. If St. Benedict set the practical rules for living, St. Augustine set the practical rules for thinking.

Nearly all his thought is derived in these things from three sources—the neo-Platonism with which he was impregnated, his own personal experience, that is his soul's experience, and thirdly, the controversies in which he was engaged, more especially those against the Pelagians on the one hand and the Manicheans on the other. From Greek thought he arrived in the Church with the certainty that the supreme prize was truth—as we have already noted. The Greeks are generally considered to have seen only one kind of freedom, that of action. Choice they thought only concerned reason[1]—any error was an error of intellect. He is aware of the two kinds of liberty; that of acting at all and that of choosing. Of the two he was at first more interested in the latter, because his own personal experience of conversion was a great battle of choice, in which the enemies of freedom were his passions. But soon his interest centred on freedom of action. He was defending the independence of the human will against the predestination

[1] A man can act or not act; in this he is said to be free; he may choose this or that thing—this is freedom of choice.

view of the Manicheans, and safeguarding it against his own arguments in favour of Grace when combating the Pelagians.

Personal experience told him that he was bound hand and foot by passion, he could not escape the clutches of his love for the mistress he had taken in his pagan days. His will seemed powerless. Then suddenly he was aware that grace had cut the bonds and freed him, so that he could go to the God he had sought. This part of his writing, therefore, seems full of the fatality of the Fall on the one side, and the gratuity of Grace on the other. In the *Confessions* themselves occurs over and over again the refrain which so angered Pelagius : 'Grant what thou dost command and command what thou wilt' (*Conf.*, x). But over and against these sentiments are the other passages defending the freedom of the will, especially against Pelagians who had said that he had jettisoned it in the endeavour to preserve grace. But typical of his replies is the one made to Hilarius[1] (*Ep.* 157): 'This freedom of the will is not removed because it is assisted, rather it is assisted precisely because it is not removed.' In the *City of God*, St. Augustine attacks Cicero for his blasphemy in denying God's foreknowledge, and although we could quote from *De gratia et libero arbitrio*, this, the more famous book, will serve. St. Augustine never worked out a system, he fashioned stones which were later to be used by St. Thomas—the latter occasionally had to refashion them more accurately to fit the mighty work he erected. St. Augustine's sources for the study of the problem of predestination, set by the opinion of Cicero, were the Sacred Scriptures and reason. From the Sacred Scriptures he is certain of God's foreknowledge, for God's providence covers all things, including the human will. From reason he is certain of the existence of the will's liberty.

In chapter ix, book V, '*Of God's foreknowledge and Man's freedom of election; against another opinion of Cicero*', he

[1] *M.L.* 33, *St. Aug.,* vol. II, col. 677.

writes, describing how Cicero led his readers into this dilemma, 'Either there must be something in the power of our wills, or else there is a foreknowledge of things to come, but the granting of the one is the subversion of the other; choosing the foreknowledge we must lose the freedom of election, and choosing the latter we must deny the former. . . . Now this learned and provident man [Cicero] of the two makes choice of freedom of election; and to confirm it, denies the foreknowledge utterly, and so instead of making men free, makes them blaspheme. But the religious mind chooses them both.' How typical of Augustine to choose both. He, Augustine, replies : 'We neither deny an order of causes wherein the will of God is all in all, neither do we call it by the name of Fate . . . for we cannot deny that the Scripture says, "God spoke once these two things : I have heard that power belongeth to God, and to thee, O Lord, mercy, for thou wilt reward every man according to his works." . . . It does not follow that nothing should be left free to our own will, because God knows the certain and ultimate order of all events. For our very wills are in that order of causes, which God knows so surely, and has in his foreknowledge; human wills being the cause of human actions, therefore he who keeps a foreknowledge of the causes of things cannot leave men's will out of that knowledge, knowing them to be the causes of their actions.'

From that there follows a vital conclusion that St. Augustine does not fail to make. Seeing that God's providence covers all, then this may be called a law, and something which men obey. 'It is in no way credible that he would leave the kingdom of men, and their bondages and freedoms loose and uncomprised in the laws of his eternal providence' (loc. cit., v, xi).

This problem occurs again and again in the writings of St. Augustine, usually in connection with the Manichean and Pelagian heresies. In one little treatise, *De Diversis Quaestionibus,* book I, q. 2, written in answer to an enquiry made by his

friend Simplicianus, bishop of Milan, successor to St. Ambrose,[1] he weighted the scales very heavily on the side of God's
foreknowledge. But in the *Retractations* he writes of that little
work as follows : '. . . *In cujus quaestionis solutione laboratum
est quidem pro libero arbitrio voluntatis humanae, sed vicit Dei
gratia*' (l.[1] 2, c. 1, *M.L.*, XXXII, col. 629). In the last
paragraph of the little work, *De Gratia et Libero Arbitrio,* it is
the pastor of souls who speaks : 'Let not the obscurity of this
question trouble you; I advise you first that you give thanks to
God for those things that you do understand' (*M.L.*, XLIV,
col. 880).

The heart of his teaching on liberty, as the heart of his teaching on law, is that he chooses both the liberty of man and the
providence of God. He had chosen to obey law, and yet he did
not think that in so doing he had lost liberty, rather had he
found it. It was the later men of the Reformation who were to
deny our freedom, and who were to lead Europe astray into
the totalitarian noose. The Providence of God, for St. Augustine, is our law, it is also our freedom. Then those other
moderns, successors of Pelagianism, who make us self-sufficient,
have led us to the brink of moral chaos; for man must depend
upon God, but he must also act freely. St. Augustine, by stressing both, laid a foundation that was to endure a thousand
years.

Love

The third element of St. Augustine's teaching to be
examined is that of love.

Love is the central theme of St. Augustine's writing, the
heart of his thinking, as Truth might be said to be the aim of
all St. Thomas's researches. What makes St. Augustine's
approach so precious is that love in all its meanings was known
by experience to him and he held this love was at root one,
if with different objects. The *Confessions* open with lovely

[1] *M.L.* 40, *opera Sancti Augustini,* vol. VI, col. 101 ff.

words '. . . *Laudare te vult homo, aliqua portio creaturae tuae.
Tu excites ut laudare te delectet, quia fecisti nos ad te, et
inquietum est cor nostrum donec requiescat in te*' (*Conf.*,
I, 1) ('Man, that little particle of thy creation, desires to
praise thee. He is roused by thee so that his delight is to praise
thee, for thou hast made us for thyself, and our heart is restless
till it finds rest in thee').

The two elements of love, Eros and Agape, are there dis-
played on the first page of the book, in which St. Augustine
describes that restless search for the object of the soul's love.
The love of God is the fulfilment of the self, that for which
each human person was made, and his fulfilment is the praise
of the Lord; it is the law of our nature, the law of praise, the
law of love.

No Christian writer has so well preserved the double aspect
of love, the desire for union and the love of giving. Many
learned articles and books have been written on the place of
each in the Christian life, chief among them that by Etienne
Gilson in his medieval studies—*L'esprit de la philosophie
médiévale*[1]—and more recently Fr. Martin ·D'Arcy, S.J., in
the *Mind and Heart of Love* (Faber & Faber, 1945).

St. Augustine has seen the distinction but not the dilemma;
the distinction is that God may be loved for one's own sake
and also for God's. He refused to substitute 'or' for 'and'. The
dilemma comes precisely by that substitution : should one love
God for oneself or for his sake ? Put so, the answer is inevitable;
but St. Augustine did not put it like that. He started from a
deeper and more embracing principle, namely, that God had a
plan, an idea for his universe, of which mortal man was a part
(portio). Being a good Platonist, he believed that the ideal purpose of life was to conform to the plan; now the plan for the
nature of man was that it should be transformed by the
divine Idea, to be filled, as it were, by God. Thus man's aim

[1] Cf. chap. xiv, deuxième édition revue, Paris, 1944.

was to seek God. That is the sublime cry of the very first page
of the *Confessions*, and many times it is re-echoed.

> '*O æterna veritas, et vera caritas, et cara*
> *æternitas, tu es Deus meus*' (Bk. 7, 10).
> (O everlasting truth and true love
>   and beloved eternity, thou art my God); or
> *O truth, truth, how the very centre*
> *of my being sigheth after thee*' (Bk. 3, 6, 10).

In the tenth book of the *Confessions* the cry, 'Grant what
thou commandest and command what thou wilt', is the cry of
the self-giving love, pure and clear. St. Augustine is there
giving himself. It is the Agape of the modern discussion,
altruistic love; it is the summit of his loving life, and is like the
prayer of St. Ignatius in the *Exercises*, 'Take, Lord, my liberty'.
It is not only giving, but also a handing over of self, not to an
abstract truth, such as the Neo-Platonic Truth seemed to be,
but to a Person, Christ-God. Here is the true love of friendship.
Christ is loved for himself, so that he should do as he wills with
Augustine.

But St. Augustine is not afraid to have the joy of that love,
the eros of the modern discussions. In the commentary on
St. John's Gospel, he waxes eloquent, almost wrathful, on the
point that people should object to divine love having joy in it,
when they would allow it for all other kinds of love. He re-
minds his reader that Virgil had said that everyone is drawn
by his own pleasure (*Ec.* 2), and therefore 'how much more
boldly ought we to say that a man is drawn to Christ when he
delights in the truth, delights in blessedness, delights in right-
eousness, delights in everlasting life, all of which Christ is?'

To prove it he quotes the Bible itself, which says that the
children of men 'shall be inebriated with the plenty of thy
house; and thou shalt make them drink of the torrent of thy
pleasure'. He knows from experience what he means, and he

affirms that any man who loves also knows what he means, but that the cold-hearted cannot. 'Give me one who loves, and he understands what I say; give me one who longs, give me one who hungers, give me one who is travelling in this wilderness, and thirsting and panting after the fountain of his eternal home; give me such a one and he will know what I mean.'

He returns to the subject a little later on, and takes the commonest of things to show that love has self in it and that that is good. He says, if a boy is drawn to a nut by loving it, 'since it is truly said that everyone is drawn by his own plea-sure; does not Christ as revealed by the Father attract us?' [1]

These passages, without the refrain from the *Confessions*, might lead one to think that St. Augustine's own love was self-regarding, but with that refrain it is seen that the two loves in him fit together : men are drawn to Christ by the delight and, having been drawn, will to give all. The sign that a man's love of God is not essentially self-regarding but Godward is the sign of obedience to God's will. St. Augustine gives the sign. 'Grant what thou commandest and command what thou wilt.'

Thus St. Augustine not only condemned the 'Civitas terreni', he evolved a Christian theory of Love and Law, and so, remotely, of society. His ideals became the ideals of the truly Christian kings and emperors, an Alfred and a Charlemagne. St. Augustine is to the social thought of the early Middle Ages what St. Benedict—as we shall see—was to become for its personal application and propagation. He defined no City of God on earth but, by his teaching on law and liberty and love, he laid the foundation upon which later men built. The signi-ficance therefore of St. Augustine in all this is that he pro-vided a reasoned application of revealed truth to society as it was dissolving and re-shaping before his eyes. [2]

[1] *Commentary of St. Augustine on the Gospel of St. John,* chap. 6,44–52.
[2] *The Political Aspect of St. Augustine's City of God,* by J. N. Figgis, 1921; specially chapters 3 and 5.

CHAPTER V

ST. BENEDICT

IF St. Antony is the father of monks in the East, St. Benedict is so for the West. While the former only experimented in the way of the hermit and the early stages of community life, St. Benedict went through the whole gamut of these experiences, and at the end summed it up in the Rule which has been a spiritual classic ever since.

St. Benedict was born *c.* A.D. 480 of well-to-do parents who lived in the town of Nursia, eighty miles from Rome. They were sufficiently rich to send him to Rome where he could pursue his studies, and to provide him with a retainer, the faithful nurse of the Gregorian stories. He fled from Rome and its vices in about A.D. 495, when he became a hermit, meeting his 'guide', as St. Antony had done his before him, in the person of one Romanus. This solitary form of life continued for three years, when his fame attracted some wayward monks to ask him to be their abbot. But while their initial intention may have been good, their perseverance was not able to stand up to the requirements of Benedict. The monks tried to poison him, and he left them, and so returned to his solitude at Subiaco. Yet again his fame attracted attention, and he seems to have instituted a form of monastic life somewhat on the lines of St. Pachomius in Egypt. There was not only one monastery, there were many—Subiaco was, as it were, a cluster of monasteries.

Only some years later at Monte Cassino did St. Benedict create the monastic family, all living under one roof, in the immediate control of one 'father of souls', the abbot. At Monte Cassino he wrote his Rule, which sums up this, the final stage of his spiritual discoveries and experiments.

In A.D. 547 he died.

Here we are chiefly concerned with St. Benedict's teaching on Obedience. Upon this matter, as in most other things, he echoes the teachers of the past, whom he willingly accepts as his masters. Obedience is useful, it is an ascetical practice, but it also is very near the ultimate aim of all religious life : the search for God. St. Benedict immeasurably enlarges the vistas thrown open by his forerunners. Nowhere in the Rule does St. Benedict give as an incentive for obeying the merely utility reason : that no community can exist as a community without some common plan. But this underlies St. Benedict's Rule far more than it does, say, St. Basil's. Nowhere do we get so minute an arrangement of the daily life as in St. Benedict's Rule. He really does lay down the law, and in this he is truly Roman. The precise time for rising is given, even if to-day we find it difficult to know what that time was; the arrangement for the Divine Office or Public Prayer of the monks is minutely laid out. The amount of food and drink is carefully regulated for lenten periods and non-lenten periods. The hours of work, the period of the siesta, the organization of the kitchen, of the serving at table, of the reading, of the receiving of guests, all are regulated with realistic care as well as spiritual insight. The reason is that St. Benedict was setting down a law, which was not a minimum below which it was rash to fall and beyond which it was laudatory to reach; but he was legislating for the absolute mean, which all his monks were expected to accept. He goes out of his way in the chapter on humility to explain that a monk was not more holy or more humble if he went beyond the Rule, but was holy only in the proportion to which he conformed himself to the normal way, that is, to the Rule as practised in the monastery. This point is a key to an understanding of his spirituality, which is based on a very acute understanding of the use of obedience in the way of asceticism and of love.

'The eighth degree of humility is that a monk do nothing except what is commended by the common rule of the monastery and the example of his superiors' (chap. 7). This degree of the Holy Rule puts obedience above austerity, and revolutionizes the technique of asceticism by advancing deeper into the citadel of man's independence than any of his predecessors in the monastic way. Obedience is the weapon of attack. That is the reason why St. Benedict is so vehement against Sarabites, 'who have not been tested as gold in the furnace by any rule. . . . Their law is their own good pleasure. Whatever they think of or choose to do, that they call holy; what they do not like, that they regard as unlawful' (chap. 1). The Gyrovagues also are castigated : 'They will not commit themselves or submit themselves to any Rule. These spend their whole lives wandering from province to province . . . ever roaming and never stable, *given up to their own wills.*'

The note is struck on the very first page of the Rule. Not terrifying lacerations of the body, not the haunting solitude of the desert, not the craving hunger or parching thirst, are to be the instruments for bringing back the soul to the law of God, so liberating it from its own concupiscences, but 'by the labour of obedience' the monk will 'return to him from whom' he has 'strayed by the sloth of disobedience' (Prologue). We owe this to God in justice.

Chap. 3 : 'Let all follow the Rule as master, nor let anyone rashly depart from it', in which he emphasizes the obedience to something outside the caprices of any man, even an abbot. Indeed, he commands the monks to have part of the Rule read aloud often (see chap. 66), which command is carried out in the twentieth century as it had been in the sixth.

He drives it home, this abandon of the *will* : 'Let no one in the monastery follow the will of his own heart' (chap. 3). One of the instruments of perfection is 'to hate one's own will' (chap. 4). He confirms this in chapter 7 by quoting Scripture :

'We are, indeed, forbidden to do our own will by Scripture :
"Turn away from thine own will" ' (Ecclus. xviii. 30), and in
chapter 5 he quotes : 'He that heareth you heareth me' (Luke
x. 16 and St. John vi. 38) : 'I came not to do my own will, but
the will of him who sent me.'

Then in the manner of the monks' obedience St. Benedict
is again direct, lucid and strong : 'not timorously, tardily, or
tepidly, nor with murmuring or the raising of objections'
(chap. 5). The monk should obey the Rule and the abbot,
'even though he himself, which God forbid, should act otherwise' (chap. 4). Not only to the abbot should obedience be
given, 'but the brethren shall also obey one another'; and
chapter 72 : 'Let them vie in paying obedience to one another.'
Why should St. Benedict dare to make this innovation?

The answer is simple in essence but complex in its ramifica-
tions. The most intimate part of man is his spirit; his body may
be lacerated, he may give all to the poor, he may say the whole
psalter every day, he may set himself upon a pillar, he may eat
next to nothing, but if this is all from self-will or vain-glory it
is nothing. Perfection cannot exist in any of these things, because the motive may be wrong. It is the motive or the will
which must be Godward. It is the will that St. Benedict attacks
by the virtue of obedience. Self-will can lead anyone to damnation, therefore he would extirpate this serpent and substitute
for it God's will. How do this? God has not, either through
Christ or the Church, laid down the routine of everyday life.
St. Benedict therefore says : put yourself under a rule and a
man, whose commands will be for you as the voice of God, and
not only as the voice of God, but be in truth his command.

It may well be asked how St. Benedict can make this jump
from the human order to the divine. In the case of the Church
the position is different, for Christ did say to his apostles, and,
so one might infer, through them to their successors : 'He who
heareth you heareth me', and 'he who heareth me, heareth

him who sent me.' But Christ made no such promise to abbots or priors or superiors of religious houses generally. What is St. Benedict's justification? As one would expect, he does not rationalize the position; quite possibly it never occurred to him to justify his doctrine at all. Obedience has plenty of other good reasons, practical and ascetic, such as increasing one's humility, without requiring this particular aspect. But St. Benedict has raised subjection to men so high in the order of virtues that one expects to find arguments and quotations, that is, grounds stated for so doing.

St. Benedict does in fact elaborate a little. 'The abbot is believed to be the representative of Christ in the monastery' (chapter 2) and chapter 5 : 'For the obedience given to superiors is given to God'; and he quotes, 'for he who heareth you heareth me' (Luke x. 16), as we have already pointed out. That St. Benedict was taking the equation, obeying superiors = obeying God, for granted, as a thing not requiring proof, may be seen from the fact that he does not bother to quote by far the best confirmatory text : 'Every soul must be submissive to its lawful superiors; authority comes from God only, and all authorities that hold sway are of his ordinance' (Rom. xiii. 1).

Could it be that in his day the sweepingness of this statement might, in view of the changing political scene, have been difficult to apply? In a stable society, such as the one within which St. Paul lived, it could be maintained that 'all authority comes from God'; but in a world of revolution and of barbarian invasions, in an age of chaos, such a statement, though true in theory, would be difficult and often misleading in application. Where was political authority in St. Benedict's day?

In chapter 7 we are given another quotation from sacred scripture to show that we should obey men : 'Thou hast set men over our heads' (Ps. lxv. 12). But this scarcely proves that these men speak with the voice of God, unless we say that as we are doing God's will by submitting to other human beings,

therefore when we obey them we obey him. Yet this passage
does not say *which* human beings, and there must be some
way of discovering this. In modern times the answer is simple.
An abbot is elected and his election is confirmed by the
Church—the mystical body of Christ—in the person of St.
Peter's successor, the Pope. Thus, to obey the abbot is to obey
the Church, and this is to obey Christ and so God. In the Rule
itself this guarantee can be found, if not for the Rule, then
for the abbot's right to rule, and even indirectly for the Rule.
In chapter 64, on the election of the abbot, it is implied
that the local bishop has controlling power; while, in the
following chapter on priors, it is assumed that the abbot is
selected by a bishop—or other abbots. He says that priors
are in certain places not appointed by the reigning abbot, but
'appointed by the same bishop, or by the same abbots, as
appoint the abbot'. He considers this bad; but from our point
of view it is evidence of the subordination of the monastic life
in St. Benedict's time to the authority of the Church.[1]

Before passing on to stability and obedience, now that we
are considering elections of abbots, it is fitting to note the kind
of government St. Benedict envisaged. This is no mere
academic study, unrelated to the main stream of history, but
of interest for the whole development of the idea of government in the West.

In the later Roman Empire, though the Emperor was
theoretically the chosen one of the people, in fact he was at the
most the chosen one of the army, of force that is, as Constantine was when he was acclaimed Emperor by his soldiers out-

[1] Abbot Justin McCann, in his book on St. Benedict, pp. 135–6
and note, says that, although from internal evidence in the Rule it is
not certain that the bishop always appointed the abbot after a choice
had been made by the community, the confirmatory evidence of St.
Gregory's letters makes one suppose that just as in the Rule the prior
was suggested to the abbot by his council and he appointed whom he
willed, so the bishop, after choice by the community, appointed whom
he thought most fitting.

side York in the year A.D. 306. If some elements of democracy
had existed in ancient times, they had vanished in the Roman
world of St. Benedict. The election of bishops and more
especially that of the popes retained some relics of this more
ancient idea of government which pertained before the imperial tyrants ruled, namely, in some form the approval of the
people. We note it in the election of St. Ambrose to the see of
Milan and in the election of St. Gregory the Great to the
chair of St. Peter by acclamation of the people, and later in
that of Charlemagne's grandfather, Arnulf, to the see of Metz.
But the power of the people in so sacred a matter was shadowy
enough even in the earliest times, and soon the Pope was
elected by ecclesiastics alone, and bishops by the cathedral
clergy, while 'Christian princes' were already busy interfering
in episcopal elections. Only the Benedictine election of the
superior by the governed survived from the ancient ideal. And
this too was much interfered with by princes. Perhaps it is true
to say that while the origin of elective practice is pagan rather
than Christian, the ideal itself is Christian, because for a Christian every human being is essentially free, and the more he
may use this power rightly the better, while pagans normally
considered many men by nature slaves. The earliest Christians,
when in practice they were faced with the problem of whom
to choose to fill the post of Apostle left vacant by the death of
the traitor Judas, did not, so we read in the Acts, proceed to a
vote for his successor, they prayed and then cast lots. Thus
Biblical example, for St. Benedict and for the Church at large,
was for trusting to the Holy Spirit to use 'chance' for his purposes. St. Benedict seems to have followed a different course,
which had an element of election or democracy, but also a new
element and one which the pagans could not have, an outside
'referee' in the person of the neighbouring bishop. St. Benedict
is forced to introduce this outsider, if for this reason only : that
he wished the one should be selected as abbot who has been

chosen by the WISER SORT, even if the wiser sort were less numerous than the supporters of a rival candidate. Who in a community will be able to persuade the rest, in such a matter, which of his brethren are the wiser sort? Only a judge from outside, supposed to be unbiased, could succeed in such a matter. In fact, all Benedictines have abandoned this first groping towards democratic election in favour of choice by majority, or two-thirds majority voting, followed by approval of the bishop and of Rome.

The monks were allowed a say in their government, at least every time an abbot had to be appointed. Yet, throughout the Rule, St. Benedict reiterates his belief in the consultative form of democracy. The monks are to be called together in council when any important matter is to be decided, each is allowed to give his opinion, but it is the superior who in the end makes the decision. In the appointment of the prior the seniors are to be called together, also on any point of minor importance their views are sought, but again it is the abbot who decides.

In one of his essays on the *History of Freedom*, it is Lord Acton's point that the ancients, the Greeks and the Romans, had no check upon their rulers, not even on democratic rulers, because the law could be changed at the will of the rulers.[1]

Consequently, the best devised safeguards could be swept away by the stroke of the pen. This could not be said of the Benedictine scheme. St. Benedict was setting out a way of living in conformity to the life of Christ our Lord, following him even in his counsels. The Holy Rule was a law which, coming from St. Benedict and very soon blessed by the head of the Church, St. Gregory, himself a disciple of St. Benedict, had a sanction, a sanctity, an absoluteness, unknown to the

[1] *History of Freedom and other Essays*, by Lord Acton (Macmillan, 1907). I. 'Freedom in Antiquity,' pp. 28–9 : 'Popular government had existed, and also mixed and federal governments, but there had been no limited government, no State the circumference of whose authority had been defined by a force external to its own.'

laws of any pagan society, except those traditional habits of behaviour in primitive and thriving civilizations, which all take for granted and whose truth no one would question. The Holy Rule stood out as an absolute and immovable thing, to which all, abbots as well as the lowliest novice, paid willing obedience.

Here was perhaps the model which would teach the young barbarian states, that were soon to spring up, the true nature of authority: a rule to be obeyed grounded upon the unshakable law of God and administered by a ruler who obtained his authority from this same supreme Being, but governing within the framework of an immutable law. Perhaps the institution we call the monastery was from this point of view the master institution of Christian Europe. Lord Acton himself, having denied to the ancient world the credit of having given the new Europe its political creed—and quite rightly, for there is little in common between the ancient totalitarian tyrannies and the complex organism of the Middle Ages which we have come to call Christendom—is forced, owing to the fact that he seems unaware of the existence and influence of the monastic unit, the abbey, spread thickly all over Europe, to attribute political freedom to the teutonic barbarians.[1]

Delisle Burns,[2] while agreeing with Lord Acton in putting aside the claim of the Roman Empire in this matter, eliminates the claim that the barbarians were any better than those they conquered. He rightly attributes political sagacity to the Church's spirit. But even he did not fully appreciate the instrumentality of Benedictinism in it all. We must agree with both in maintaining that the Church in its own constitution is not democratic. It holds delegated power; it administers a revelation. Yet it does not repudiate democracy as a political

---

[1] *History of Freedom and other Essays* (Macmillan, 1907). Cf. such phrases as 'the collective supremacy of all free men', p. 32, to describe the teutonic body-politic.

[2] Cf. *The First Europe,* by C. Delisle Burns, pp. 273-4 (Allen and Unwin, 1947).

institution, and in its own spirit the Church is democratic, that
is, defender of true liberty, firstly because it recognizes the
rights of all men to be equal before God, rights which go
deeper than the state, and secondly because it claims for itself
and for the state only limited power.

It was this conception of authority which became a visible
entity, a 'going-concern' all over Europe, and partly through
the sowing of abbeys in every corner of it.

It is sometimes maintained that the only originality that St.
Benedict showed was in the choice that he made of the precepts
of the ancients, especially of those of Cassian and St. Basil. This
power of selection—which he undoubtedly had—would, on
account of its prudence, certainly put St. Benedict in a class
by himself among monastic legislators; but there is more than
that, and it is precisely concerned with obedience and the vow
which he called stability.

Some kind of permanence in the monastic life was requisite
in order that those who had taken it up should not return to the
world. St. Basil, as we have seen, was clear on the point. We
might add this from his Longer Rule : 'He who has consecrated
himself to the Lord, and who then passes to the life of the
world, is a sacrilege. He has snatched himself from God : he
has taken back a present which he had given to him' (*Regulæ
fusius tractatæ,* interrogatio xiv). Thus we see that this permanence or stability was rather one to the life than to a place
or to a particular superior. Before St. Benedict no one expected
stability of place. This was, as Abbot Butler points out in his
Benedictine Monasticism, St. Benedict's greatest contribution
to the history of the institution. 'It is felt on all hands that the
introduction of this vow was St. Benedict's most important and
characteristic contribution to the course of Western monasticism' (p. 123).

Abbot Butler is keen to prove that the stability intended
by the Rule is one of locality : 'I accept as St. Benedict's mind

what has been called local stability in its most rigid sense, the idea of strict local stability' (p. 126). Abbot Butler overstressed the 'local' aspect. When the idea of permanence is taken in conjunction with other ideas in the Rule, for instance, the fundamental nature of St. Benedict's notion of obedience, his clear views on bad monks, his whole ascetical outlook, it is clear that the substance of 'stability' is perseverance in the monastic state.

If a monk could leave his monastery when obedience had become intolerable for him, then the whole system would break down. While St. Benedict abandoned much of the outward show of mortification, he substituted this deeper and more inward one of surrendering one's own will. If this personal will could be snatched away again at any time, then there was no complete giving, no real sacrifice. Stability therefore meant for St. Benedict obeying a superior or his successors until death.

In St. Benedict's day this special vow was patently needed. Even in the Code of Justinian we find the echo of the same problem. It legislates against wandering monks. In the Rule itself the sternest condemnations are reserved for 'the third kind of monks . . . that detestable one of the Sarabites, who, not having been tested, as gold in the furnace, by any rule or by the lessons of experience, are as soft and as yielding as lead. . . . They live in two or threes or even singly, without a shepherd . . . their *law is their own good pleasure*'. Or later : 'The Gyrovagues . . . these spend their whole lives wandering from province to province . . . never stable, *given to their own wills* . . . of the wretched life of all these folk it is better to be silent than to speak' (chap. 1).

The above throws light on the incident in the life of St. Benedict when he attempted to govern some unruly monks (cf. Bk. 2 of the *Dialogues of St. Gregory*). It is a strange story : Benedict was still in his twenties, he had been a hermit three years, and he was called by this group of monks to be their abbot. What did they expect of him? Perhaps all they wanted was little more than the prestige of having him about the place. But they soon found their error; he wanted to reform them, or make them keep a rule. Their second decision was as unexpected as their first: they decided that the simplest way out of the difficult situation into which they had led themselves was to poison the holy man. A miracle saved St. Benedict.

St. Benedict had learnt his lesson, and from subsequent events it seems to have been this, that no ascetical life is of avail for spiritual advancement without obedience. For instance, Lenten penance must be submitted to the abbot. Withdrawal from the world is only the first step on the road; the second must be an approach to God by obedience (see the first degrees of humility). He, a man of extreme austerity, saw through the snares of that way, and consciously abandoned it for the safer and more penetrating one of sacrifice of the inward will. Those bad monks had perhaps done all the rest: penance, fasting, vigils and prayers; but this last they would not do. It was the pearl of great price, and they were not ready to sell all to obtain it.

In his later life, surely, St. Benedict is working on a system of asceticism based partly on that fearful experience—they had been disobedient, so his monks were to be, before all else, obedient.

If a monk has the right, at will, to quit his monastery and choose another superior, he is still seeking his own will, even though he has submitted to another, because he only hopes that the new superior will agree with him. It is not so much leaving the place which constitutes instability, but the leaving a superior. Stability, as it were, blocks up the holes by which the fox, self-will, might escape.

Enough has been said to show that in the Rule of St. Benedict obedience, supported by its strong ally stability, is the essence of his ascetic teaching. But by that very fact of con-

centrating upon the will, he turns asceticism into love, for the
will is the human instrument of love. Obedience is not only
ascetical, but an act of love. This we shall proceed to show is
St. Benedict's own idea.

In the Prologue he states what the aim is : 'We shall run
with unspeakable sweetness of love in the way of God's commandments.' There, placed side by side, are the two keys : love
and God's commandments. The method for attaining this end
is also stated in the Prologue.

'By the labour of obedience thou mayest return to him from
whom thou hast strayed by the sloth of disobedience.'

He links the Rule with God's will : 'To fulfil God's commandments daily in our own deeds' (chap. 4). While obedience
to superiors without delay 'becometh those who hold nothing
dearer to them than Christ . . . receive (the command) as a
divine command (chap. 5). The third degree of humility is 'that
a man for the *love of God* subject himself to his superior in all
obedience, imitating the Lord, of whom the Apostle says : 'He
was made obedient even unto death' (Phil. ii. 8) (chap. 7). He
quotes Christ's own words, 'He that heareth you heareth me'
(Luke x. 16), and remarks in the same chapter 5 : 'Obedience
given to superiors is given to God.' St. Benedict, then, had no
doubts about the matter.

What precisely has St. Benedict done here? Has he substituted for the love of God himself a love for God's will as mani-
fested in the Rule? No, emphatically not; he has, however,
extended the operation of our love over a wider area of our
life than was normally envisaged perhaps by the Fathers of
the Desert. For them love for God meant the love in prayer :
they went to the desert in search of that quiet and abstraction
from earthly things in order to find God himself in their
souls. St. Benedict did the same; he and his monks seek God
in himself. But over the everyday activities of a monk he now
extends the mantle of love, for he has explained that the rule

and the voice of the superior are indirectly the voice of God. Therefore they can be obeyed from love.

St. Benedict therefore may be said to have added to the Eastern ideal of contemplative love—which he never abandons —the love in obedience, or active love, and thus set his monks upon a trail of practical activity for the benefit of the Church and of all mankind of which he little dreamed.

While the Rule became an instrument of charity towards God, it did not cease to be also the safeguard against natural backsliding and the instrument of asceticism preferred before all others. The whole spirit of St. Benedict in this matter is summed up in his concluding words on humility :

'When all these degrees of humility have been climbed, the monk will presently come to that perfect love of God which casteth out all fear, whereby he will begin *to observe precepts* which formerly he did not observe without fear, no longer with the fear of hell, but *for love of Christ*' (chap. 7).

Obedience in the eyes of St. Benedict is no longer only a means of freeing oneself from the slavery of self-will in order that one may give oneself to God; it is part of that very giving of oneself to God. Giving is love. That is why he can say, 'Let him (the monk) obey out of love' (chap. 68).

This point of love is borne out by the special character of the superior. The superior is called abbot, a word derived from abba, meaning father. The monk obeys his abbot as a son his father.

It is unnecessary to labour the point that everywhere in the Rule the abbot is considered as the *paterfamilias,* the monks as brothers. Now, obedience to a father is first of all a loving obedience—we shall go into the idea of understanding obedience later. It should be without that element of fear, which would have been so common in the obedience at the time of St. Benedict, in that typical relationship of master and slave. Just as God is our true father, from whom all fatherhood is

named, so the abbot derives all his authority from God, the
Father of all. Indeed, it would be to miss the whole point of
monastic obedience to imagine that obedience when given to
the superior was given to any other than God himself, an
obedience of love given by a son to his heavenly Father.

But a monk not only obeys the command of the superior, he
obeys the written rule. The holy Rule, or any Rule for Religious,[1] is not some invention of a holy man, such as that of a
Buddhist monk; the people trust the holy man to lead them to
God. The Rule is much more than that; it is a codifying of the
teaching of Christ for a particular set of circumstances. It,
however, not only includes the application of the commands of
Christ, but also his counsels. Christ said, pray; St. Benedict lays
down periods for so doing. Christ said, be the servant of all;
St. Benedict says obey the abbot, the lesser superiors, one's
fellow monks. There is nothing new there, it is only an application of Christ's injunction to a particular way of life. We
are following therefore the Rule of Christ. A sure way of
proving our love of Christ and his teaching is to put his teaching into practice.

We have examined the Rule as a law and as an opportunity
for love; there remains liberty.

A willing obedience is a free one, for what we do willingly
is given freely. There we find liberty. This is reinforced by the
relationship that St. Benedict wishes to see between the monks
and the abbot. The latter is the father, the former sons and
brothers one with each other. A father's commands are not
irrational; there is a sense of understanding between a father
and a son. Benedictine obedience is not a military business, it
is not at its best a blind obedience, but an understanding one,
such as a son would give to his father. Understanding implies

---

[1] 'Religious' is a term used for any monk, nun or friar who submits
to a Rule approved of by the Church, in the person of its Head the Pope,
living under the three vows, poverty, chastity and obedience.

reasonableness and the command is reasonable if it is understood. It is the reasonableness of commands which makes them most highly free. The will naturally obeys what is rational to do. That we should obey at all is a reasonable thing : it is commanded by Jesus, we must be servants of all, and as he is the Truth, that is most reasonable. The Rule is a reasonable scheme of life; the superior's commands are within the framework of that ordered scheme.

Liberty has never been unreasoned action, but the capacity to follow what is reasonable to do. A monk sees that it is reasonable to obey both on natural and supernatural grounds. By obeying he is free.

But it would have surprised St. Benedict, one ventures to think, to find that he was supposed to be defending liberty. He was attacking licence; his was a reaction against the excess of sin and vice, against lawlessness in all its forms, a return to obedience to God. Therefore the discussion of liberty in relation to obedience will come later, specially when examining St. Thomas and later the teaching of Leo XIII. And yet, as we saw, when examining his teaching from the point of view of Law or the Rule as such, by implication St. Benedict was laying the foundation of true liberty, which we call ordered liberty. The Rule maps out the skeleton of the Christian life within which the individual is free. Just as the ruler cannot therefore act arbitrarily, so also is the subject freed from the fear that he might; and, provided that the law is in accordance with the nature of man, then each is free to follow the way to his perfection. St. Benedict was not liberating man from the law of God, but from the slavery of sin. Once that liberation had been more or less achieved in society—i.e. when society was based upon Christ-given principles, even if not always obeyed—then the sense of liberation was tremendous; and we see the immense aliveness of the High Middle Ages in every branch of art and of learning. But the early monks had to do the laborious work of helping to restore order out of chaos; only later could the relief of freedom from the thrall of sin be really appreciated.

The outward expression of all this doctrine on obedience, law and love is to be found in the social prayer of the Church, particularly of the monastic choirs; but this we shall deal with in discussing its mighty growth in the Cluniac revival.

We shall now proceed to show how gradually, very gradually, this institution—the Benedictine abbey—and its master-ideas of loving obedience to the abbot and the Rule, spread throughout Western Europe. We must always remember that, owing to the belief that men were 'all one in Christ', this obedience was considered to be given to Christ, and it is still so considered in the Church.

CHAPTER VI

THE DIFFUSION OF THE RULE

It is frequently said that the Benedictines were the civilizers of that post-Roman Europe which had been overrun by the barbarians; and this assertion is so rarely explained that it will not be out of place, in a book whose thesis is to show how the spirit of Benedictine Obedience was certainly one of the formative influences in that process, to give a short survey of the facts, taken from approved sources (see note at the end of the chapter).

The Benedictine centuries are usually said to be the eighth to the eleventh inclusive. But in order to make the story intelligible, we must pick up the threads at the time of St. Benedict's death in A.D. 547.

This survey is undertaken, not as an end in itself nor with the aim of giving any new information, but to make manifest, by collecting the outstanding data together, the amazing spread throughout Europe of the ideas expressed in the last chapter, namely, the Benedictine and Christian ideas of law, liberty and love. These monk-missioners and bishops were to apply to stricken Europe the principles which had built their monasteries and which may be summed up in the verse of the psalm, *'Nisi Dominus aedificaverit Domum, in vanum laboraverunt qui aedificant eam'*.

At St. Benedict's death his rule, as far as we know, was in use only in those monasteries which he himself had founded: the cluster of monasteries at Subiaco, that of Monte Cassino and the one at Terracina.

The generations of men who lived under the misrule of the later Roman emperors and their minions had no love for their rulers, since the latter were so often ruling, not for the benefit of the ruled, but for their own advantage. When the barbarians came marching into the Empire, the slaves, who had been expected to do the fighting and the dying in defence of the Old Order, went over to the enemy. The best-known example of this is on the occasion that the host of Alaric arrived before the city of Rome in 410. The slaves, instead of defending Rome from the invading horde, joined it, flocking from the city to return as conquerors and to share in the loot.

When a civilization has within it such a split between the rulers and the ruled that those who lead are no longer loved by those who are led, that civilization has broken down. This state of affairs existed in the Roman Empire when St. Benedict withdrew into the wilderness. The obedience given by the common man was no longer a loving obedience, for he saw nothing lovable in the decrepit thing incapable of command.

A new love was needed to rouse that common man from the torpor of inaction. It was kindled by the sight of great saints attending to the needs of the poor. St. Gregory stands out as an example of that type in a superlative degree. He was a patrician, he was the Prefect of the City of Rome; but he saw that the civil service had not the secret of salvation. He withdrew to find God first; he became a monk in the monastery he himself founded at his ancestral home on the Cœlian Hill. Against his will he was dragged from his retreat, first to be a legate of the Pope at the court of Constantinople, then to be elevated by the spontaneous love of all the populace and clergy, who had witnessed his practical good works to the poor of the city as seventh Deacon, to be Head of the Church in the Chair of Peter itself. The rest of his life, one of chronic ill health, was devoted to rebuilding what he could of civilized life in the West.

By the action of such men as St. Gregory, the love lost to the Empire was transferred to the Church, and more particularly to the centre thereof, the Papacy. With love went obedience, and with obedience the possibility of rebuilding a shattered society, for no society can survive without co-operation nourished by esteem and gratitude.

An analogy perhaps is not out of place. In our own days we have seen the breakdown of that loving obedience of the governed for their rulers. In the epoch of the Iron Law of Wages the proletariat had been ground down by unbelievable hardship. Into their hearts they had got a feeling of rancour against the governing class. They were not wrong to condemn their rulers, even if they were wrong to nurture rancour. That rancour persists; nothing on earth will give back that link of love between the two sides, the leaders and those who refuse to be led. What is required is a change of heart in both; but the spirit of religion has very largely vanished from the minds of rich and poor alike, so that we see two armies in array, the armies of the capitalists and those of the proletariat. The outcome of that struggle will be the same as that which ended the Roman Empire; neither side can triumph, for it is a question merely of hate. The only victor in the end will be he who, like St. Gregory, carries the wounded man as it were in his arms, nurses him, feeds him, and by belief in and love of God gives Europe hope once more.

The activity of this great shepherd of the West was to be exerted also through the spread, at his instigation, of the Rule which he as a monk had observed. He himself had gained insight into obedience through this Rule, and he was convinced that if he could, as it were, shower sparks of its torch, reviving flames of loving obedience and activity through the West, he would revive Christendom. And he did.

It is now generally agreed that, when St. Gregory the Great (540–604) turned his patrician palace into a monastery on the Cœlian Hill in 573, he based its life on the Rule of St. Benedict. It would indeed be surprising if the Pope, who so loudly praised the Rule, should not, when he became a monk, follow it himself. Almost certainly, then, the first conquest made by the greatest of monks was the greatest of the popes, St. Gregory.

St. Gregory's enthusiasm for the Rule did not stop there. He wrote letters on the subject; he wrote a life of his Father in God, which forms the second book of the *Dialogues,* and it became one of the favourite pieces of spiritual reading throughout the Middle Ages. The details of that life he learnt from the lips of trustworthy witnesses, chiefly, no doubt, from monks of the abbey of Monte Cassino, now refugees in a monastery by the Lateran. Gregory also founded six monasteries upon his family estate in Sicily.

But his greatest contribution to the spread of the Holy Rule was his sending the band of forty monks, headed by St. Augustine, to England in 596 to convert its barbarian conquerors, the Anglo-Saxons. They passed through Gaul, and their exploits would be avidly related from abbey to abbey. Besides, here was the model Benedictine action upon Europe's life at a most critical moment. In England, the influence of the Catholic Church was exerted almost entirely by monks, so that it may be called the type. If any country may be said to owe its religion to the Benedictines, it is England. The English sees were set up by St. Augustine, so that to this day in the Anglican Church the metropolitan sees of Canterbury and York rank above all others. St. Augustine founded the first and his fellow monk St. Paulinus the second. From these two centres and from many others the missionaries spread. Monasteries sprang up everywhere, and often they became episcopal sees : Winchester, Durham, Rochester, Norwich, Coventry, Ely, Peterborough, Gloucester, Worcester, Bath and Chester, to mention those kept to-day in perpetual remembrance by the English Benedictine Congregation.

When the question became acute between the Celtic and Saxon Christians as to the right of Rome to lay down disciplinary laws—it was no question of divergence of doctrine—

the Benedictines, who were trained in discipline, became the strong upholders of Rome. It is to be noticed that, at the time of the crisis, the monks were not Roman born but English. True, St. Wilfrid did go to Rome and lived in the very monastery of St. Gregory's for a time. Yet he had been educated by the Celtic monks in their most famous monastery of Lindisfarne. His biographer tells us that he specially brought back from Rome a copy of the Rule of St. Benedict; this he brought into use at his own monastery of Ripon.

Essentially the dispute was concerned with whether the English Church was to be autonomous in discipline or not. It would be an error to think that previously there had been any conscious schism in the Celtic or British Church. The Celts of Wales, Ireland and Scotland had become isolated from the rest of Christendom when the barbarians broke through the Roman defences and so divided the Celtic Church from the Church of Rome. During that interval of isolation, the sixth century, they lagged behind in the reforms concerning the dating of Easter, and on some other more trivial matters. But it never entered their heads that they were not members of the one, visible, Catholic, Apostolic Church. It was only in the time of St. Augustine and St. Wilfrid that the matter of Easter was brought to a head, and it naturally disturbed the peace of their minds.

The decisive moment came when King Oswy convened a council at Whitby. After much talk on both sides, he cut it short by quoting the words of Jesus to St. Peter, 'Thou art Peter and upon this rock I will build my Church'. He asked whether Christ had ever said anything like that to St. Columba —the patriarch of the Celtic Church in Scotland—as he had said it to St. Peter and his successors in Rome, the popes. The answer could only be, no. That said, the King for his part decided in favour of Rome, and all, save a small section, did likewise (A.D. 664).

Those are the bald facts to be found in any textbook. The facts are very well known, but the significance has often been ignored. Besides linking the English Church once again with the discipline of Rome, the struggle was part of a vast one between the forces of disintegration and those of order. St. Wilfrid fought for order within the Church at the Council of Whitby, and that victory was to have immense effect in the later years when missionaries from England were to roam the Continent and establish new nations in Christ. Wilfrid also fought valiantly for order between the civil power and the ecclesiastical, between king and bishop, just as Pope Martin was doing in Rome against the contemporary emperor. St. Wilfrid twice went to Rome to defend the rights of the Church, once against King Oswy who had intruded another bishop in his place, and a second time to defend the right of the bishop against the arbitrary action of another bishop, on this occasion the indefensible action of St. Theodore. In vindicating his own rights St. Wilfrid was vindicating the rights of the Church at large.

Thus in the struggles of St. Wilfrid we have summed up all the later struggles that the Church had during the Middle Ages. He defended the right of Rome in her office of Head of the Church in matters of discipline; he defended the Church against intrusion into her affairs by the secular power; he defended the bishop in his position against the intrusion of another bishop who had no jurisdiction.

Though the Danes came to destroy most of the Saxon Church, more especially that Northumbrian Church with its centres of learning at Wearmouth and Jarrow, ever memorable for the names of Bede the Venerable, the schoolmaster of his age, and for that of St. Benet Biscop, second only to St. Wilfrid in importance as the introducer of Roman ways, yet the spirit of that Church survived, so that the later Saxon, Norman and Angevin England still continued to be largely Benedictine in

ecclesiastical government. Just as the early Saxon kings had
had monks as their advisers, so did the later Saxon ones and
the Normans. A St. Paulinus stood by King Edwin of North-
umbria, a St. Dunstan by Edgar and a St. Anselm by King
William.

(The missionary effort under St. Boniface and his companions will have to wait until the telling of the story of the
Frankish Church.)

To sum up in the words of the acknowledged master in this
subject: 'Under Edgar and Dunstan the revived monasticism
had been the very heart and soul of the rebirth of the country;
from the monasteries came the rulers of the Church for two
generations, and the same men were the controlling influence
in the social and political life of their times . . . they were
indeed especially between 950–1000 the very core and kernel
of the nation' (*The Monastic Order in England,* vol. I, p. 680,
by Professor David Knowles, 1940, C.U.P.).

In those formative years of English history, the two Saxon
epochs, divided by the Danish incursions, from 597—when St.
Augustine landed—to 840 when the Danish attacks were at
their most furious (the Vikings sacked London that year) and
from 878, when the treaty of Wedmore was signed, to the
death of St. Dunstan in 988, the Benedictine influence was
paramount: the schools were monastic schools, the scholars
were monks, their chief, St. Bede; the ministers of the kings
were monks; the hierarchy was made up of such famous monks
as: Augustine, Mellitus and Paulinus, Wilfrid and Wili-
brord, Aldhelm of Malmesbury, and later Dunstan, Wulstan
and Oswald. All these were also saints. The purveyors of the
Roman material civilization were monks. It is scarcely surprising that to this day the English love both liberty and law,
and see nothing incompatible in these two concepts.

In Spain, whose monastic history is obscure, the early growth
of medieval European culture was arrested and then crushed

by the invasions of the Moors in A.D. 711 and the following centuries. This kept the country in turmoil and revolt; at first with the invaders having it all their own way, but after 1212 —to take a symbolic date—with the victory of Navas de Tolosa, the Christian kingdoms took the offensive. But until the arrival of the Cluniac monks in Castile (A.D. 1033), apart from the earlier monasticism of St. Leander and St. Isidore his brother and many others, there is perforce a gap of hundreds of years.

It is sometimes maintained that the Benedictine influence in the Visigothic period in Spain was nil. Yet that would be a very wrong impression to give. The Spanish monks may not have been Benedictines, but the Rule of St. Benedict was not unknown to them. St. Isidore of Seville is a case in point. He was born in 560 at Cartagena, and like his brother Leander he became a monk in Seville. We know little of the rules for monks in vogue in Spain at this time, but St. Isidore was himself to write a 'Regula de los monjes', full of that moderation and prudence so characteristic of St. Benedict's. It is generally supposed that he was aware of the latter's Rule, though it is difficult to discover the relationship between the two rules. But we know that St. Isidore had an almost unbounded admiration for St. Gregory, writing, for instance, that he was to Europe what St. Augustine had been for Africa. Anyone with such a profound admiration for St. Gregory could scarcely fail to note his love of the Holy Rule.[1]

While we cannot, then, call St. Isidore a Benedictine, we may claim that he was imbued with the spirit of the Patriarch of Western monachism and with the spirit of that greatest of St. Benedict's sons, St. Gregory. It was he who inspired the early Councils of Toledo, organizing the faith, the discipline

---

[1] St. Fructuosus (seventh century) in North Spain quotes from the Rule of St. Benedict but without mentioning his name. By the ninth century both the Rule and St. Benedict were well known in Spain.

and liturgy within the Church in Spain through its decrees. The key-note of his life was Order. If the acts of the Councils of Toledo may be said to be the work of any one man, that man is St. Isidore, the monk of Seville. And all are agreed that those Councils were the formative instrument in the creation of the first Christian culture in the Iberian peninsula.

The great Spanish historian, Rafael Altamira, however, would put us on our guard against thinking that the influence of the Church at this time was paramount. The King alone could initiate legislation, and he could veto any decision taken by the assembly. However, we must not forget that the king was elected by the bishops and nobles, his was no hereditary post; further, he was anointed and crowned by the bishop— a fact which gave power to the Church if it also gave moral authority to the king. So perhaps we may say that honours were evenly divided between the king and the Church, with the nobles coming a poor third; and when the Church was led by a St. Isidore, the power of the Church could be almost supreme.

France's polity differed essentially from that of England and Spain, chiefly because the old Roman framework of city bishops had survived the invasions of barbarians. The ecclesiastical atmosphere, though tinged with monachism, was not in itself monastic. This differed from England where no bishop survived the inrush of the Anglo-Saxons, and the Benedictine missionaries, as we have seen, became local pastors, bishops, schoolmasters, everything to the new Anglo-Saxon Church.

Thus Clovis was baptized by St. Remi, archbishop of Rheims, and not a monk; and there was a spirit of independence in those early Frankish kings which soon reduced the Church to something little short of anarchy; a state against which St. Columbanus notably fought, but which was only finally brought to order by St. Boniface, the English monk, whose activities received their symbolic completion when he crowned and anointed Pepin as king in 752 at Soissons.

To return to the beginnings. Gaul already had its quota of monasteries, long before the passage of St. Augustine on his way to England in A.D. 596. There was the ancient tradition at Tours, where St. Martin had established something akin to the Egyptian monachism—tradition has it that St. Patrick was trained at Tours, which fact might explain the very Egyptian spirit of Irish monasticism. To the south lay the famous island monastery of Lerins, nursery of saints and school for bishops, while at Marseilles was the monastery of Cassian. All these traditions were Eastern in spirit.

But strongest of all was to be the tradition of St. Columbanus in the north. He was an Irish monk who had left his monastery of Bangor, that nursery of apostles, in about 590 to evangelize the Burgundian Franks in the lands we would now call north-eastern France and western Germany. His travels did not end until he reached Bobbio in northern Italy, having gone via St. Gall in Switzerland, founding abbeys in his path. The greatest of these was Luxeuil in the mountains of the Vosges. He wrote a rule for his monks; and like so many of the early monastic rules, it was more a collection of ascetic lore than a scheme for the daily round. It is doubtful whether we have the original text of this rule, but we know that it was of extreme physical severity. His monks were to eat only before retiring to bed; often they were expected to recite the whole psalter in one night. Every failure of discipline had a penalty attached: should a monk not make the sign of the cross over his food, six stripes; should he fail to sign himself when blessed, twelve stripes; should he answer back, fifty stripes. (Cf. Mabillon, *Annales,* liber I, cap. viii.) Obedience was a mortification and an occasion for practising patience. Death to self was the great lesson of St. Columbanus, the essential practice of monks.

It is hard to-day to realize the strange fascination that both this almost farouche monk and his violent ascetical doctrine had for men of the seventh century. Yet monasteries clamoured to have his rule, and men flocked to those monasteries. A mere list of the names is alone impressive : Coutanse and Jouarre, Rebais St. Gall and Solignac, Jumièges and Fontenelle, the famous Corbie, Sithiu Grandval and Remiremont, Hautvilliers, Montiérender, Leuconaus. Besides these for men there were others, comparable to that of Whitby, for men and women, and others again for nuns only. The general conclusion to draw is that in the middle of the seventh century the Rule of St. Columbanus seemed to have come to stay. But that was not to be.

In the mountain monastery of Luxeuil, which one might almost call the mother house, though it was not the first, Agrestius, a lawyer turned monk, raised the standard of moderation, not, it is true, during the rule of St. Columbanus himself, but certainly in that of his immediate successor, St. Eustace. The latter, loyal to his master, resisted, but his successor, Waldebert (629–670), perhaps more wise if less loyal, seeing the reasonableness of Agrestius's ideas, tempered the austerity of the Columban spirit with the moderation of the Rule of St. Benedict.

Very soon, not only Luxeuil but many other abbeys of this 'family' adopted a 'Rule of St. Benedict according to the manner of Luxeuil'. The manuscripts which contain the two rules in one volume are very early. Dom Mabillon, in the chapter referred to above, says that these were, however, later than St. Columbanus himself, and that he could not have been aware of the Benedictine Rule when writing his own. Yet the dates of the two founders do not make this impossible (St. Benedict died *c.* 547 and St. Columbanus 615) and, after all, St. Augustine had passed through France in 596. It remains true, however, that St. Columbanus had behind him the Irish tradition, itself perhaps derived from Gaul, and that in its turn from Egypt; consequently one might expect his spirit to be congenial to the natives at least for a time.

Once Luxeuil had fallen under the spell of St. Benedict, the rest soon fell into step, not excluding Fontenelle and the abbey of Bobbio itself, which was the final resting-place of St. Columbanus. It was part of this enthusiasm for Benedictinism which sent some monks from Fleury-sur-Loire to bring to France the precious relics of the Patriarch from his abandoned monastery of Monte Cassino. This was accomplished in A.D. 673.

By the end of the seventh century the monasteries of Gaul are Benedictine in spirit. St. Leger, martyred bishop of Autun, for instance, prescribed in his diocesan councils, held between the years 663–680, that the abbeys within his jurisdiction should observe the Rule of St. Benedict (*Hist. de l'Eglise*,[1] vol. V, pp. 506–42). An edict of Pepin, commanding all monasteries within his domain to follow the Rule of St. Benedict, may be said to be the final act of the preliminary stage in the spread of the Holy Rule. It thus became the official and all-embracing rule. If one wanted to be a monk, then one became a Benedictine.

We now return to the English scene, which could not have been understood until a preliminary excursion had been made into Gaul, one future field of the English Benedictine activity. The peoples north and east of the Rhine were to receive their faith from the spiritual descendants of St. Augustine of Canterbury. The Irish had passed over the lands some years before, notably St. Columbanus and St. Gall, but only to move on. The English went to stay.

St. Wilfrid, in his various peregrinations to Rome, became aware of the apostolic work still to be done, and, with characteristic energy, began to evangelize the Frisians who lived in

[1] For full title, see p. 116.

that part of the Low Countries we call Holland. St. Willibrord, who had been a monk in St. Wilfrid's own abbey of Ripon, was fired by a like enthusiasm, and with eleven companions set off from his Irish monastery, the abbey of Rathmelsigi. He made the characteristic English gesture of going to Rome for authorization. He was to be the real founder of Dutch Catholicism, setting up the primatial see of Utrecht. The tomb of this great man may still be seen in the magnificent romanesque and monastic church of Echtenach,[1] in a secluded valley of Luxemburg. He died in 739.

But the greatest of the English monk-missionaries, and the one rightly called the apostle of Germany, is St. Boniface of Crediton in Devonshire. He was born *c.* 680, and as a young man he became a monk, and after some years teaching in a monastic school, he persuaded his superiors to allow him to follow the footsteps of SS. Wilfrid and Willibrord, and go to convert the pagans of Frisia. His first sally occurred in 716, but he had to return owing to unfavourable political conditions. He then went to Rome in 718. There Gregory II gave him the commission to evangelize the Germans, but before doing so he returned to Frisia, where under his predecessor he preached successfully for three years (719–722). Then he turned south again and had remarkable success in Hesse and Thuringia, so much so that he sent word to the Pope. The latter recalled him to Rome and consecrated him bishop. Boniface took a special vow of obedience to the Holy See. In all this he stands out as typical of the Benedictine tradition. Now his energies knew no bounds; he founded monasteries and dioceses, and called upon England to send him more monks and nuns to help him in his task. The most famous see is that of Mainz, of which he became archbishop; the most famous monastery was Fulda, where finally he was to be buried.

[1] It was very gravely damaged in the War of 1939–45.

In 741 Pope Zachary made him legate and gave him the commission to reform the Frankish Church which had sunk into almost unbelievable chaos under the late Merovingians. His work here was crowned with success, when in 747 a synod of Frankish bishops sent a written act of submission to the Holy See. At this date, therefore, chiefly through the gigantic energy of this great man, the whole of the Western mainland of Europe excluding the Scandinavian countries and Spain— already swamped by the Mohammedans—were in loving union with the Mother of Churches, Rome, one in doctrine, one in discipline, one in worship.

There is one other deed of St. Boniface which is worthy of special mention.[1] It is generally admitted that he crowned Pepin III king of the Franks, though some are found to deny that he actually performed the ceremony. The important thing is that he was the instigator. Pepin had wanted the Pope to do so, but Pope Stephen had deputed his faithful Boniface. This great event in a sense set a seal of divine approval upon the new dynasty of the Carlovingians.

The desire of Pepin to have his authority recognized by the Papacy rather than by the Byzantine, distant, emperor, and also the performance of the act by the greatest monk of the day, St. Boniface, are of great symbolical and doctrinal significance. This desire linked kingship and ruling, in the person of the most powerful monarch of the West, with the Church; it turned power into moral authority, so that no matter how often men might be led to snatch away this power, all knew and admitted that unless this same power were consecrated by the Church, it was merely an usurpation. The anointing of the king by the bishop, of course, represented in the eyes of all the fact that the new ruler had God on his side, that the ruler's authority came from God. We have travelled a long way in this

---

[1] *The Lives of the Popes in the Early Middle Ages,* by Horace K. Mann, vol. I, pt. 2, p. 271; and *Histoire de l'Eglise,* vol. V, p. 364.

act of the year 752 from the despairing cry of St. Augustine
of Hippo concerning the origin of all worldly kingdoms, which
he declared was theft.

The origins of the coronation ceremony, a rite which included anointing as well as the placing of the crown on the
head of the new king, is obscure; but it is generally agreed that
the Gallic rite, as used by St. Boniface when he anointed Pepin
in 752, was derived, as one would expect, from the country of
his own origin, England. The coronation ceremony, as found
in the Egbert Pontifical (Egbert was archbishop of York in the
early eighth century), survives in one precious manuscript preserved in the *Bibliothèque nationale* of Paris. The MS. itself
dates from the tenth century, but Dom Cabrol, in the *Dictionnaire d'archéologie chrétienne et de liturgie,* in an article on
the point is quite certain, in view of the thoroughly eighth-
century nature of the contents, the purity of the Roman liturgy,
the recurrence of early Northumbrian saints' names, that we
have here perhaps the most precious relic of liturgical interest
of the Saxon Northumbrian Church of the eighth century.
Archbishop Egbert was a friend of Alcuin and of St. Boniface.
It is not improbable therefore that he sent a copy of his pontifical to St. Boniface for the very purpose of the ceremony of
Pepin's coronation. Whatever our view on that particular point,
it is agreed that this tradition of the anointing of kings and the
very ceremonial used throughout the Middle Ages are derived
from the English originals.

The importance of this act can scarcely be exaggerated in
considering the re-establishment of law and order, of obedience,
after the Roman Order had vanished in the blood and flames
of the barbarian invasions. The only ground for the authority
of all these petty kings and conquerors was their strong arm,
and that was not enough. They found, in the alliance with the
Church, a better ground than that. Doubtless many a king
failed to fulfil his bond and acted against Christian law. If he

did so, all recognized the act as an infringement of the rights of God and of his subjects. The basic principle remained firm, and that is all we can expect in an imperfect world, but at least we should expect that.

Once again, however, the work so laboriously done was undone. The flourishing condition of things under Pepin did not continue. Many monasteries became canonries, many were deserted, religion languished. One of the chief causes of this lamentable state was that recurring nuisance : the descendants of kings and nobles, who founded an abbey, wanting to impose their nominee upon the monks at election time. Often the intruder was unworthy and discipline soon crumbled.

The accession of Charlemagne (*regnabat* 768–814) did much to restore order, but we must not exaggerate. Charlemagne too made use of monasteries as presents for his friends, used their wealth for his many wars, used the monks to help him create what he hoped would be a Christian culture. We notice the reaction of the monks, against being 'used' for social ends, in the restrictive legislation of the reforming St. Benedict of Aniane, who forbade his monks to teach !

The name associated with that of Charlemagne in the noble endeavour to restore learning to the Western world is that of Alcuin of York, he also a monk. Alcuin, disciple of St. Bede, became during this brief interlude of learning—whose extent and depth we should be unwise to exaggerate—the minister of education to Charlemagne; he became the trusted adviser on every matter, a veritable encyclopædia of learning. It was he who re-established the system of teaching in schools based on the divisions of Cassiodorus, the trivium, or first three stages, and the quadrivium, or later four stages. He was the schoolmaster *par excellence* of the Franks.

All this, or nearly all, was swept away by the terrible Age of Iron which was to follow; but the fragrant memory of learning remained to give courage to later generations to imitate and excel that first Christian renaissance.

Just as the Franks were helped by the English monks, so were the Danes and Scandinavian peoples helped now by the Franks. St. Anschar was to Denmark and Sweden what St. Boniface had been to the Franks. Yet, in spite of his devoted labours, St. Anschar failed to get a firm foothold upon the Scandinavian peninsula. His apostolic zeal bore fruit after his death. But it is Hungary which shows perhaps almost as well as England the power of the Benedictine impetus and its particular spirit.

In Hungary, as in England, success was complete. The Magyars were late comers into the plains of Europe. They conquered the lower Danubian plain of Pannonia only in A.D. 906 —the traditional date for the decisive victory of Arpad over his opponents. Strategically they were placed between the Germans on the north and the Byzantine empire to the south. Only when they had been severely beaten at the battle of Lechfeld in 955 did they begin to consider conversion. It seems that Duke Geza, who sent to Otto II in 973 for missionaries, did so partly from political motives. But his successor was of a different stamp; we mean St. Stephen, king and saint, who had married a Catholic Bavarian princess. He, who has been called 'one of the great constructive statesmen of history' (*Encyclopædia Britannica*, 11th ed., vol. XIII, col. 902), appealed to the West for missionaries.

Already St. Adalbert of Prague and St. Wulfgang of Einsiedeln had ventured there in 971; but now monks from many monasteries, from France and from the Low Countries, flocked to Hungary to fill the monasteries the king was constructing. The chief of these was Pannonhalma, begun under Duke Geza in 966. Anastasius was its first abbot, but was soon raised to the dignity of Primate of Hungary; Astric, the abbot of another great monastery, Pecsvarad, was sent to Rome by Duke Stephen to ask for the title of king and for a crown. It was fitting that in this typical and symbolic act the Pope should be a Benedictine, Sylvester II.

To quote the words of Dom Philibert Schmitz in his history of the Order (vol. I, p. 237):

'No nation, we think, unless it be the English, owes more to the Benedictines than Hungary. It owes them its conversion and its cultural development. The Order of St. Benedict gave spiritual and intellectual birth to Hungary. Its first missionaries, its first educators, its first bishops, its first saints were Benedictines.'

Other Benedictines of the same period went to other lands, to Poland, to Dalmatia, to the Near East; but we have said enough to show that their spirit, which is one of ordered liberty, of loving obedience, had by the eleventh century helped to permeate Europe with the spirit of Christ, not only individual men, but society as such. It was a spirit which encouraged loyalty to and love of the Papacy as an institution of order; it was a spirit of a holy alliance between the two powers, spiritual and secular. Is there not something symbolical in the fact that the tombs of kings are in the great monastic cathedrals and minsters of England, France and Scotland: Westminster, St. Denis and Iona?

The work of bringing some order out of chaos was progressing in the reigns of Charlemagne and his successor, Louis the Pious. But already the Danes were harrying the coasts of England and France and Ireland; the Vikings were spreading their tentacles up and down the river-ways of Europe, and as far as the gates of Constantinople. Consequently, at the death of Louis the Pious in 840 the darkness is once again almost entire; and the mighty work done by the monks seems to have been done in vain. Yet when the clamour and the cruelty were over, once more the monks set to work to restore the broken thing; chief of these were St. Dunstan and the monks of Cluny (foundation charter, 910). Gradually, what appeared lost was restored, and Europe entered at last into her age of glory, the Age of Faith.

To conclude, in the words of Professor David Knowles: 'As a great and formative influence on the civilization of the West, the monasteries of Europe are perhaps the most important factors in the spiritual and cultural life of the Church and society from the days of Gregory the Great to those of Bernard' (loc. cit., p. 692).

It is one of the special characteristics of the Benedictine centuries that Europe was linked by bonds of love as well as by those of truth and law with the Papacy. A St. Wilfrid and a St. Boniface organized the discipline of the Church in the West, with the Papacy at its head; but this was only possible on two conditions. The first was that men believed in the divine commission of the Pope to teach and guide. This men certainly did believe. Rome, for men of that age, was the home of the successor of St. Peter, as is clear from the speech of King Oswy at the council of Whitby. Men believed that the popes had the keys of the kingdom of heaven. The second condition was that the men of that age loved the Papacy, and the reason for this love is obvious from the preceding pages. England had been converted and civilized by messengers from Rome; France had been restored from anarchy by monks from England, themselves in love with the Papacy; Friesland and Germany had been converted to the faith by monks from this same island; Hungary had gone straight to the Papacy to receive its spiritual life.

No wonder, then, that a king, Alfred, made pilgrimage to Rome, that Pepin asked to be crowned by the Pope himself, that Charlemagne in fact was so crowned in the year 800, that St. Stephen should request to be made a king by the Pope and be sent a kingly crown to wear. True, the monks created order, as is so often said, but it was an order impregnated with love, esteem and gratitude. Europe felt that it owed its very life to the Papacy, and Europe was duly grateful. It would take centuries of slow decline before this all-pervading union should be dissolved. We enter into that stage of the story in the succeeding chapters. The change of atmosphere is slight at first, almost imperceptible, but by the fourteenth century the signs of decay are visible, and in the fifteenth century collapse seems almost general.

SOME AUTHORITIES CONSULTED

1. The various encyclopædias found in libraries.
2. *Histoire de l'Eglise depuis les Origines jusqu' à nos jours,* Bloud et Gay, vol. IV, par A Fliche; vol. V, par Louis Bréhier et René Aigrain; VI, par E. Amann.
3. *Histoire de l'Ordre de St. Bénoît,* vol. I, par Dom Philibert Schmitz (Maredsous, 1942)
4. *St. Benedict,* Dom Justin McCann (Sheed and Ward, 1938).
5. *The Monastic Order in England,* Dom David Knowles (C.U.P., 1940).
6. *The Ecclesiastical History of the English People,* St. Bede.
7. *St. Wilfrid, Life of,* by Eddius, ed. B. Colgrave (Durham Univ. Press).
8. *History of England,* Lingard.
9. *History of the Anglo-Saxon Church,* Lingard.
10. The usual manuals of early European history: Bede Jarrett, Previté-Orton, etc.
11. *The Decline and Fall of the Roman Empire,* Edward Gibbon, ed. Bury.
12. Mabillon, *Annales.*
13. *Los monjes españoles en la Edad Media,* by P. Justo Pérez de Urbel, 2 vols. (Madrid, 1934–5).

CHAPTER VII

CLUNY

THE little town of Cluny lies unobtrusively not far from Mâcon to the north-west on the River Grône in Burgundian country. Nothing now remains of that most spacious of medieval churches except an inconspicuous turret and a side chapel. The grandiose style of the surviving eighteenth-century monastic buildings gives the traveller no idea of the atmosphere the place must have had when St. Odo or St. Hugh or Peter the Venerable or Abelard lived in it. The Cluny of the High Middle Ages has vanished for ever.

Baronius called the ninth and tenth centuries the Iron Age; of all the centuries of movement and of slaughter, of invasion and of devastation, those centuries are most surely the darkest. In the first place the Empire of Charlemagne was too grand in scale to survive efficiently after the death of that 'strong man armed'. Merely the physical difficulties of holding it together, in an age when communications were bad, must have been insuperable. Order over so huge a tract of country, which included all Western Europe except the Iberian peninsula, was impossible. In the second place, three strong and virile enemies were beating at the gates: the Saracens, the Norsemen and the Hungarians.

To the south the Saracens had a foothold in Italy— they sacked Rome itself in 846; they were supreme in Spain and Portugal, they held Marseilles, they had devastated Lyons. In the East they stood at the gates of Constantinople.

From the north came the Vikings in their warships, burning and looting. Ireland was the first to be overcome; soon it was

England's turn: Lindisfarne was sacked, then London in
842 and Canterbury was burned to the ground nine
years later; then they would stealthily creep up the great
rivers. Up the Seine they went to plunder Paris in 845.
It was by rivers that they even reached to the heart of the
Byzantine empire, Byzantium itself. Here they were repulsed
in 860.

From the slopes of the Urals the Hungarian horsed archers
swept down upon eastern Europe, swift and ubiquitous. We
think of their descendants as peaceful Europeans, but to the
men and women and children of the tenth century they were
the 'Ogres' who ravaged their homes, reaching even farther
than Attila, for they saw the Atlantic shore; but they turned
back. The year after the papal confirmation of the charter of
Cluny, in 932, the Hungarian hordes swept over Gaul for the
last time, returning to the banks of the Danube and the vast
Hungarian plains.

Such was the political scene when Duke William of Aquitaine, Count of Burgundy, gave his hunting lodge—a place
where he kept a pack of hounds—and all the adjacent land, to
his friend the Abbot Berne of Gigny. This was the entry of
Cluny into history, and its end came in 1790, when the Revolution destroyed it and dispersed the monks, forty of them, who
had carried on the tradition.

Cluny, it is true, was only one of many revivals after the
blizzard of the invasions. In England King Alfred had begun
a restoration—the treaty of Wedmore had been signed in 878.
On the Continent at St. Gall and at Fulda men were struggling
to restore religious life. But Cluny, for all that it was not alone,
remains by much the most important, the most famous and the
most typical. Besides, Cluny became the mother house, indeed
the mistress, of a host of dependent priories throughout Europe.
The English revival under St. Dunstan, though independent,
was closely allied to that of Fleury; and Fleury was

one of the abbeys earliest influenced by Cluny and reformed by it.

Hildebrand, in the words of Professor Arnold Toynbee, 'the greatest man of action in the history of our Western Society hitherto' (*A Study of History,* vol. IV, p. 528), though perhaps not a monk of Cluny was a monk, and a monk of the daughter house in Rome, St. Mary's on the Aventine. And his association with the Cluniac reform, with the great abbots, with all its associated monasteries, was so close that the Hildebrandine reform has even been said to be the Cluniac reform.

Furthermore, Cluny stood at the centre of things, between the Frankish kingdom of Gaul on the one hand and Germany on the other, besides being on the road to Rome from the north. It became a neutral ground for Pope and King and Emperor to meet; there they did once meet with all their retine. Cluny at its height was a Rome of the north.

Therefore we take Cluny as the type for the restoration of order after the chaos of the ninth century and during the ensuing chaos of the early tenth.

The first and most obvious prize won was the exemption which Cluny claimed from all secular and even religious authority outside the Pope. This point is preserved in the famous charter which Duke William signed when he presented his friend with the villa of Cluny. We cannot do better than put it here in full.

The Charter of the Founding of Cluny

'All the world knows that God has only given much wealth to the rich in order that they may merit eternal reward by making a good use of their earthly inheritance. This is the meaning of the divine word and its evident counsel, when it says: "The riches of a man are the redemption of his soul" (Prov. xiii. 8). I, William, count and duke, and Ingelberga, my wife, after serious consideration, while there is yet time, and desiring to provide for my own salvation, have deemed it good and indeed necessary for the profit of my soul to dispose of some of the belongings which have come to me during my life. For I do not wish, at my last hour, to merit the reproach of having only considered the increase of my earthly riches and the health of my body, and not given a thought to the supreme moment which must take me from all my possessions. In this matter I cannot act better than by following the precept of the Lord, "I shall make myself friends among the poor" (Cf. Luke xvi), and by prolonging perpetually my good deeds in a house of religious whom I shall feed at my expense; in this faith, in this hope, that, if I cannot myself reach that same contempt for the things of this earth, yet I shall receive the reward of the just, when the monks, contemners of the world, and whom I believe to be just before the eyes of God, shall have received of my liberality.

'For this reason, to all those who live by the Faith and implore the mercy of Christ, to all those who shall succeed them and who follow, unto the consummation of the world, I let it be known that, for the love of God and of our Saviour Jesus Christ, I give and deliver to the holy apostles Peter and Paul all that I possess at Cluny, situated upon the river Grône, together with the chapel which is dedicated to the Blessed Virgin Mary, Mother of God, and to Saint Peter, prince of the apostles, without excepting anything of all that depends upon my domain of Cluny (Villa), farms, oratories, slaves of the two sexes, vines, fields, meadows, forests, waters, streams, mills, rights of way, cultivated and uncultivated land, without any reservation. All these things are situated within the county of Mâcon, or in its neighbourhood, and enclosed within their confines, and I give them to the said apostles, I, William, and my wife Ingelberga, first for the love of God, then for the good of the soul of king Eudes, my overlord, for my father and mother, for me and for my wife, that is for the salvation of our souls and of our bodies; for the soul also of Albana (Ava) my sister, who left me all these possessions in her will; for the souls of our brothers and sisters, of our nephews and of our relations of both sexes; for the faithful men attached to our service; for the upkeep and integrity of the Catholic religion. Finally, and as we are united to all Christians by the bonds of the same faith and the same charity, let this gift also be made for all orthodox Christians of times past, present and future.

'But I make the gift on condition that a regular monastery be constructed at Cluny in honour of the apostles Peter and Paul, and that there the monks will live, according to the Rule of St. Benedict, possessing, holding and governing in perpetuity all the things given : in such a manner that this house become the true home of prayer, that it should be ceaselessly full of faithful vows and pious supplications, and that there men should desire and ever seek with strong fervour and interior zeal the wonders of intercourse with God. Let petition and prayers be offered ceaselessly to the Lord, both for me and for those whom I have named. We ordain that our gift should serve always to provide a refuge to those who, coming poor from this world, should only bring to it a good will; and we desire that our superfluities should become their abundance.

'Let the monks and all these belongings be under the power of abbot Bernon who will rule them regularly so long as he lives according to his knowledge and power. But, after his death, let the monks have the right and power freely to elect as their abbot and lord a member of their order, according to the good pleasure of God and the Rule of St. Benedict; without our power, or any other, being able to countermand or prevent this ecclesiastical election from taking place.

'Let the monks for five years pay to Rome the yearly sum of

ten gold coins for the lights of the church of the apostles; and putting themselves thus under the protection of the aforesaid apostles, and having as their defender the Pope of Rome, let them themselves build a monastery at Cluny, according to the measure of their powers and of their knowledge, out of the fulness of their hearts.

'Further we desire that, in our own time and in the time of our successors, Cluny should be, in so far as the opportunities of the times and the situation of the place will permit, open every day by good works and merciful intentions, to the poor, to the needy, to strangers and to pilgrims.

'It has pleased us to insert in this will that, from this day, the monks of Cluny in congregation shall be completely free from our dominion and from that of our relations, and shall be subject neither to the emissaries of the regal might, nor to the yoke of any earthly power. By God and in God and all his saints, and under the redoubtable threat of the last Judgement, I pray, I implore, that neither secular prince, nor count, nor bishop, nor the Pontiff of the Roman Church himself should invade the possessions of the servants of God, should sell, diminish, nor give to anyone as a benefice anything which belongs to them, nor take it upon himself to establish over them a superior against their will.

'In order that this prohibition may restrain more strongly the wicked and the rash, I insist and add, and I conjure you, O holy apostles, Peter and Paul, and you, pontiff of pontiffs of the apostolic see, to cut off from the communion of the holy Church of God and from eternal life, by the canonical and apostolic authority that you have received from God, all thieves, intruders, sellers of what I have given freely and by my evident will. Be the guides and the defenders of Cluny and of the servants of God who will live and sojourn there together, as also of all their domains given to our most pious Redeemer, for alms, clemency and mercy.

'Should anyone, kinsman or stranger, of whatever condition or authority he might be (a thing which I hope God in his mercy and the apostles by their patronage will forestall); should anyone in any way or by any subtlety try to violate this will, which I have desired to sanction by the love of the all-powerful God, and by the respect due to the princes of the apostles, Peter and Paul, let him first incur the anger of the almighty God, let God carry him off from the land of the living and efface his name from the book of life : may he be with those who have said to God : depart from us; may he be with Dathan and Abiron, beneath whose feet the earth opened and whom hell swallowed up fully alive. May he become the companion of Judas who betrayed the Lord, and be buried like him in eternal torture. May he not, in this present world, show himself with impunity before the eyes of men, and may he experience in his own body the torments of future damnation, a prey to the double punishment of Heliodorus and Antiochus, one of whom barely escaped half dead from the continuous blows of the most fearful flagellation, and the other expired miserably, struck by the hand of the Almighty, his members rotting away and gnawed by innumerable worms. Let his place be finally with all those other sacrilegious persons who have dared to steal the treasures from the hand of God; and, if he show not repentance, may the key bearer of all the kingdom of the Church (and to him be joined Saint Paul) lock him out for ever from the joys of paradise, instead of their being, had he wished it, most eager intercessors on his behalf.

'May he be taken in charge by the civil law and condemned by the judiciary court to pay 100 pounds of gold to the monks whom he would have presumed to attack in order that his criminal design may not be put into effect.

'And let this Will be clothed in full authority and remain for ever firm and inviolable in all that it stipulates. Done publicly in the town of Bourges.

'Signed by : William, duke of Aquitaine,
           Ingelberga, his wife, daughter of Boson, Duke of Burgundy,
           the Archbishop of Bourges,
           etc., etc. . . .'

September 910.

N.B.—The modern editor of the Cluny Charters is Bruel, *Recueil des chartes de Cluny,* I–V. No book I have been able to consult gives this text, not even Mabillon in his *Annales,* nor the *Cambridge Medieval History,* nor *The Monastery of Cluny,* by L. M. Smith, but only the *Essaie historique sur l'Abbaye de Cluny,* by M. P. Lorain, pp. 20–24 (Dijon, 1839).

It will be seen from the above that Duke William offered the villa of Cluny, not to the monks, but to SS. Peter and Paul and to the Holy See. This in itself was symbolic, showing that his thoughts and hopes were turned, not to his overlord in Gaul, but to the spiritual power in Rome.

There was, of course, nothing new about this devotion of Duke William to the Papacy; it was the common inheritance of all Western Europe since its conversion through the monks sent out from Rome or authorized by it. The Papacy had long been recognized as the centre of Christendom. But, in view of the appalling condition of the Papacy at the beginning of the tenth century, the survival of that devotion does amaze one. Never in the long annals of the Holy See had its representatives been so subject to the thrall of political factions. A woman, Theodora, ruled Rome, and forced upon the Chair of Peter whom she willed.

Sergius III (*regnabat* 904–911) was said by his enemies to be the lover of Theodora and father of John XI; and, though Mann says that this is libellous, that it should be whispered gives us an idea of the depths to which the prestige of the individual popes had fallen. Yet, the strange thing is that this degradation did not diminish the devotion of Europe for the institution. Indeed, in their distress, as is shown so completely by the Cluny Charter, it was to these pathetic successors of Peter that men of all the nations turned.

The contrast between this attitude and the one in a similar situation six hundred years later is most striking. In the year 900 the Papacy was more sinned against than sinning; in the year 1500 the Papacy had offended Christendom almost to estrangement. In the tenth century the Papacy was seen to be the only safeguard against tyranny, in the sixteenth century it seemed the only obstacle to national progress.

The English, in this dark period, with their native loyalty continued to send their practical aid, their Peter's Pence. Duke Mieszko (*regnabat* 962–992) gave in gift his whole domain of Poland to St. Peter—to free it from the domination of the Germans (Mann, *Lives of the Popes,* iv. pp. 383–4). The Hungarians were to appeal to the popes in order to be free from all foreign rule, and they received a crown. Now Duke William handed over to the Papacy his precious abbey of Cluny.

Thus the aim of the pious founder was to make Cluny both free from secular interference and bound to the Holy See, to wrench it from the grip of the princelings and kings, who were always meddling in the rule of religious houses at that time, and to bequeath it to the popes so that no one could touch it, not even the local bishop, often enough a noble in disguise and with no pretensions to spiritual virtue save that of ordination. In this one instance, therefore, we have in miniature the whole quarrel and the answer to the urgent problem of lay control in church matters.

There is a legal side to this bequest. The old Roman law had recognized three forms of ownership—the individual form, the collective form and the state form. In the tenth century the Germanic custom in regard to ownership was that the lord owned everything and everybody on his land. If he founded a monastery, the land and the people were still his. It was this over-simple legal view which partly caused such a distressing collapse of religious life in the abbeys of the north; for a lord would interfere at every turn, especially in elections.

According to Germanic law the Church, as such, could not own property. According to the Roman law she could. The item in the Charter of Cluny which arranges for an annual sum to be paid to the Holy See is a legal token recognizing the abbey as a corporate body with legal status. (Cf. Professor David Knowles, loc. cit., p. 251.)

The exemption that Cluny had won from clerical or lay interference was not mere words. This is proved almost immediately by the protection given it by the Holy See in regard to some dispute over land which belonged to it. In A.D. 928 Innocent X wrote to the Frankish king, Rudolf, and to Widom, archbishop of Lyons, that Cluny was under the protection of the Holy See, that therefore some land which it claimed from the abbey of Gigny—in fact the parent house—should be restored to it. (Cf. *M.L.*, vol. 132, col., 812–13.)

This great victory of exemption was confirmed by successive popes and first in order came John XI (931–936). On the political plane he was completely effaced by his mother, Marozia; but there was little harm in that, provided that on the spiritual plane he held his own. Cluny he recognized as important and issued for it a privilege.

Such privileges were not uncommon; examples may be found dating several centuries earlier. But there are points in this one which are of considerable interest. It is the irrevocable link between the Papacy and Cluny; it modifies the Benedictine vow of stability in its favour; it recognizes Cluny's exemption from the lay power and the Papacy's own protective mission in its regard. The monks may mint coins.

As it forms the complement to the charter given above, it is here given in full (*M.L.*, vol. 132, col. 1055 ff.).

Letter of Privilege from Pope John XI to the Monastery of Cluny

March, A.D. 931.

'Pope John, servant of the servants of God, to Odo, venerable abbot of the monastery of Cluny, built in honour of the holy Apostles Peter and Paul and situated in the Matisconensian country, greeting, and through you to the same monastery and all your successors.

'It seems fitting for us, in our Apostolic power and having a fatherly concern for you, to give our speedy and loving assent to what you have so long desired. For in this way especially shall we merit a reward from God our Creator.

'Therefore, since you have asked us to decree by our Apostolic power that your monastery should remain for ever in the same status that Duke William decreed in his Will, the matter has been brought before the Holy Roman Church which with the help of God we serve.

'We have heard your prayers and now grant our permission for the monastery to be governed by you. And so, let that selfsame monastery, together with all that it now possesses or that may be given to it in the future, be completely free from the dominion of any king, any bishop or his associates, or any relation of the same Duke William. And at the same time, let no one take it upon himself to appoint a ruler for the monks against their will when you die, but let them have their own choice, free from the direction of any temporal power, as to whom they may wish to govern them, according to the Rule of St. Benedict : that is unless perhaps they should prefer to elect a person who will condone their faults. Whoever wants to prevent this let him for the love of God do so.

'Let that monastery known as the Roman monastery, which the mother of our son King Rudolph bequeathed to Cluny, be subject to it, and also the farm of Vaningum, as she laid down when she made the bequest in her will.

'And if, at the wish of those whose business it seems to be, you think it right to take over the control of some monastery for its betterment, from now on you have our permission to do so. Furthermore, we completely restore to you those tithes, which formerly pertained to your chapels, and which were removed by the new so-called authority or caprice of some bishop. We will also allow you to keep the chapels, if any have been built or are soon to be built, so that no tithes will be lost to your abbey. Also we decree that what our beloved son bishop Berno granted concerning your chapels mentioned above is confirmed for ever. Besides that, we allow you to set apart for your guest-house a portion of any tithes from the crops or vineyards which you put to your own use, and similarly those tithes you may acquire in the future. Also you may use the property left by Leobaldus to your monastery in his will. Similarly, in our Apostolic power, we restore to you and confirm as yours the property in Agiona or anywhere else which should belong to you, and also the chapel of St. Martin in the farm of Maceium. Also you have our permission to mint your own coinage, as our son Rudolph, King of the Franks, allowed you.

'And since, as is very well known, almost every monastery is troubled by its abbot, if a monk from any monastery wants to join your community, providing his only reason for doing so is that of leading a better life, and if his abbot has clearly neglected to provide him with sufficient means to keep him from having his own property, you may receive him, until the government of his own monastery is put right.

'Therefore, to remind you that the aforesaid community is under the continual care and guardianship of the Holy See, let ten solidi be paid for five years. And if anyone tries to resist this our most righteous decree, or act against any of its clauses,

or fails to respect everything we have sanctioned, let him know
that unless he repents, he will be bound by the chains of ex-
communication under the invocation of the Divine Justice, cast
out from the Kingdom of God, and will suffer the pains of
damnation for ever with Satan himself. But may he who stands
forth as the guardian and upholder of this our most righteous
decree be blessed by Christ Our Lord and obtain forgiveness
of his sins now and hereafter from the Holy Apostles, the
judges of the world.

'Copied by Andrew the scribe in the month of March, at
the fourth indiction.'

CLUNY AND THE HILDEBRANDINE REFORMS

The first victory was won. Cluny was free. It remained now
to free the other monasteries, and then to free the whole
Church. The first of these two works was to be done by Cluny;
the second was to be done by Hildebrand. That network of
monasteries throughout the West associated with Cluny played
no small part in assisting him.

The empire of Cluny was not built in a day. At first those
monasteries in the immediate vicinity submitted to be reformed; Baume, Déols, Massay and Gigny were the earliest.
Then followed Fleury, one of those which already had a rich
tradition and possessed the relics of St. Benedict himself.

The example of Fleury [1] is instructive, for it was to be the
source of inspiration to the English monastic revival under
St. Dunstan. Thus the English monasteries, though not for-
mally within the orbit of Cluny, were of a kindred spirit. When
it is sometimes said, even by such authorities as Dom Henri
Leclercq in *L'Ordre bénédictin*, that, in the great days of St.
Hugh in the reign of Gregory VII, there were nearly two thousand monasteries under the sway of Cluny, it can only be

---

[1] *M.L.*, vol. 132, col. 1075–1077, for Leo VII's privilege to Fleury after
being restored by St. Odo.

understood in the sense that most of them followed the customary of Cluny, not that they were subject.

Yet Cluny, according to most authorities (cf. Abbot Butler, *Encyclopædia Britannica,* Cluny), at its zenith had about three hundred dependent priories or abbeys, which looked to the mother house for a lead, which sent every monk for a long stay at Cluny, whose superior was chosen by Cluny. This network was spread over Spain and France, England and Germany, Switzerland and Italy, and even as far as the Holy Land. Cluny was truly European, helping to weld nations in a supernational unity of Faith.

In Rome itself there were two Cluniac monasteries from the very early days : St. Mary's on the Aventine, founded by the Consul Alberic who gave it to St. Odo, the second abbot of Cluny. The other was St. Paul's without the Walls. A third in Italy was in Salerno. Monte Cassino itself was restored to fervour by Cluniac influence but was never subject.

The uncle of Hildebrand was abbot of St. Mary's on the Aventine; there the future Gregory VII went as a youth and became a monk. The fact of his being a monk is recorded on the great doors he had made for St. Paul's without the Walls and can still be read there. He is called a monk even by his enemies, and we know that he lived as a monk at Cluny after his friend and patron Gregory VI had died, and that he attended a general chapter of the Order which was held at the time.[1]

Hildebrand's association with Cluny was very close. He never ceased to praise it. In 1080 he made this speech to the Council assembled in Rome : 'I would have you know, my brethren of the priesthood, each of you who compose this holy synod, that of all the noble abbeys founded in transalpine Europe to the glory of almighty God and of the Blessed apostles

[1] Cf. Mabillon's preface to *M.L.*, vol. 133, col. 26; cf. Mann, loc. cit., vol. VII, p. 14.

Peter and Paul, there is one which is the particular property of St. Peter and united to the Church of Rome by a special right. I speak of the monastery of Cluny, vowed specially from its foundation to the honour and for the defence of the Holy See. By divine mercy and grace it has reached under its holy abbots such a height of greatness and sanctity that it outstrips all other monasteries of transalpine Europe in service of God and in spiritual fervour; no other is its peer.' (Quoted by Dom H. Leclercq, loc. cit., p. 48.)

At Cluny Hildebrand met one who was to be his fast friend, St. Hugh, abbot of that monastery for sixty years, Godfather of Henry IV. In his mighty wrestling with simony, Gregory VII could turn to St. Hugh and write asking for a list of monks from his abbey who could be made bishops. (Mann, loc. cit., p. 53.)

When the clash came between Henry IV, the Emperor, and Gregory VII over the rights of the secular power in ecclesiastical matters, it was Hugh of Cluny, friend of both, who acted as mediator; indeed, it is surmised that in the final scene at Canossa Hugh brought reconciliation and at least temporary peace.

The successors of St. Gregory VII in the Chair of Peter were, first, the abbot of Monte Cassino; then the prior of Cluny, Odo, who chose the name Urban; later Paschal II (1099–1118), who was also a monk of Cluny.

We may conclude therefore that Cluny was intimately linked with the great reform of the Hildebrandine popes. The reform itself was one of the outstanding achievements in the Church's history. Control had, for reasons already outlined, fallen into the power of the lay folk, unworthy persons were being chosen and men bought benefices openly. Even worse was the almost universal concubinage. These twin evils it was Hildebrand's glory to extirpate. The issue in this age had been narrowed down to a recognition of the Church's right to independence in her own life. But soon it was to take an unfortunate turn when the popes, in order to assert their right, used the weapons of the world and claimed supremacy even in secular affairs. This, however, belongs to a later chapter.

As in the case of the first Gregory, so in the case of the seventh we witness a great increase of loyalty and gratitude to the Holy See. Obedience came easily from the faithful towards one who had saved the thing they loved from dying of corruption.

Cluny and the Liturgy

Anyone who has examined those old engravings showing the vast church of Cluny cannot fail to know that this was the centre of the life there, even if he cannot explain to himself what this life meant. The church was the masterpiece of Burgundian romanesque architecture, with its immense nave and groined roof : a high altar with tall, slim, round pillars standing behind it in a semicircle like sentinels, and at their top little round arches; behind the pillars, apses and innumerable chapels for the private Masses of the monks. The choir was the centre of the life. Here the liturgy was performed as it perhaps never had been before nor was to be since.

Besides the divine Office as laid down by St. Benedict, the monks of Cluny followed the liturgical customs of the great Benedictine reformer, St. Benedict of Aniane. Consequently, they also sang or recited every day the divine office of the Blessed Virgin and that of the Holy Souls. It seems likely that, instead of getting through the 150 psalms in the week, as the holy Founder of Monte Cassino had laid down, they often sang 100 psalms in one day.

To a Protestant or Liberal of the twentieth century this huge expenditure of time and energy may seem love's labour lost. To a Catholic this devotion to prayer may seem extreme, but he can understand. This is a suitable point at which to pause

in order to show how the divine Office is linked with the ideas
we are examining.

Two points may make the Catholic ideas intelligible. In the
first place a Christian, believing in God the Creator of the
universe, realizes that there is the closest possible relationship
between it and its Creator. Being endowed with intelligence,
he feels he is the representative of creatures before the Creator,
and spontaneously would show recognition of this fact by word
and action; this is the natural origin of the liturgy.

As men of all ancient times considered that of their nature
they were social beings, this worship of God was done, not
only in private, but also in public. In the Middle Ages monks
were looked upon as that part of society which performed this
duty to God for the community. The status of monk included
in its duties the praise of God and thanks which were his due
from his creatures.

But on a different plane was the specifically Christian form
of worship, namely, the Mass. Round this sacrificial act, believed to a be a sacramental representation of the sacrifice of
Calvary, were grouped all the liturgical prayers of the day,
Matins, Lauds, Prime and the rest. Besides, the Mass added to
the element of justice, or dutiful praise, the further element of
charity, or the love of God. Christ's death was an act of
supreme love both towards God his Father and towards men
his brethren; to his Father because he was doing his divine
Will, and to men because by his death he was saving them.
That is Catholic doctrine, and so the Mass naturally became
the centre of this liturgical life.

Add to this the belief that their prayers were Christ's prayer
—for were they not *one* with him in the Mystical Body of
Christ?—and it becomes plain why they gave such solemnity
to their praise of God.

The Cluniac monks may have prolonged unduly the services
in church and neglected other sides of the normal monastic

life, manual work and the like; but their insistence upon the worship of God certainly taught, not by words but by performance, that men, both as individuals and as members of the Christian society, had a duty to perform towards God, their creator and their Saviour.

We can scarcely restrain our minds from picturing Cluny as the Cluny of the old etchings : the domed roof, the mosaics or frescoes, the great apse, those towering pillars keeping vigil round the high altar, the immensity of the 'enceinte', the walled gardens, the noble medieval monastic buildings; we visualize the Church councils held within its walls, its abbots, friends and advisers to emperors and popes. But Cluny began as a forgotten villa, scarcely cultivated, wild and remote. It was accepted, not for its wealth, but for its poverty. Truly one might find God there as St. Antony had found him in the desert.

The essence of Cluny is not even in the magnificence of its liturgy. At the beginning it was not so. The early saints went there to find God, but finding him they found all else besides. Love came before obedience, yet as ever overflowing into obedience, and, in this famous instance, into an ordered liturgy of unparalleled grandeur.

So great a triumph was not without its dangers, which St. Bernard did not hesitate to expose. The pioneers in their virile and austere life could not fail to seek God and only God; but with time, and the early fervour cooled, the liturgy, from being the flower, was taken for the root, and the Order of Cluny went into a decline. '*Nisi Dominus ædificaverit domum, in vanum laboraverunt qui ædificant eam.*'

CHAPTER VIII

ST. FRANCIS OF ASSISI

'Love is not loved.'—St. Francis

St. Francis of Assisi was something new in saints. He came from the business world, the son of a clothier, a citizen of one of those new-fangled prosperous city-states. He was gay, he was a troubadour, the leader of a boisterous band of young men; he loved life.

Austerity is the mark of most saints previous to him; they seem almost dour; St. Francis was happy and care-free, a poet. Yet Francis in his own way was austere, but delicately and with spontaneity; the poverty, the wounds, the labours and bitterness were sweet and beautiful as transformed by his spirit.

The burghers of Assisi were opulent and not a little proud of their free city; they were making money in trade; they loved luxury. This city life was a new thing, and it seemed that the inhabitants might be forgetting the Cross and the next world in the process of enjoying this.

Peter Bernadone was one such business man, rich, efficient, self-respecting. He did not like waste, he had an eye for profit and a head for figures. Business was his life, and he travelled widely, for those days, in search of it. The name Francis was given to the saint in memory of one of those journeys to France. For all that, Peter was a good Catholic, bringing up his son in the Faith and in the fear of God, but also in the delight of this world. Francis himself enjoyed it all and, though he led the revelling and the singing, he remained unsullied in his purity.

It is worthy of note, in passing, that many of the earliest followers in the movement were from the same class : Bernard of Quintavalle, who gave Francis a bed in his room in the early days of his disgrace, was a merchant; Peter Cathanii, a lawyer of Bologna University and a canon; Sylvester was a priest, and Giles, on the other hand, was a farmer's son.

From that world Francis had first to be set free. God was beckoning as he sat in a soldier's prison in Perugia, as he lay sick with fever in Assisi, as he marched to war in Apulia. He began to see Christ in this outcast of his society, in this beggar, in that leper. He kissed the wounds of the leper and, as he found himself free, the wonder world of Francis was created. He had stepped across the frontier of the city of Servitude into the kingdom of true Liberty.

The spontaneity of Francis is characteristic, and on the natural plane a reaction against the heavy stereotyped life of Assisi. This element appealed so much to the Romantics: Francis was breaking the rules, freeing himself from the meshes of mediocrity. They were wrong to imagine that Francis was endeavouring to free himself from all restraint; it would be to misunderstand, not only Francis, but the very nature of sanctity. Yet the conventionality of the Bernadone home may be safely assessed from the violence of the reaction evoked when Francis did break away from it. Peter, his father, honest clothier that he was, stood appalled : he struck Francis on the face, he beat him, he locked him up; finally, he was so enraged that he braved the gossip and would have had him brought before the magistrates, had not the case been transferred to the bishop. Francis was not conventional; he was by nature free, leading his own life as he saw it under God.

In the last fifty years, ever since the publication of Paul Sabatier's work upon St. Francis in 1894, there has been a flood of literature and scholarship on the saint. The questions which have occupied many minds are : the value of the sources (and that on the whole has ended in the vindication of the most famous and the discovery of several important early writings,

especially Thomas of Celano's work, which had been super-
seded by St. Bonaventure's careful piece of hagiography);
next, the relationship between St. Francis and authority,
especially the Papacy; and then the problem for the saint, in
love with God, of a group of disciples who were not—at least
not all the time. These last two problems are exactly the question this book is studying, namely, the relationship between
law, liberty and love. St. Francis, without being a theorist, is
perhaps the best example of the true outlook in regard to them
all. He is universally acclaimed as the very embodiment
of love and of liberty of spirit, yet he is, though few have
bothered to notice it and even some have denied it, the
embodiment of true Christian obedience. How can this last be
denied?

The theory runs that at the first stage in his spiritual progress
the idea of law never entered his head except as something
from which to escape : love and law were to him opposites. He
was afraid of law because it might hinder the flight of the
spirit. Love needed no law. Or put in another way : Francis
had wanted to lead his followers by love and not drive them by
commands. It is even held, and with some justification, that
this is the crux of human civilization : a few seers follow their
vision and a few catch the enthusiasm and the vision, but the
rest follow mechanically by drill; so the Russians may drill
Eastern Europe into conformity. St. Francis had a vision, but
the disciples saw none, nor did they hear a voice; and soon the
excitement died down, to be followed by the dullness of every
day; novelty ceased, and many were inclined to drop out from
the march. St. Francis had naught wherewith to enchant
them; he would not drive—that kind of obediential drill was
useless—they refused to be led.

There is a tremendous amount of truth in all that. The fact
is attested; but it should not lead us into the error of thinking
that this kind of obedience was the only one, nor that, because

Francis rightly rejected it, therefore he rejected every kind. His attitude to obedience needs very close study and a great reward awaits those who undertake it.

St. Francis was too intent on loving and on imitating the Crucified to analyse his motives or to describe the process by which he came to be the central figure in medieval spirituality. But motives there were, and an analysis is possible because his companions have left us most precious records of his doings and of his words. In the first place there are the legends of Thomas of Celano—these go to confirm the accuracy of the later documents: the *Life* by St. Bonaventure, the *Mirror of Perfection* and the *Little Flowers of St. Francis*. Then we have a few writings of the saint himself; chief among them are the Rules.[1] The teaching of St. Francis on the relationship between the letter and the spirit, between law and love, liberty and obedience, may be studied there.

On one of the walls of the upper church in Assisi there is a fresco by Giotto depicting the meeting between Francis and the Pope, Innocent III. On the one hand the visionary, poor, alone; on the other the practical man. Innocent's face is seen strong and decisive yet burdened with care, the poise of the body is that of a man searching for an answer, groping into the future, his fingers anxiously gripping the edge of the pallium. The artist seems to have had an intuition of the complexity of that great moment.

Innocent was not exactly a worldly man as we would understand that term; he was grappling with the world, and without being a politician he had to take politics seriously. The burden of Christendom was upon his shoulders; not that he had imposed the burden himself, but rather the Christian peoples expected the Pope to be judge as well as teacher and leader. It is a tragedy of Christian history that the world expects to find

---

[1] For the reliability of the sources see Fr. Cuthbert's *Life of St. Francis,* pp. 492–527.

the Vicar of Christ impeccable as well as infallible. He never
is so.

Innocent hesitated, not because he had no understanding of
sanctity, but because there were all too many visionaries
reforming the Church after their own ideas. On the one hand
were the Waldensians and on the other the Albigensians, both
pointing fingers of condemnation at the corruptions in the
Church. Innocent was the implacable enemy of these twin
heresies. Might not this strange individual be yet another? He
too spoke of love and the counsels of perfects, a return to the
Gospel.

In fact, the Pope gave Francis his blessing; he did more, he
confirmed by word of mouth the Rule that Francis had
brought with him. Perhaps it was this Rule which turned the
scales. Francis was a visionary with a rule. The story of the
arrival of Francis in Rome is as follows, given in the words of
Thomas of Celano:

'Saint Francis, seeing that our Lord was increasing every
day the number of the brothers, wrote simply and in few and
fervent words a formula and rule of life for himself and for his
present followers and those to come, using principally sayings
from the Gospels whose perfection was their only aim. However, he added to it also some other regulations necessary for
the practice of the religious life.' [1]

St. Bonaventure, in his *Life*, goes on: 'But he was anxious
that what he had written should be approved by the Pope; so
he proposed to approach the Apostolic See, together with his
company of simple men, trusting on the divine guidance'
(chap. 3).

This fact of obedience to the Holy See is attested by all the
early witnesses. The Legend of the Three Companions reads:
'Let us then go to our Mother, the holy Church of Rome, let

---

[1] Quoted in *San Francisco d'Assisi*, by P. Vittorino Facchinetti, O.F.M.,
Milano, 1921, pp. 96-7.

us tell the Supreme Pontiff what God has told us to do, so that
with his approval and by his command we may continue on
the road we have begun.' [1] While Thomas of Celano himself
wrote : 'He ardently desired to see what he had written confirmed by the lord Innocent III.' [2]

Perhaps it was natural for anyone seeking perfection to obtain a guarantee from the Father of Christendom; it certainly
proves, by the way, Francis's complete orthodoxy; but it might
still be objected that Francis, having secured his religious
superior's sanction, then proceeds to live a life of pure love
unalloyed by the brutal and mundane element of law. True,
the rule he made out, as we have seen, was almost entirely
composed of passages from the Gospels, but Rule it remains.
The evidence, however, on Francis's early spirit is more complete on this matter than one might think.

No sooner were he and the twelve companions on the way
to Rome than he made them choose a leader, and he ordained
that it had to be one of his own disciples, not himself. So they
chose Bernard of Quintavalle. He wanted to obey all the time
and with a personal obedience; a rule was for him not a
regulation but a stripping of himself.

The devotion of St. Francis to the Holy See and his
obedience to the Church in her least minister is so typical and
yet so understressed that here we must pause to examine it.
Throughout his life his attitude to the Holy See was like that
of a child for its mother, loving, trustful, loyal. Perhaps he is
the last in whom that childlikeness remained; ever after there
has been the ring of battle, of defence. For Francis it was the
most natural thing in the world to nestle, as it were, under the
wing of mother Church.

'Under obedience I charge the ministers to ask the Lord
Pope for a Cardinal of the holy Roman Church as governor,

[1] *San Francisco d'Assisi,* p. 97.
[2] Loc. cit., p. 97.

guardian and corrector of this Fraternity, so that ever subject and prostrate at the feet of holy Mother Church, firm in the Catholic Faith, we may observe poverty, humility and the holy Gospel of our Lord Jesus Christ, as we have firmly promised.' (Cf. Rule confirmed by Honorius III.)

On his death-bed, leaving the thing he had made and going to him for whom he made it, St. Francis wrote a final Will and Testament; it contains the following :

'The Lord gave me and gives me still so much faith in priests who live according to the rules of the holy Roman Church, on account of their Order, that if they persecute me, yet I would have recourse to them. And if I had as much wisdom as Solomon had, and I found priests of this world, poor and lowly, I would not preach against their will in the parishes in which they live. And these and all other priests I desire to fear, love and honour as my lords.' (Cf. Fr. Cuthbert's *Life of Saint Francis,* p. 451, Longmans, 1927.)

This is the final expression of that heroic submissiveness in love to the Holy See, not only in the person of the successor of St. Peter, but also in that of its lowliest minister. Now he would accept the authority of the least of Christ's priests.

Yet, did St. Francis change his attitude towards obedience as the weary years wound on? It is thought that he began with an enthusiasm which scarcely had a use for this virtue, and that he ended by being forced through the backslidings of his followers to impose the old round of obediential performances. It will be useful therefore to examine the growth of his ideas, if we can, through these years.

In the most primitive Rule, the one verbally approved by Innocent III, we have—if we can rely upon the reconstruction made of it by Fr. Cuthbert—the best statement of his early attitude to the subject. 'Neither shall any brother do evil or speak evil to another; nay rather by charity of the spirit shall they voluntarily serve and obey each other. And this is the

true and holy obedience of our Lord Jesus Christ' (Fr. Cuthbert, loc. cit., p. 104).

The first step away from this absolute simplicity may perhaps
be discerned in the Chapter of 1217, when friars from all over
Italy converged upon Assisi. There and then it was decided to
have local superiors; but even at this step we can see the heart
of Francis grow anxious. He would not have them called
priors or masters, but only custodes, guardians : 'Let no one be
called prior, but universally let all be called friars minor, and
each wash the other's feet' (Rule 1, chap. 5).

Later, it hurt him to see disobedient friars, and he knew not
what to do. 'Since I am not able to correct and amend them
by preaching, warning and example, I refuse to become an
executioner, punishing and flogging, like the magistrates of
this world' (*Mirror of Perfection*, chap. 71). Now he compares obedience to a sword, the symbol of force; 'an order,'
he thought, 'should be seldom given under obedience
. . . the hand should not be laid ready on the sword' (*ibid.*,
chap. 49).

But most astonishing of all comes the simile of the corpse,
which rings more true of the writers in the sixteenth century
than of the sweet reasonableness of the Franciscan spirit. But
here it is : 'Take a lifeless body and put it wherever you like,
you will notice that it will not resist being shifted, nor change
its place, nor ask to be sent away. But, if it is high on a throne,
it gazes, not at high things, but at low. If it is dressed in purple,
it grows twice as pale. He therefore is truly obedient who
does not criticize why he is moved, does not mind where he
is put, nor ask to be moved; promoted to an office he keeps
his former humility . . .' And yet the former fervour comes
back to him as he speaks. Holy obedience, he admits, is to do
something commanded which has not previously been sought.
But the 'highest obedience' is to follow the inspiration of God
in the command 'in which flesh and blood had no part to

go to the infidels, for their good or for the desire of martyrdom'
(*Mirror,* chap. 48).

This 'highest obedience', which reads like the annihilation
of all order, is really not a revolution, but an extension of the
Benedictine ideal. St. Benedict had saved monasticism by his
vow of stability; St. Francis was attempting to save the world
by confining the vow to its true essence, stability of rule and
superior, but extension of place. He was not concerned that
his Friars roved from Assisi to Peking and back, they still had
the stability of Rule and superior—he breaks the bounds of
stability of place to send his sons the world over in search of souls.
He created the modern order, world-wide, flexible, centralized.

St. Bonaventure writes in the first chapter of his commentary
on the Rule of the Friars Minor ('Expositio in regula Fratrum
minorum,' quoted by PP. Huby and Rousselot in *Christus,*
chap. 17, p. 1161, Paris, 1927). Friars are people 'who may not
decline anything imposed on them by obedience, on the
grounds that it exceeded the rule, except in the case when it
tended to the harm of their soul'.

Unless Francis had taken as his foundation the traditional
view of obedience, his superstructure would not have survived.
We find him echoing the words of St. Benedict : 'Fulfil a command at the first word . . . do not argue or judge, for there
is no impossibility in the command, for even if I were to order
you anything beyond your strength, holy obedience will not
fail to help your weakness ' (*Mirror,* chap. 47).

In his end was his beginning; as he began, so he ended.
He clung to that complete surrender in which he would strip
himself of all. 'Wishing to remain in perfect humility and
subjection, he said to the Minister-General, "I would be
pleased if you would hand over your rule over me to one of
my fellow friars, whom I may obey in your place, for as
obedience is so rich in merit I desire that in life and in death
it should abide with me".' Then he goes on to give the secret

of his obedience. 'God grant me this grace, to obey as carefully the novice who enters the order to-day . . . if he were
set over me as Guardian, as the most outstanding or ancient
in the Order. For a subject ought to consider his superior, not
as a man, but as God for whose love he is subject to him'
(*Mirror*, chap. 46). (Cf. also St. Bonaventure's *Life of the Saint*,
chap. 6).

The world loves the heroic poverty, that abandonment to the
providence of God which St. Francis showed. But perhaps it
has not dug right deep into the nature of the thing Francis
was doing, for it would not then have thought obedience alien
to his mind. Obedience is essential to his spirituality, and it
derives from his love of Christ, as all true obedience must. Yet
in his case it came from the love of the Crucified Christ, the
Christ of poverty. We shall understand the nature of his obedience if we understand the spirit of his Poverty.

On 24th February, the feast of St. Mathias, Francis was
assisting at Mass in the little Benedictine chapel of Our Lady
of the Angels, presented to him by the abbot of Subasio and
restored with his own hands. As the priest read the Gospel,
which came from St. Matthew's tenth chapter, the saint's
mind and heart were flooded with light and fire. 'Cleanse the
lepers'—yes, he had done that; Jesus was then speaking to him
—give as you have received the gift, without payment. Do not
provide gold and silver or copper to fill your purses, nor a
wallet for the journey, no second coat, no spare shoes or staff.
. . . You must be wary, then, as serpents, and yet innocent as
doves. (Cf. Matt. x. 7–19.) After Mass he asked the priest to
read him the passage again. Suiting the action to the words of
Christ, he took off his shoes and laid aside his staff. He had
begun his courtship of My Lady Poverty.

When Bernard of Quintavalle first joined Francis and they
shared a room in Bernard's house, the two went one morning
to Mass at Saint Nicholas'. It was the day Bernard resolved to

take the final step, so they sought a sign from God, and like St. Augustine before them, who did as the child's voice instructed, *tolle, lege,* they opened the book of the Gospel three times and read :

The first : Matt. xix. 21 : 'Jesus said to him, if thou hast a mind to be perfect, go and sell all that belongs to thee; give it to the poor, and so the treasure thou hast shall be in heaven; then come back and follow me.'

The second : Luke ix. 3 : 'Take nothing with you to use on your journey, staff or wallet or bread or money; you are not to have more than one coat apiece.'

And the third : Matt. xvi. 24 : 'If any man has a mind to come my way, let him renounce self, and take up his cross, and follow me.'

The outward manifestation of these texts is the spirit the world knows and recognizes as Franciscan : the simple serge, the friend of the poor, personal and community poverty. But the inward poverty eludes them, the poverty of spirit, without which the outward sort would be worthless. Francis did not only strip himself of his clothes before the bishop of Assisi; he stripped himself of himself. Nothing made Francis so poor as the giving up of his own will. This he did by submitting his most cherished ideas to the Court of Rome, by giving up his daily will to another friar. That was true abandonment, true poverty.

In the story of St. Francis, love conquered in the first battle. So obedience for him was never aught else than love. But his followers were made of commoner clay; their life did not always portray the ideal they had fixed their heart upon. So we have the struggle between the idealistic attitude of Francis and the legalistic view of Elias. Was St. Francis's ideal an impossible one and was the practical man, Elias, misunderstood ?

The answer seems to be that Francis, for all his sanctity and spiritual insight into the ways of God, was not in fact very

clever at running a large Order of men made up of all sorts.
He made little or no allowance for original sin, which requires
a rule as a brake as well as a rule as a spur to high things.
Francis was afraid of the legalistic spirit of the times, that
very spirit which had sent many a good man into the arms of
the heretics, Waldensians or Albigensians. In the long view he
was right, if in the short view Elias seemed to have all reasonableness upon his side.

On the one hand were the heretics who sought the spirit and
felt themselves encumbered by the hair-splitting lawyers; on
the other the place seekers, keeping the letter but not the spirit
of Christ's law. Between stands St. Francis, the supreme example of those who know how to combine both spirit and
letter, law and liberty, love and obedience. He was obedient
to the Papacy and, indeed, to the lowliest priest; yet who in
the whole sweep of history was ever more free in love?

Francis wrote his rules as an aspiration to the life of perfection. To love was to be perfect, therefore any motive less
than love was unworthy; and, for those who aim always at
perfection, St. Francis is right.[1]

[1] Since writing all the above, the book, *Saint Francis of Assisi, the
Legends and Lauds,* edited by Otto Karrer, Sheed and Ward, 1947, has
come into my hands. Better than anything I have read, it gives the spirit
of that wonderful lover of God, the little man of Assisi, because it gives
the earliest accounts and all gathered together.

CHAPTER IX

ST. THOMAS AQUINAS

'Christus præcepta caritatis ex obedientia implevit, et
obediens fuit ex dilectione ad Patrem præcipientem.'
(*Summa Theologica sancti Thomae*, III,
Q. xlvii, art. 2, responsio ad tertium.)

THE aim of this chapter is to show how the ideas of Law, Liberty and Love are linked together, and, by so doing, to throw light on each and on the thought of the High Middle Ages on these subjects. The revolt in the sixteenth century cannot be understood except in the light of the Thomist position.

St. Thomas is the inevitable choice. No other man so completely embraced his Age or moulded it as he did, with the possible exception of Dante; and he built upon St. Thomas's foundations. Few men have had a more ordered mind than St. Thomas (and what is order but law?), few have defended so whole-heartedly the reasonableness of all things, and more especially the reasonableness of law, thus lifting law out of the realm of force into that of freedom; few have succeeded so well as he in applying a rational approach to love.

Born in A.D. 1225 near Naples, St. Thomas was related to the Emperor Frederick II sufficiently nearly for his imperial majesty to intervene in his schooling at Monte Cassino. On reaching early manhood he joined a new and almost vagabond order, the Order of Preachers, but not before he had been kept under lock and key by his outraged relations in the hope that he might change his mind. He did not.

St. Thomas thus had ample occasion to consider over a

period of months, in a personal context, the nature of justice, law, liberty and coercion, true love and selfish love. If his thinking did become sharpened by personal trial, these things were never intruded into his writings, which remain always objective and unmoved.

We may sum up St. Thomas's view upon law thus[1] :

1. At the summit of all law is the *Eternal law,* which is the plan that God has in his mind for the universe he made. It is not merely a 'dictat', a will of God, though of course God's will comes into it. It is the mind of God in regard to his creation. God's law, for all that it is his will, is not irrational. St. Thomas, one might almost say, at this point joins hands with the Stoics, who imagined a logos or law in the universe. For St. Thomas it is a law *of* or *for* the universe in the mind of its Creator.

2. The *Natural Law,* again for St. Thomas, is that part of the eternal law which concerns men and which can be discerned by them with their own native wit. Thus, when men obey the natural law, they are really obeying the eternal law; they are obeying the law of their own nature, but they are also obeying the will and the mind of God in their regard. This raises such an obedience from the purely human to a divine level.

3. *Human laws* are governmental legislation. They are to be obeyed only in so far as they conform to or derive from the natural and divine law.

4. *Divine law* is the name given to God's commands which have come to us through revelation, whether in the Old Testament or the New.

Law, in a simple way, has been erroneously viewed as nothing more than the arbitrary will of the ruler, whether it be that of one man, many, or of all the people. But the

---

[1] This may all be found in the *Summa Theologica,* I, II, Q. xc, and following.

Ancients, particularly the Romans, had a theory that law was somehow connected with reason and was not arbitrary. St. Thomas makes use of that idea, and so lays the foundation for true liberty. For arbitrariness in a ruler, even if it be the people, cannot be called true liberty; only what is reasonable can be truly free. Though an arbitrary law might, by chance, be rational, it would not constitute a basis for freedom, since at any time this just law might be rescinded. The idea that Law had nothing to do with reason, and was merely the will of the ruler, was a theory which lay as yet unborn in our world when St. Thomas wrote that little treatise on law which can be found in the first part of the second part of the *Summa* (Q. xc, and following). Luther reversed the history of thought on this matter, as we shall see later.

According to St. Thomas, only those laws were just which laid down the way to the common good. As the object of speculative thought was 'being', so the object of practical reasoning or of action was 'the good'. The means for procuring the good were to be found by applying this practical principle of reason : that good is to be sought and evil avoided. Thus, St. Thomas had such confidence in reason in this matter of the natural law that he compares the conclusions drawn from the above principle to those which a philosopher draws from the first principles of metaphysics. Good is to be done and evil avoided, *'et super hoc fundantur omnia alia precepta legis naturæ'* (*S.T.*, I, II, Q. xciv, art. 2).

Not that St. Thomas imagined that all the laws men make, or the traditions by which they live, are reasonable. He was too much aware, as Pascal was, of the diversity of laws and traditions among peoples, to be such an optimist. He accounts for this diversity by admitting that in the remote conclusions from the first principle of the natural law men might by faulty reasoning err, and might also err because they wanted to do so (*ibid.*, art. 6).

Yet he clings to his principle that no law is just unless it is derived from the natural law, and is therefore reasonable. He quotes St. Augustine to the same effect: 'In temporal laws nothing is right and legitimate which is not derived from the eternal law' (*De libero arbitrio,* lib. 1, cap. 6 *ad finem*). (Cf. *S.T.,* I, II, Q. xciii, art. 3.)

If true law must be reasonable, then it becomes reasonable to obey. Therefore, in obedience, reasonableness is essential. To obey an arbitrary law would be slavery, but to obey a rational ruling is to behave as a man and not like the beasts of burden. Man's highest activity is to act from reason; any other action is a slavery to something, whether one's own passions or the dictatorial will of another. Rational obedience is therefore freedom.

Thus, in a roundabout way—the way of reason—St. Thomas comes to the same conclusion as St. Paul, that obedience, far from being a servitude, is a free act.

Human Laws and Obedience

In religious orders it may be easy enough to obey. In the case where the obedience is difficult or unreasonable, a subject may go to the superior and expostulate in all reasonableness and humility; this is not so easy for the citizen of a state, and for several reasons. Firstly, it is difficult for an ordinary citizen to see for himself that a law is necessarily derived from the Natural Law; secondly, he may have a rooted objection to his ruler, who may belong to a party of which he approves little; thirdly, a law may seem very oppressive without being positively unjust. Lastly, the law may appear thoroughly wrong.

St. Thomas, in the 104th question (*S.T.,* II, II, Q. civ, art. 5) is clear on the last point. In this fifth article he asks and answers that very question: whether a subject is bound to obey his superiors in all things. Rulers have not a right over the minds of their subjects. He quotes Seneca, *'mens quidem est sui juris'*;

they have a right over the bodies of their subjects, but even this is limited; for, in those things which concern the very nature of the body, man is not bound to obey man but only God. He makes the brave statement that all men are by nature equal and therefore are in this matter subject only to God: '*Quia omnes homines naturâ sunt pares*'. He refers to the preserving of one's own life and the propagation of the species, marriage and virginity and such like. There remain the actions and belongings of men which may be governed by men for the common good. Therefore, for a ruler to require obedience in any of the things above enumerated would be wrong and he should not be obeyed.

St. Thomas sums this up in the reply to an objection in the following article (6): Man is obliged to obey princes (rulers, governments) in so far as the order of justice requires. Therefore, if their authority is not just or is usurped, or if the authority commands unjustly, its subjects are not bound to obey, except perhaps for some other reason (*per accidens*) to avoid bad example or some danger.

It is not necessary for a subject to see the reasonableness of every law before obeying it. The general line taken by St. Thomas is that, provided a government has 'the consent of the governed', that is, provided the governed consider, by their acquiescence at least, that the rulers are ruling for the common good, then it follows that the laws they make are for the common good, unless they are, on the face of it, not so.

The question of likes and dislikes in regard to rulers and ruled probably never entered St. Thomas's mind as a reason for obeying or not obeying. However, in modern times and here in Europe, when the rulers are party men, it is inevitable, especially as they come forward as party men, that those not of their party should have a dislike of their very names, and a consequent unwillingness to obey. The dislike is really only a symptom of a rational judgement that came earlier in the process, by which the citizen has concluded that the rulers are no longer ruling for the common good but for the sectional good of the ruler's party. At this point the question of obedience becomes truly difficult. Probably the answer to an objection quoted above is the only solution, namely, that one has to obey for extrinsic reasons, such as avoiding perils, i.e. worse evils. But, of course, a time may come when the rulers rule so unjustly that it becomes a duty not to obey.

LIBERTY, according to St. Thomas, is twofold. There is the natural liberty and there is the moral liberty. The former consists in being able to will or not to will at all. The latter consists in being able to choose what is right. The first, most people would be prepared to admit, was a form of liberty; the latter presents more difficulties, especially since liberty is often understood to-day as simply being able to do what one likes.

According to St. Thomas the will necessarily wants goodness itself in general. Even if we choose death, we choose it because we think it good for us or for somebody. Even if we choose something we know to be wrong in some way, we in fact choose it because in another way we see it as good—if only up to a point.

The good is the universal object of the will. If we saw God face to face, says St. Thomas, we could not refrain from choosing him, because he is the All-Good. And yet we shall see later that this necessary choice is free. Since we do not see God, but only have indirect knowledge, which is very limited indeed, some pale reflection of him, we can turn away from him and choose some other good, or apparent good. In regard, then, to limited good, we have a special kind of freedom, namely, *liberty of choice.*

The power to choose occurs when the object presented to the will is only a limited good and therefore does not completely satisfy the desire for the all-good of the will. For every limited good has a side to it which is a lack of good; for instance, a friend lacks the charm of some other friend, one picture cannot have the details of another picture. It both contains good and lacks good. If one looks at the thing desired from the latter angle, then the will is not drawn to it. Thus the will is left free either to go forth for that thing in so far as it is good, or to refrain from doing so for the reason that it lacks some good. This is the liberty of choice, or moral liberty. (Cf. *S.T.*, I, Q. xix, arts. 3 and 10.)

It will be seen from the above brief analysis of St. Thomas's approach to this subject that for him the act of the will is not an irrational act, spontaneous and inexplicable; indeed, the will would not stir at all unless some object was placed before it as desirable. This is a judgement of the mind, a rational business : that thing is good, or that thing is not good; or there is more good than bad in that thing, and so forth. Such judgements are the ordinary stock-in-trade of the intellect. Indeed, until the intellect has done this spade-work of thinking, the will cannot start to function. The act of the will, therefore, according to St. Thomas, is grounded on reason. The reason may be a bad one, the man may have got his facts wrong, he may choose the lesser good, but he does follow a judgement.

It is in this power of choosing the lesser good, one indeed which on the broad view will do harm, though on the short view will give pleasure, that sin, as moralists understand it, enters in.

The fact that, on such an occasion, a man does as he likes, though not following his better judgement, proves that he is free; but he is less free according to St. Thomas than a man who does follow his better judgement; for the one who 'does as he *likes*' is not really being reasonable but submitting to a passion, and in a sense being a slave. To do something that is unreasonable may prove our liberty; but if, in order to be free, one has to be unreasonable, then freedom has come to have a meaning which makes one wish not to be free.

It would seem therefore that men could be free on this earth, but could not be free in heaven. This, however, is not St. Thomas's view. On earth we are free because every good presented before us appears limited, and so we may take it or not take it according to whether we look at its good side or its bad side. In heaven we shall be confronted with the all-good. We shall be bound to go towards it, for there will be nothing, outside of God, the infinite Good, which could satisfy us; nor would there be any flaw in that supreme Good which we see.

But to say that we are bound to go towards the supreme Good is not the same as saying that we do so under duress; we can, and do, still do so freely. This should be clear from all we have said about the rational nature of the will. There, in heaven, God himself is the object of the human mind transformed by divine grace. He is there, as Truth, as Beauty, and Goodness. The mind, however the beatific intelligence works, will see that God is supremely Good. The will at that point acts, not because it is forced to do so by some exterior influence, but because here is its object without alloy. It is free because nothing outside of it is impelling it to move, but only its own object, which is the Good.

In this way God himself is free, for he wills according to his infinite wisdom and understanding. No extrinsic thing could influence the Will of God. Essentially, freedom is the will acting according to its nature, spontaneously going to the good presented to it by the reason. The freedom of choice, which adds to this the element of being able to choose between two limited goods, is really a separate thing, though dependent upon the first. God is also free in this sense; for instance, he was not bound to make our world.

In the *Summa Theologica* St. Thomas seems to say that

God, in willing his own divine Goodness, does so necessarily (I, Q. xix, art. 3). In modern English this term 'necessary' has the sense of not freely. But to take this as the meaning of St. Thomas would be to misunderstand him. He means that God, from the nature of the case, wills his own goodness, and yet he does it freely. He says :

'Everything is that which belongs to it naturally.' By this he means that all beings are their essence and not any excrescence which is there by accident, e.g. a man is his nature and not the hat he is wearing. 'When therefore a being acts through a power outside itself, it does not act of itself, but through another, that is, as a slave. But man is by nature rational. When therefore he acts according to reason, he acts of himself and according to *his free will; and this is liberty.*'[1] (Quoted by Leo XIII in *Libertas Præstantissimum.*)

Liberty, then, for human beings, is not merely being able to do as one likes, though this would prove our freedom to us, but being able to follow right judgement without interference from outside, from emotions, from pride, from force. But as law is the expression of God's mind, his plan for us, then our right judgement will dictate that we should follow it and submit to it, for that would be reasonable. If, then, it is reasonable to submit to law, and freedom is eminently to act according to our reason or judgement, then to obey what is reasonable is to be eminently free. This is St. Thomas's standpoint.

LOVE is the summit of St. Thomas's teaching. Though the vision of God is the final end of man, yet, in this life, love of

---

[1] The same, *mutatis mutandis,* may be said of God himself. He cannot be influenced by anything outside his own knowledge and will, and therefore to that extent he is supremely free, even in loving himself, with a freedom from compulsion from without. But by the very nature of the case, being infinite-will faced with infinite-goodness, he cannot fail to will it with a love of perfect complacency. '*Quando ergo movetur secundum rationem, proprio motu movetur, et secundum se operatur, quod est libertas*' (Commentary on chap viii. St. John's Gospel, section iv).

God gets us nearer to him than faith (*S.T.*, I, II, Q. xxvii, art. 2, ad. 2; and cf. II, II, Q. xxiii, art. 2, c.).

He would say that there are three kinds of love : the instinctive love of the senses, as among all animals, then this same love in men but under the control of the will, and lastly, the love in the intellect, that movement of the will to the lovable things put before it by the mind, and the chief of whose objects is God. This last is the concern of St. Thomas, and ours.

Normally speaking, love is a passion, in the old sense of that word, a reaction to a stimulus, instinctive and fundamentally irrational; but love is used, and has been used for centuries, in the sense of the will's going out to its object, and this, being reasonable, is neither instinctive nor inevitable but free. (Cf. *S.T.*, I, II, Q. xxvi, arts. 1 and 2.)

Even in this type of love, St. Thomas lays down two main divisions. There is the division between natural and supernatural. Our concern is with the latter. The other division is between love, which is love of desire, *amor concupiscentiæ*, and altruistic love, a movement outwards; this he calls sometimes *amor* and sometimes friendship (if mutual), or charity. The supernatural kinds of these are not something quite new, but an infusion of Christ's life into the natural love.

What is this love? Is it union? If so, then union of what?

He is never tired of distinguishing. Love, which is the act of the virtue of charity, according to St. Thomas, is something more than benevolence or wishing good to the person loved, though it does include that.[1] The act of the virtue of charity has as part of it the desire for union. (*S.T.*, II, II, Q. xxvii, art. 2, corpus). Its nature seems to include a link between the lover and the beloved. One could perhaps imagine a form of love which was purely well wishing and had no element of

---

[1] 'When a man loves another with the love of friendship, he wills good to him, just as he wills good to himself.' (*S.T.*, I, II, Q. xxviii, art. 1, corpus.)

union. But this St. Thomas does not consider to make up the whole of Christian love, and this apparently because it includes *amor* and desire. Thus, in St. Thomas's analysis, the two loves live side by side within the virtue of charity. Friendship is the key because, there, love is mutual and each wishes to give good to the other, each wishes good to the other, each wishes to be joined to the other. In the case of the friendship between men and God, this is only possible because, according to the revelation of Christ, men have been raised up to be sons of God, and, in the phrase of St. Peter, given natures by grace like unto God, and so have been granted a certain equality with God.

The union between lovers is one of those strange and mysterious things that love forces upon those who love; but between mortal men that union cannot get through beyond the barrier of personality. In the love of friendship with God that barrier seems to have been lifted and Christ lives by grace in the soul. 'God is love, and he who remains in love remains in God and God in him.' That statement of St. John the Apostle will remain for all time the perfect expression of what the love between men and their Creator and Redeemer can become. Or St. Paul's, 'Now, not I live, but Christ lives in me'.

Thus the love that St. Thomas is describing is one of the whole being of man through the instrumentality of his will.

OBEDIENCE, which has such a high place in the teaching of St. Benedict, seems, in the *Summa* of St. Thomas, to be relegated to a very minor position as a subdivision of the virtue of Justice. In the main, for St. Thomas, obedience is an ascetical virtue by which we mortify our wills. Man, he says, contemned God by cleaving to created things, and those virtues which directly make us cleave again to God—faith, hope and charity —are more important than those which 'are only means to this end'. Obedience is one of the latter sort (*S.T.*, II, II, Q. civ. art. 3). But in the second part of the same article St. Thomas seems to modify his position, and this is of great moment for the clearing up of a possible misunderstanding concerning the relationship between obedience and love, and brings St. Benedict and St. Thomas into agreement in thought on the subject.

These are his words : 'St. Gregory says that "obedience is rightly preferred to sacrifice, because by sacrifice another's body is slain, whereas by obedience we slay our own will". Wherefore even any other acts of virtue are meritorious before God for being performed out of *obedience to God's will.* For were one to suffer martyrdom, or to give all one's goods to the poor, unless one directed these things to the *fulfilment of the divine will,* which pertains *directly to obedience,* they could not be meritorious; nor would they be so without charity, which CANNOT EXIST WITHOUT OBEDIENCE. For it is written (1 John ii. 4, 5): "He who saith that he knoweth God, and keepeth not his commandments, is a liar . . . but he that keepeth his word, in him in very deed the charity of God is perfected"; and this because friendship makes the two friends like and dislike the same things.'

In fact, neither St. Benedict nor St. Thomas equate love with obedience. St. Benedict, when he fled from Rome to the wild country of Subiaco and to solitude, sought not obedience but God himself. St. Thomas was many times wrapped in contemplation of God, in a love which had nothing to do with obedience to man. But that love would not be far removed from the idea of obedience to God. Some distinctions are necessary, and this is the place to make them.

St. Thomas divides the life of the human soul into three compartments : there are the powers of the soul, knowing and willing; there are various ways of acting, or capacities, and there are the acts themselves. These capacities, when formed and easy to put into act, are called dispositions; if good, virtues, if bad, vices. Again, following the standard teaching, he lays down that we distinguish different kinds of dispositions by the different kinds of acts—the power to act in one way requiring one virtue or perfected power, another requiring a different one. He goes farther, and says that acts themselves are distinguished by their objects.

According to St. Thomas, obedience is a virtue or good habit. What, then, is its act, which distinguishes it from other human acts? The act of obedience is the submission of the will to the command of another, to a superior. It comes under the general heading of justice, because we presume that the superior has the right to command and, therefore, the subject has a duty to obey. The object of the act is the command of a superior.

Where, then, does love come in? It comes in with the motive from which we obey a superior or anyone else. Obedience to a superior could be done out of routine, it could be done from fear, it could be performed in order to ingratiate oneself with the giver of the command. From this it is perfectly plain that of itself obedience cannot be said to BE love. Yet obedience can also be done *from* love, just as any other human act may. A man might sing for the love of God, or like the pious jongleur go into the crypt of the minster and perform his antics for the glory of God. Obedience may be an act of love; and indeed, unless it becomes so, obedience is mere legalism and as deadening as any letter that killeth.

Love of God, as the Gospel has it, is to be done with the whole of man's soul, with all his mind, with his whole will and with all his strength. It is a matter for the whole man, a holocaust. Now, obedience to a superior is only part of the life of any man, and therefore it cannot be called co-extensive with love, even when done out of love. When we obey a civil or a religious superior out of love of God, whose mouthpiece we consider them to be—for all authority comes from God—that is an act of love, and it is of a kind that we can do many times a day; but there are other acts of love. God, in his wonderful love, desires to approach each one of us in the inmost recesses of our souls. He is ready to speak to us in our own consciences, guiding us many times to what is right, leading us without any command from without. That too is a command from God, an obedience, a submission to the will of God. This too is love, but it cannot be said to fall under the virtue of obedience in the strict St. Thomas's sense, though in the broadest sense it is obedience to God; it is submission of will to Will, oneness of purpose, of soul, with God.

Then there is the essential act of prayer itself, that undifferentiated act of love in which we give our whole being to God unconditionally, to be his and do as he wills with us. That too is love; indeed, it is the spring and source of all else, it is the essential love, the heart of the matter, the central fire of the Christian life, it is love *tout court*.

Can this primary act of the human soul before its God be said to be obedience in any sense? Only in this sense that love is an act of the will, a conforming of the will to God. In this sense all human acts are obedience or disobedience. It was thus that Adam and Eve sinned by disobedience; they refused to submit themselves to God, and they set themselves up as distinct entities, not willing as God willed; they neither loved God nor were obedient to him.

Therefore we say in answer to this problem, firstly, that obedience to a superior is a means to an end. Loving obedience to God through a human superior is only one of the ways of showing our love for God. Secondly, even obedience to God's will is also only one of the ways of loving God, the more fundamental one being prayer, or the love of God in contemplation, the abandonment of the whole self to the infinitely loving God. That is the reason why the Church has always held that the contemplative life is the higher—in the abstract—of the two. Mary did choose the better part by loving her divine Master in contemplation. In the third place, it remains true that without the love of obedience there is no true contemplative love, for to fail in one is to fail in them all, seeing that to disobey God, or those he has set over us, proves that one does not love him in that way. Not those who cry Lord, Lord, enter into the kingdom of heaven, but those who do the will of God. What sort of love of God has a man who says in his heart that he delivers over to his divine Master his liberty, his mind, his will, his all, and who refuses to do what he knows his God wants him to do? He is merely loving God with words and not with his whole will.

Appendix

St. Thomas's masterly analysis of friendship, particularly in regard to the union created by it between the two friends, has immense value to-day, when the philosophies and theologies of India are beginning to percolate through to the West.

These systems, to speak very generally, are based on two principles:

(i) The fact of mystical experience, which is interpreted as an apparent absorption of the mystic into the All or the Nothing.

(ii) This absorption, they say, proves that we are not, and only seem to be; only the All, or No-thing, is.

The ordinary, practical Western man, who deals all day with earthly particular problems and who sleeps at night, has a profound belief in his own identity and distinctness from all other beings. The fact that he makes his own living by his own exertions and skill also tends to make him forgetful that he does depend upon God; the ordinary Western man has a tendency to assert in practice that he is an autonomous being. He is blissfully unaware that he is poised in existence by the will of

God, that he is enveloped in the power of God, who keeps him in existence, that in a word he is impregnated through and through with the might of God's power. In fact, far from being autonomous, man is utterly dependent.

Many Eastern minds seem to work in the opposite way. In India men are more conscious of their physical dependence on Nature. They are each a part of a system, that of caste, which holds them firmly in its grip. They are far from autonomous. This sad reality of miserable dependence has led many thinkers to find ways out; there is the way of the Hindu philosophers, such as Sankara and Ramanuja, the way of mystical absorption in the All; there is the way of the Buddha, a negative way, Hinayanan Buddhism.

That these doctrines are not irrelevant to the West to-day is proved by the immediate success of two books, both taking the view that we should learn the solution of our grave problems from Indian thought; they are, *Grey Eminence,* by Aldous Huxley, and *The Yogi and the Commissar,* by Arthur Koestler.

The point at which we have arrived in our generation seems to be this: man does not live by bread alone, he needs a spiritual food, religion. Is this spiritual food to be by way of Buddhism or by way of Christ? Is it to be by way of union with God or by extinction? St. Thomas has, we think, given us the clue to the answer, on the philosophic plane, in his analysis of the union of love.

The reason perhaps why his answer is so apposite to the twentieth century may be that in his thought on mysticism he was conscious of the mystical teaching of the Moslems of his own day. He had learnt the first news of Aristotle, the metaphysician, from the Moslems of Spain; that same Spain was alive with the Sufiist, pantheistic theories of such masters as Algazel (cf. Altamira, *Historia de España,* vol. I, p. 504), and Sufiism was certainly by this time fundamentally pantheistic (cf. *Encyclopædia Britannica,* 11th ed., art. 'Sufiism', by Prof.

Nicholson; also *The Legacy of Islam,* p. 223). 'The existence of created things is not other than the very existence of the Creator. Everything emanates from the Divine Essence and will finally return to it' (Ibn Taimiya). (Cf. A. Vincent, *Islam,* p. 31.)

Though St. Thomas was fully aware of how a being was apparently 'placed out of itself' (*S.T.,* I, II, Q. xxviii, art. 3) in ecstasy, he does not confuse this intellectual and voluntary phenomenon with the completely different thing of ceasing to be.

'The first of these ecstasies is caused by love dispositively, namely, in so far as love makes a lover dwell on the beloved . . . and to dwell intently on one thing draws the *mind* from other things. The second ecstasy is caused by love directly; by love of friendship, simply . . . because he wishes and does good to his friend, by caring for him and providing for him, for his sake' (*ibid.*)

It is this seeming withdrawal from normal thinking and willing which gives a person the impression that he is not existing, for we only know of our existence through our activity, having, if at all, only the very haziest awareness of our underlying being in itself.

Thus having disposed of the first principle upon which the Indian philosophy is based, namely, that in ecstasy we cease to be, by showing that all we have a right to state is that we cease to be aware of our own thought and will, St. Thomas preserves our identity and so our morality also; for, if we do not really exist, why worry at all?—and yet at the same time he shows how, without being absorbed into God, we are closely conjoined to him in love.

CHAPTER X

ANAGNI AND MARSILIO OF PADUA

AT dawn on Saturday, 7th September, 1303, the gates of the little town of Anagni, temporary abode of Boniface VIII and the Papal Curia, were traitorously opened, and Nogaret, agent of Philip of France, burst in at the head of 600 horsemen and over a thousand men-at-arms. The citizens were terrified to hear the clanging of the great city bell and the shouts—'Long live the King of France and the Colonna'.

The attackers wasted no time; they looted the palaces of several cardinals, and some, with Sciarra Colonna at their head, attacked the palace of the Pope himself. They burnt down the doors of the cathedral, plundered the church, killed those who resisted, and finally broke into the palace by the treachery of one of Boniface's own men. Sciarra rushed to the Pope's room, and striding forward struck him on the face, threatening to kill him. Boniface remained calm, kissed the crucifix, and offered his neck for the blow Sciarra threatened to make : *'Ec le col, ec le cape'*, was all he said. At that moment Nogaret arrived and prevented Sciarra going farther. Sciarra promised the Pope his life on three conditions : that he would restore the Colonna cardinals, resign the Papacy and hand himself over to Sciarra. The Pope refused and the truce was over.

All next day, Sunday, Boniface was kept under guard, but that night the citizens secretly arranged to save him from the clutches of his enemies. At dawn on the Monday (9th), they in their turn rose, and after a short fight, Nogaret, now wounded, and with 'Long live the Pope, down with the foreigner' ringing in his ears, escaped disguised. His soldiers took to flight and the Pope was free, but in two weeks he was dead.

This episode, in its vivid, dramatic and tragic sequence, stands as a symbol of the collapse of the medieval and papal political system. It was the hammer-blow which smashed the delicate structure of spiritual rule. Such a thing would not have been dreamt of in the days of Hildebrand or of Innocent III. It shocked Christendom at the time, as well it might; it shocks us still. How could these things be?

The history of the relationship between Church and state may be stated shortly for the present purpose thus. In the beginning the Christians obeyed the civil power in all save sin; the sin which particularly occurred to upset the harmony was the sacrifice citizens were bound to offer to Cæsar. Christians refused, and for this they were persecuted. They nevertheless remained loyal and rebutted charges levelled against them. The second stage came when the Empire became officially Catholic and the Emperor a Christian. At that point a new situation arose, for the Emperor was supreme in the civil sphere, yet as a Christian he was subject to the Church.

Conflicts were not slow in coming. St. Ambrose resisted the Emperor Theodosius. A pope was dragged to Constantinople (St. Martin). The emperors, inheriting as they did the title of Pontifex Maximus, felt themselves in some way officials in the Church. Many times their aid was called for by the Church: to suppress heretics here, to call a council there. At Nicea, Constantine was at least in a seat of honour—though of course no one thought of him as head of the Church. The later Frankish emperors again took much on themselves in Church matters, from Charlemagne in the ninth century to Henry in the eleventh. There was a danger that a Christian emperor should think himself above the law, or at least above any earthly spiritual authority, owing allegiance to his conscience and to God alone.

On the other hand, the Church, and naturally the popes,

claimed authority in the doctrine, behaviour and worship of all Christians, emperors and kings not excluded. In this they had all good men with them. But after the struggles of the Dark Age and the beginnings of the investiture quarrel, a new situation arose, and this we may call the Third Stage in the relationship between Church and state, one in which the Church was supreme and tending to interfere in secular affairs.

The story is too well known and easily accessible in any history book for it to be stated in any but the most general terms here. It has itself three stages.

The first is the one we have examined in some detail with regard to Cluny. There the Church is freeing itself from the control of laymen and using only spiritual threats to preserve that freedom. But when this idea had spread to the universal Church, owing to the Cluniac monk Hildebrand becoming Pope, the problem of freeing the Church from simony and lay control was so urgent that the popes used not only spiritual anathemas but threats of deposition and finally force. These are the second and third stages within this third stage. Thus we find Hildebrand, now Gregory VII, excommunicating Henry IV and freeing his subjects from their allegiance to him (1076). Gregory succeeded in this way in bringing Henry to heel at Canossa. But the implication was this, that the Church was supreme in secular as well as in religious affairs, at least indirectly; for a man who can depose a sovereign has the ultimate authority. No Pope, not even Innocent III, would claim control of kings in mundane affairs, but the medieval popes certainly claimed the right to depose kings who transgressed the moral law; and this in itself is control in the most fundamental aspect of government, namely, the obedience a subject owes to his sovereign. But, almost inevitably, this led to the use of force, as the only sure means of seeing that the excommunications and depositions were carried out. Hildebrand had

cleared the Imperialists out of Rome by force, later popes were
to fight bloody wars with the emperors, in order to have their
own way; and they did have their own way, the victory of the
Papacy was complete. The failure to realize that the popes
were also feudal lords has led many an historian to misjudge
the actions of the great medieval popes. Not all their acts were
done as spiritual overlords but many simply as secular ones.

What are the rights and wrongs of this third stage? In this
England, with its state religion and its 400 years of Erastian-
ism, the tendency of historical writing has been to excuse the
supremacy of state over Church, and to condemn the supremacy of Church over state. The Protestant Churches arose as a
protest against the worldly power of the Papacy and its taxes,
which it levied to preserve that medieval power. But, now that
we have passed into a new age where the dangers of state
tyranny are increasingly evident, the approach to the old
problem is more sober and less filled with the passions of long
ago. Let us, then, consider the problem in the light of the
events at Anagni.

The view that the Papacy from Hildebrand to Boniface
upheld in the Middle Ages, as has been expounded above,
would be held to-day by any theologian, though the procedure
if a sovereign acted tyrannically would most certainly be different. The Church then and now considers that all authority
comes from God, and anyone holding authority, but not keeping the laws of God in his relationships with his subjects, is
ipso facto in those respects not to be obeyed. Indeed, he could
be deposed by peaceful means and in the last resort by force.
Thus, when the popes deposed emperors or kings, they were
only expressing the teaching that the Church, being guardian
and teacher of morals, can state when a ruler ceases to have a
right to the allegiance of his subjects.

But two points must be noted. In the first place, the medieval
popes, from the time of Innocent IV, claimed that the authority

of emperors, and therefore even more so that of kings, came directly from the popes. 'He who denies that the temporal sword is in the power of Peter, misunderstands the words of the Lord, "Put up thy sword into the sheath". Both are in the power of the Church, the spiritual and the material. But the latter is to be used for the Church, the former by her; the former by the priest, the latter by kings and captains, but at the will and by the permission of the priest. The one sword, then, should be under the other, and temporal authority subject to spiritual' ('Unam Sanctam').

This, as Professor Powicke points out in his book, *Christian Life in the Middle Ages*, Oxford, 1935 (p. 56), was only one of the alternative views held in the High Middle Ages, and was accepted by Boniface. The other view, and the one generally held now, was that each is supreme in its own sphere, and the secular power gets its authority immediately from God and not through the Church. The democratic principle we shall examine later.

The second point is that the medieval popes themselves used force in the interests of what they considered right, keeping an army, waging war; but the Church has abandoned that for good. The Papal Guard is an ornament and a relic, not a threat to world peace. In the time of Pius IX its members made a token resistance to the troops of Garibaldi, and no more.

The outrage of Anagni described above was the almost inevitable result of the medieval extreme view as upheld by Boniface. This stroke of extreme violence really put an end to that order of things, shattering the fragile Papal polity.

Because the balance has changed, we are not bound to hold that this is all for the best. A century ago a defence of the medieval papal states would have been received with shouts of derisive laughter. To-day, when the secular power, now emancipated from moral and ecclesiastical tutelage, has emerged as the Leviathan, steel-fisted, absolute, and ruthless, we are less inclined to minimize the usefulness of any check upon this new colossus. Historically speaking, the breakdown of the medieval order was undertaken by the nation-states which grew during the struggle between pope and emperor, using spiritual reformers as their tools. Anagni was the first blow struck in the interests of the Absolute State, and by those who believe in such things it must be treated as a red-letter day. But for those who see, in the rise of national absolutism in economics, culture and religion, the re-birth of slavery, that day was the first lightning flash of the storm overhead, prelude to a cataclysm, the striking down of true liberty.

The wars between the popes and the emperors had left the Empire exhausted and impotent, the Papacy burdened with a vast machinery of taxation and a worldly spirit; but above all it left France powerful as the *Tertium Quid*; somewhat as the U.S.A. waxed rich and fat after the first World War and the South American states likewise after the second. This new power and prosperity was dazzling to those who governed France. When the Pope claimed that the kings had no right to tax ecclesiastical property, the reply of Philip was not obedience but rebellion and, with rebellion, insult. He could say in his own defence that the matter of the dispute was not in its essence religious, that it was a matter of economics. But the medieval mind worked somewhat differently from ours; it saw in everything a principle. Here was a matter of principle; was the Church in France inside or outside the jurisdiction of the lay power? In Philip's eyes the temporalities of the Church in his kingdom were within his jurisdiction, and he proceeded to tax them as he thought fit. Boniface, in a bull 'Clericis laicos' (1296), prohibited this procedure in as far as it included collecting money for waging wars. When Philip, as a reprisal, forbade the sending of money out of France into the coffers of the Papacy, the answer was the famous bull, 'Unam Sanctam' (1302), which stated unequivocally the position of Boniface :

Philip and every other civil ruler derived his right to rule from God via the Pope. Philip's reply to this, as it seemed to him, supreme act of pride was to send his emissaries to Anagni, the native town of Boniface, where he was residing, with instructions to seize his person; the results we have already described.

And so came to an end, in fact if not in theory, the wonderful edifice of Papal supremacy by which the world would be governed by the Church through spiritual and lay authority. In the Dark Ages the popes had indeed led Europe and saved it from collapse. The Church was the matrix whence came the medieval order, its schools and guilds, its universities and laws, its governments and its pleasures, its arts and its theatre, liturgy and architecture. But at Anagni a new spirit is alive : it is the spirit of nationalism and secularism, the spirit of the Renaissance princes, of the Reformation, and of the eighteenth century.

At Anagni the extreme views on authority came glaringly into violent conflict. It was in the interests of all men to find a compromise. No one could claim absolute certainty for his own view, it was not in the deposit of faith, though many a strange allegorical interpretation was given to texts from the Gospel. Here were the two powers, each supreme in its own order—that was conceded by all—but the precise relationship between them was in doubt because both claimed jurisdiction, though in different respects, over the same persons : the Pope over citizens as souls, the kings over clerics as citizens; the Pope over temporalities as tools for a spiritual purpose, the kings over spiritualities, i.e. ecclesiastical property, because they were needed for their wars. Where did the frontiers lie ? The popes had a tradition of authority; they had won the day against the emperors; Boniface tended to overplay his hand; while on the other side, the French king was fresh in the experience of power, and he resented any sign of constraint.

While Boniface VIII was stiffening the view of Papal supremacy, a friend of Nogaret was writing a book which proved to be a most potent weapon against the Papal theory. Little is known about the man save that his name was Marsilio or Marsiglio or Marsilius, and he is said to be of Padua. But his book, the *Defensor Pacis*, survives, and it is the book that matters. Between 1312 and 1313 Marsilio was Rector of the University of Paris. Whether he was a lawyer, a medical man, or a theologian is unknown. He seems to have had a hankering for the soldier's life. But it is clear that, whatever else he may have been, he was no philosopher; as Dr. Hughes writes, 'He was not of that elect company, possessed of the metaphysical intuition of being' (*History of the Church*, vol. III, p. 146, Sheed & Ward, 1947).

His theories may be tabulated in the following manner :

   i.   The Church must be kept out of politics.

   ii.   Law is not a matter of reason, but of Will; what the state wills is law and so right.

   iii.   The Church must be subject to the state.

His aim was to transfer to the state the power wielded by the popes. He therefore not only denied that the clergy had any right to interfere in civil matters, but even claimed that they had no legislative rights in ecclesiastical affairs. All the clergy had a right to do was to administer the Sacraments. The only authority within the Church was the faithful; and what they wanted at any time was right.

On the other hand, having eliminated the Church's authority, he proceeds to hand it over to the state. By maintaining that law had naught to do with reason, and that it was nothing more than the will of the state, he presented to the latter a weapon, the extent of whose power we know very well to-day.

The arguments he used were not very profound, but they

proved very congenial to his patrons and to the makers of the
English Reformation—Cromwell had his book translated into
English. He held that a state should be a unity, and therefore it
should have one government, for division would create weakness. In this way he could not only eliminate Church authority,
but also hand over to the state whatever authority was needed.
What a tremendous weapon this became, with the rise of the
Reformation worthies, with which to strike down the Papal
power. The arguments of this medieval schoolman became the
arguments of the Reformers.

Following Prof. Previté-Orton in his introduction to the
Defensor Pacis, we give the argument of Marsilio for ousting
the Pope from his supreme position as follows : the authority
in a state must be one, whether an individual or a group. This
he takes from Aristotle. Consequently it is against Nature for
there to be two authorities, lay and ecclesiastical. But this
opinion seems to be against the Christian faith. He therefore
proceeds to show that Christ never laid down a rival authority
to the secular power. As the Pope is the centre of that usurped
authority, he shows that Christ never instituted a vicar to himself, nor made any apostle senior to any other, that in any
case St. Peter succeeded St. Paul as bishop of Rome, and that
in the early Church there was no difference between priests
and bishops. Besides, their function is only to administer the
Sacraments. His final shot is that, now that peace is provided
for the Christians, they are the ultimate authority and should
elect their pastors.

The driving power behind this monumental attack upon the
Papacy and all its works was, as M. de Lagarde points out on
page 53 of his book,[1] the experience and memory of the inter-
necine strife between the city-states of northern Italy, fomented
by papal 'policy'. Marsilio turns to the popes: 'The disgrace of

---

[1] *La naissance de l'esprit laïque au déclin du moyen âge*, II, Marsile
de Padoue, Georges de Lagarde, Paris, 1948.

your political activity in Italy is the wars that you have strewn over it. Thousands of the faithful have been killed; death has surprised them with hate or wickedness still in their hearts, consigning them thus to eternal damnation; the survivors, unfortunate wretches, have no hope of escape from an equally miserable fate except some miraculous intervention of God. Quarrelling and hatred and wrangling fill their minds and drive them into war. Men and women are equally corrupted, and live for vice, sin, crime and debauchery. Families, utterly exhausted, die out from sterility, the greatest houses in the land and indeed the most famous have been abandoned by their inhabitants, the fields remain untilled, and as the final stage of misery, divine worship is almost everywhere abolished, the churches deserted, having been abandoned by their pastors' (*Defensor Pacis,* II, chap. xxvii, 19, p. 422, Previté-Orton ed., C.U.P., 1926, quoted by de Lagarde).

He calls upon all to join him in his attack against 'these Roman bishops with their horde of clerks and cardinals' (*ibid.,* II, chap xxv, 18, p. 395). He is the father of anti-clericalism, and for one brief period he had his reward. In the struggle between Louis of Bavaria and the Papacy he is at the side of Louis. In 1328 he is in Rome with his master, assists at his coronation and becomes spiritual vicar of the Emperor. The Emperor is not crowned by the Pope, but by the head of the 'people', Sciarra Colonna. He reached the height of secular bliss on 18th April, when the Emperor, together with all his clergy and his knights, deposed the Pope, John XXII, and the 'People' were called upon to elect another.

But the triumph was ephemeral. If any example be needed to prove the truth of the saying, '*qui mange du Pape, en meurt*', the subsequent story of Louis will provide it. He soon had to withdraw from Rome, his army dwindling to nothing, his popularity fast vanishing, and, never recognized as emperor by successive popes, he died of apoplexy in 1347.

Marsilio went North with his master in the retreat from Rome, and seems to have stayed by him; but after that brilliant opening to the secular state, the sequel was nothing but disappointment. The fortunes of his imperial master did not prosper, even Marsilio's fellow imperialists began to turn against his own extreme views, notably William of Ockham. And the possibility of a peaceful settlement between the Empire and the Papacy, though more than once attempted, broke down precisely because he, Marsilio, was still at court, and the Pope would have no reconciliation until the heretics, such as he, had been removed. He died some time before 1343. (Cf. de Lagarde, op. cit., pp. 36–41.)

As M. G. de Lagarde points out in his book,[1] the *Defensor Pacis* was greater than the man and the doctrine greater than the book. Few facts are known about the man, few have the inclination or the leisure to read the book, but the doctrine pervaded the later Middle Ages and became common doctrine at the Reformation. In any case the problem Marsilio tackles is a fundamental one for a Christian society, the only society perhaps where the spiritual and temporal powers have been divided, in the sense of being independent of each other in their own sphere of action.

Lord Acton, in his *Essays on Freedom*, maintained that the greatest safeguard of men's liberties was that these two powers were separate, and that so long as neither party had absolutely the upper hand, men were able to grasp some degree of freedom. The age of Boniface VIII and Marsilio saw the supremacy of the Papacy. The natural reaction to it occurred; men revolted against the totalitarian nature of that power. But Marsilio and his following, unwittingly no doubt, attempted to throw us out of the papal frying-pan into the state fire. Whatever the true answer is, it is not the Absolute State. At least, the Church claimed to act upon the principles of Christ, and it

[1] Loc. cit., p. 172 n.

could be censured if it did not live up to its claim; but the state has no mandate from on high, no sense of obligation; the slaveries that have descended upon many peoples of eastern Europe in recent years are a direct result of the laicizing of government.

CHAPTER XI

AUTONOMOUS MAN

'Take but degree away, untune that string,
And, hark, what discord follows! each thing meets
In mere oppugnancy: the bounded waters
Should lift their bosoms higher than the shores,
And make a sop of all this solid globe:
Strength should be lord of imbecility,
And the rude son should strike his father dead:
Force should be right; or rather, right and wrong,
Between whose endless jar justice resides,
Should lose their names, and so should justice too.
Then every thing includes itself in power,
Power into will, will into appetite:
And appetite, an universal wolf,
So doubly seconded with will and power,
Must make perforce an universal prey,
And last eat up himself. . . .'

WILLIAM SHAKESPEARE, Ulysses in
Troilus and Cressida, Act 1, scene iii.

WITH the explosion of Anagni and the publication of the *Defensor Pacis,* we pass from the formative centuries of Christendom into a world of uncertainties among actors who know their parts, but these are not all parts of the same play. The Europe of Christendom no longer spoke with one voice; there is the sound of conflict, of doubt and a sense of disunity. The fissures are at first only just discernible, but the shock of Anagni certainly disturbed the very foundations themselves.

This is meant as a constructive essay in that it attempts to show the nature of the principles which created Christendom, their growth and their application to the whole of medieval and modern life. Therefore those who broke it, consciously or unconsciously, only concern us in so far as they explain the problems with which the traditional writers and thinkers were faced. Each new problem produced a new solution, but based on the traditional premisses.

We shall therefore consider in chronological order the following representative persons, who each in his own way is a symbol of the collapse of the thing we call Christendom. They are Machiavelli, Luther, Rabelais, Rousseau. Having done that, we can then return to the upholders of the old ideas and examine the way they attempted to support the mighty structure. Each will not treat of the whole of the subject, nor did each person treat our subject in a new way, so our task will be eased. They are Thomas More, martyr saint and Chancellor of England; Ignatius Loyola, founder of the Jesuits, a Basque; Newman, an historian and philosopher; the series of popes beginning with Leo XIII and reaching the present day with Pius XII, then finally St. Thérèse of Lisieux.

In each branch of human life there were now, in the dusk of the Middle Ages, signs of a rising autonomy; each department was freeing itself from the restrictions of the moral law. There is a sense in which autonomy is good, every science and art has its own object, its own method—theology has nothing to say about making telescopes—but there is a sense in which autonomy can become disastrous, namely, when a science becomes an end in itself and ignores the wider requirements of the whole man. The reason for this pervading restlessness does not seem to lie in any deep-seated rational position; almost in every case it arose through abuse of the theological authority wielded by the Church; for as usual, one extreme in human affairs leads to its opposite. As we have seen, in the case of the quarrel between Philip of France and Pope Boniface VIII, the extreme papal view induced in the opposition the extreme secular view as expounded by Marsilio of Padua. The same is true in economics, science, religious orders, indulgences. The breakdown of medieval life as governed by the Guilds was primarily due to the failure of that glorious medieval institution to adapt itself to changing circumstances; the masters in the later Middle Ages were commonly more interested in their own protection than in that of the whole trade. From being city units they should have become nation units, but this only partially succeeded. Traders and bankers, tied to no guild, took advantage of their freedom, breaking the restrictive regulations of particular guilds, thus making it impossible for honest men to earn a living honestly. Here to-day, gone to-morrow, no one could control their nefarious dealings or call the culprits to book.

In the Middle Ages the craft guilds regulated the economic life of their members according to the moral law; thus the conditions of work were inspected, the hours, the number of employees; the finished article was also examined, this time to provide a guarantee to the general public; supplies of materials were shared out evenly : for instance, the millers of Southampton each received a due proportion of the corn that came in on the ships; the price of the corn would be set fairly, the price of the finished article likewise. Each master craftsman was limited in the number of employees, of journeymen and apprentices he was allowed. The aim in this was to give each craftsman in the town the chance of a livelihood, otherwise one man might squeeze out all the others, or goods flood the restricted market. Though no one would maintain that conditions were perfect, it is now generally admitted that the guilds in the Middle Ages were based on sound moral principles, and that on the whole they worked for the good of the community.

When masters began to make it difficult for others to be

admitted to the guilds, and only because they wanted more profit for themselves, disgruntled journeymen or enterprising masters left the towns and set up their primitive factories in the country, where no restrictive laws existed.

Before the age of the eighteenth-century economic nationalism there had first arisen the break-away from the guild system. This break-away is but one of the many examples of the rise of autonomous man, in this case the autonomy of economics. And when the mercantile system of the eighteenth century began to break down in its turn, the movement was not a return to the moral law as opposed to nation necessity, but towards the complete autonomy of *laissez-faire*.

It is only with the rise of Christian social teaching, particularly Papal doctrine, that a return to justice has become apparent. That will be discussed later.

(i) MACHIAVELLI

One's natural impulse, after reading Lord Acton's essay on Machiavelli, would be to preserve a discreet silence on the man and his work. The number of authorities quoted in that article is staggering, and that was eighty years ago. What is the number now? Machiavelli is in the news, for it is certain that the lessons he taught have been assiduously learned by more than one would-be dictator from Henry VIII onwards.

But Lord Acton was, as it were, after ethical game; he wanted to know what Machiavelli's views were, *in foro interno,* in the depths of conscience. Lord Acton wished to discover— no two writers before or after seem to have agreed on the point —'Was Machiavelli disclaiming any moral responsibility for the views he was expounding in the little book, *The Prince?* Was he merely saying what would succeed in this wicked world of ours?' It is difficult to say. Nor need we bother. We may take the stand that the Church takes when judging a book, which is to ask what does a writer say, not what does he mean to say?

That is between him and God. We want to know the impression
that he makes upon the ordinary unprepared reader.

Il Principe, written by Nicolo Machiavelli (1469–1527)
during that period of enforced retirement from the very exacting and exciting business of Florence's city-state international
politics, gives the impression that it does not pay to keep the
moral code in international affairs. In other words, we have
here in blatant undisguised language the advice to abandon
the rule of law in international relations and to resort to the
rules of guile or force. Now, no sensible man would deny that
force plays a large part in international politics, quite as great
indeed as the police force does in home politics. But our concern is that it should, like the police force, be put to the service
of right.

After describing in some detail how Cæsar Borgia rose to
power by the most unscrupulous means, Machiavelli sums up
in chapter 7 :

'When all the actions of the duke are recalled, I do not
know how to blame him, but rather it appears to me, as I have
said, that I ought to offer him for imitation to all those who, by
the fortune or the arms of another, are raised to government.
Because he, having a lofty spirit and far-reaching aims, could
not have regulated his conduct otherwise. Therefore, he who
considers it necessary to secure himself in his new principality,
to win friends, to overcome either by force or fraud . . . to
exterminate those who have power or reason to hurt him . . .
cannot find a more lively example than the actions of this man'
(chap. 7, p. 62. Everyman ed., trans. W. K. Marriot); or see
the passage in chapter 18 (loc. cit., p. 143) : '. . . a prince,
especially a new one, cannot observe all those things for which
men are esteemed, being often forced, in order to maintain the
state, to act contrary to fidelity, friendship, humanity, and
religion . . . not to diverge from the good if he can avoid doing
so, but, if compelled, then to know how to set about it'.

In fact, many a ruler had so acted even before *Il Principe* was written. But the difference between the Christian king acting against his conscience and the renaissance prince acting according to the rules of Machiavelli is that the former knows he should not and perhaps repents, while the latter is convinced that he should and does it. Machiavelli's *Il Principe* was a kind of salve of conscience to rulers, it gave them an excuse. If others acted by it, how could they survive without doing the same?

Once it was generally admitted that morality or law, *Lex Gentium*, did not really rule in relationships between states, but only 'combinations', then a new method had to be invented to preserve the peace. The idea of a supreme court of appeal, the Pope or the Emperor, being abandoned, truces of God being outmoded, it became imperative to find some other stable force to preserve the peace. This was the principle of the balance of power; not force in the service of law, which is justice, but power and brute force had become paramount, and they are still. That has been one of the most fatal steps in our decline. The situation, of course, in this matter was much worsened by the break-up of Christendom at the Reformation, for then there was no centre to which to appeal, no authoritative voice. The failure of the Thirty Years War to end with a clear victory for one side or the other, and the Treaty of Westphalia which followed (1648), sealed and signed the contract of pathetic Europeans to agree on one thing only, to agree to differ. The divisions have grown deeper ever since.

The disciples or admirers of Machiavelli might with justice remark that it is not surprising he wrote such a book at such a time. Did the Papacy show many signs of giving spiritual leadership in the affairs of Europe? That is the crucial point, and we Catholics must face it squarely. We will admit that the Papacy and the great ecclesiastical feudal lords were little better than their neighbours in their schemings and their unscrupulous diplomacy. We beat our breasts and admit the shame. *Quis custodiat custodes, quis custodiat custodem?* He, the successor of Peter, has no equal upon earth, no man to keep him in check, he is responsible to God alone; and that must be a burden which few men can bear. Yet, when we examine the list of popes, how few have been bad, how many good, how many saints and martyrs.

We recognize that the Renaissance Papacy gave an excuse to those lay princes and their advisers for not trusting to the honesty of others, and for their breaking away altogether from morality in world affairs. Yet this admission does not justify their acts, though it excuses and explains them. And once we see that, it becomes our business to-day in the twentieth century to put our world right in this respect. We must set up a court of international law, abide by its decisions, and give it power.

But the disorder has become so great that we find it difficult to establish a court which all will trust and respect and still more difficult to give it the force necessary to ensure that its decisions will be upheld. For our world has become the whole, and contains within it many millions and many nations whose views of right and justice are not ours.

There is but one solution, and that is for those who live by the old Christian ways to unite in forming some such court for themselves. Otherwise we will be forced to admit the terrifying dictum of Pascal, who, though a Catholic, echoes in this respect the spirit of Luther. They seem to despair of human nature and of finding the natural law, let alone of keeping it.

(This *pensée* is often mistranslated, so I give my own version.)

No. 298 (Brunschvicg edition, Hachette):

'Justice, force. It is right that what is right should be followed, it is bound to be that the strongest should have his way. Justice without force is powerless; force without justice is tyrannical. Justice without force is gainsaid, because the wicked will always exist; force without justice is condemned. Therefore we must bring together justice and force, and to this end either make what is just strong or what is strong just. Justice is subject to dispute, force is very evident and not subject to dispute. Thus, it has not been possible to make justice strong, because force has gainsaid justice and said that it itself was just. And so, not being able to arrange that what is just should be strong, men have agreed that what is strong should be called just.'

(*On a fait que ce qui est fort fût juste.*)

(ii) MARTIN LUTHER

The second name on the list and by far the most important is Luther. It would be foolish to attempt in this place a full-length account of Luther's thought. Much of that, in any case, would be difficult and controverted; here we shall undertake a simpler task, namely, describe the stages by which he broke with Rome, provide the background for that act, and then examine his views on liberty. On these points the opinion of scholars is more or less unanimous, and in our subject these points are vital.

The story of Luther's break with the Papacy is simple. Luther began by attacking the sale of indulgences, that is, the promise by Rome that, for giving money to build the new St. Peter's, any member of the Church would be excused a certain number of days of Purgatory. Note that the particular 'sale' which Luther took exception to was specially commercialized, but also that he did not primarily condemn the turning of alms-giving and indulgences into a business concern; he condemned indulgences in themselves. Thus in his sixth thesis he wrote :
'The Pope has neither the desire nor the power to remit any penalties except those he has laid down by his own will according to the will of the canons.'

The behaviour of pardoners was a great scandal in the

Church. We are all familiar with the rascally pardoner of Chaucer's *Canterbury Tales*; the technique of hawkers of indulgences has often been described, especially the farming out of the collecting to moneylenders. But to show the universality of the abuse, an incident in that vivid picaresque novel, *Lazarillo de Tormes* (*c.* A.D. 1554), may be recalled.

Lazaro was a vagabond youth, serving his apprenticeship in begging under a blind man; he later joined a priest, next a friar, and then a pardoner and his mate, a seller of bulls or indulgences. In one town in the archdiocese of Toledo the man's wares were not selling at all. On the third evening he and his mate had a quarrel over a bet, and the latter shouted that the pardoner was a fraud. This got to the ears of the parishioners, and next morning, when the pardoner was in the pulpit and at the height of his oration, the disgruntled assistant entered the church crying out, 'He is a fraud'. The pardoner thereupon made an impassioned appeal to God from the pulpit to strike him and the pulpit through the floor if that were so. But if the assistant were lying, he implored God to strike him down instead. No sooner had he uttered the prayer than the assistant fell down foaming at the mouth. After much excitement the pardoner agreed to pray again, and his mate came back to his senses, confessed his fault, with the result that the bulls or pardons were all sold in a trice.

As the three left the town, Lazaro heard his two companions congratulating each other on the ruse. Only a story, it may be said. Yes, but it shows which way the wind was blowing. It is incontrovertible, the sale of indulgences was much abused. It was this extreme example of merit and good works that infuriated Luther and moved him to act.

Luther had had enough and the revolt began. Its stages may be easily discerned; first he refused to obey the summons to Rome made to him by Leo X; next, in his interview with the Cardinal Legate, Cajetan, he refused to retract. Then he wrote to the Pope, appealing from the Pope ill-informed to the Pope better-informed. But in all this he only wanted an endorsement of his own views by Rome, not a submission of his views to Rome. This is clear from the next step he took, for Luther actually wrote a letter of submission to Rome at the instigation of Charles von Miltiz, but in it he did not retract his heresy, he reaffirmed it, and of course the letter was unacceptable to Leo X.

The disputation held at Leipzig in 1519 between Luther and the Ingoldstadt professor of theology, John Eck, is the epitome of Luther's subsequent history. Luther now maintained that the Pope's authority was only of human origin. When Eck appealed to the Fathers of the Church, Augustine, Jerome, Chrysostom and the rest, Luther contradicted them without a blush. Tradition therefore for Luther held no certainty. When Eck appealed to the Councils of the Church, Luther replied that, as they were composed of men, they could err. Thus there remained the Sacred Scriptures alone. But they too were arrayed against him. He denied several of the books whose texts were produced to disprove his theses. He finally appealed to the authority of his own conscience and private inspiration. Having appealed to the Pope as his authority and found the Pope against him, as he refused to retract his views, he was forced from one defensive position to another, until the only authority or obedience left to him was his own will. That is the core of Protestantism.[1]

Luther's contempt for the authority of men and for the human reason is a symptom of the age in which he lived, more especially of the Nominalism of the Augustinian Friars and

---

[1] In the case of England, the Anglicans have denied the authority of the Pope and therefore of the living voice; they have to admit a divided Christendom, in which there is no teaching authority. In their appeal to tradition and to sacred Scripture, they cannot agree among themselves. We say this, not captiously, but as a statement of fact which is not unconnected with the assault on authority by Luther at Leipzig in 1519.

other thinkers, chiefly Franciscans, of the later Middle Ages. (Cf. Paquier, art. 'Luther', in the *D.T.C.*)[1] But for our purposes it is the fact which is of importance. It was this Nominalism which helped Luther to escape from controversy and retire behind the blind walls of a voluntarist faith.

Luther's attitude to Law was vitiated by the same distrust of reason. Luther's rejection of reason as a tool for finding truth had the most disastrous effect. It meant that if one could not see the reasonableness of a law, the only justification for it was the WILL of the ruler.[2] Luther in this way played into the hands of the princes, those aspiring tyrants, flourishing in his day and flourishing yet.

The rise of the autonomous states was almost contemporaneous with the rise of Luther; they had emerged a century earlier, after the exhaustion of Empire and Papacy. The kingdoms of Spain, France and England were the chief beneficiaries of that struggle, and were well on the road to glittering power. They could not resist the advantage of such a theory as Luther presented to them; and all, even the Catholic ones, only in varying degrees, absorbed this virulent idea. The sovereign is above the law, for it emanates from his will. The king can do no wrong : the divine right of kings. Though there is a just meaning to the last phrase, it was much abused.

Thus Luther's innovations did not end at the break with Rome. Having cast aside the anchor of authority, he swept out into the open sea of religious experience. He abandoned nature as in any sense good, and with it inevitably the human reason for which he kept some of his choicer sayings, for instance, a passage in the final sermon at Wittenberg, quoted

---

[1] *Le dictionnaire de théologie catholique,* ed. Vacant, Mangenot, Amann.

[2] This might be reasonable in the case where the ruler was guided by God; but who, to-day, would assert that of secular rulers?

by J. Maritain in *Three Reformers* (p. 33. Sheed & Ward, 1941): 'Reason is the devil's greatest whore; by nature and manner of being she is a noxious whore; she is a prostitute ... who ought to be trodden underfoot and destroyed. . . .'

It may be kind to excuse Luther's vulgarity and vehemence on the grounds that he was a vulgar and vehement man; but, having reduced the idea to its elemental form, the truth remains that he abandoned reason in the same way as he had given up authority. And as confusion became worse confounded, with the Peasants' Rising, the monks and nuns leaving their monasteries and convents, he leant more and more on the civil power, to put it bluntly, upon force, in order to safeguard his reform.

'What kind of Christian doctrine is this, that the Temporal Power is not above the Spiritual?' (*Appeal to the German Nobility,* 1520. Cf. Bettenson, loc. cit., p. 273).

If reason was impotent, then how could men discover what should be done? So the Natural Law, which had been discovered by human reason, also had to go. And so the intellectual slaughter went on. But in any case Luther held that man was too corrupted in his very nature ever to do a just act. Men were not saved by good behaviour, works were of no avail. Men were saved by trust in God, by faith alone.

Luther, far from being a person congenial to the Humanists of the age, appears as their very antithesis—he cast aside the two things they cherished, reason and human nature. This we shall see when studying Rabelais, who, while being destructive, is a typical humanist and held views the complete opposite of Luther; for the very things he prized were his own capacity for thought and his own body and its powers, all of which he saw were good, and all of which Luther saw as bad.

Obedience was as much a red rag to Luther as were reason and law. He cast aside his monk's habit, he married a nun, he encouraged with all his eloquence the flight from convents and

monasteries; religious life had no meaning now that salvation
depended on faith alone.

Luther was also angered at the idea of obeying a foreigner.
Obedience to an Italian Pope was unworthy of a German, 'the
Master race', to use his own words. So he is also at the source
of nationalism or even racialism in religion, and stands con-
victed of that crime against Europe, the attempt to split its
soul. Europe was no longer one thing.

A civilization is a common way of life which means that
all the men and women in it live by commonly accepted principles, not of course in trivial matters, but concerning marriage,
property, right and wrong, sanctions, law. These in their turn
will depend upon the religion or faith common to them all.

Every civilization up to date has been based on a religion,
or set of ideas, which is accepted without question as coming
from an infallible source or tradition. It is with truth that we
speak of a Hindu or a Buddhist or Confucian or Mohammedan
scripture. Each of these was taken without question as true;
every child would be taught it as the Way. Even the Russian
experiment has its Scripture which no one would dare to contradict.

The Western world of to-day is not based on any infallible
Scripture; yet we know, if we examine closely enough, that for
fifteen hundred years it was; and even now half Europe, if
not geographically at least numerically, holds to that Scripture, that tradition and that living interpretation of it, which
are the Bible and the Roman and Catholic Church. When
Luther broke with that millennium and a half of tradition, he
broke something in a day which it had taken all those years
to create.

How could this thing be? Leaving aside the political
motives, which were as we have seen fairly prominent, what
could have induced so many, those who had the interests of
the Church at heart, to break that most precious unity, to rend

the seamless garment? If we can find the answer to that, we may find the answer to the riddle of how to bring their spiritual heirs back into the unity of the One, Catholic and Apostolic Church.

This question of obedience gives us a clue. If Christian obedience follows immediately on love, as we have been at pains to show, then obedience went when love went. We know that obedience went with the refusal of Luther to conform to the rulings of the Diet of Worms. Had Luther loved the Papacy, perhaps he might not have broken with it.

Of course, there are the polemic arguments by which Luther and his confederates ventured to prove that the Papacy was a man-made thing. But the fact remains that he hated the Papacy—which emerges from examining his sayings and his propaganda, particularly a little book of drawings in which he shows the Papacy as the fount of evil, the Scarlet Woman.

We know only too well that when a quarrel has once started, particularly an international one, both sides vilify each other in order to keep up the morale of their own side. For by showing how wicked the other side is, fuel is fed to the fires of self-righteousness. This was certainly the case in the quarrel between the Reformers and the Popes. But still the question remains, how could it be that they allowed themselves to vilify this once sacred thing, this very heart of the Christian world, this Mother?

One might reply that they had found her out, that it was a great hoax, built up on false Decretals and on false Donations of Constantine. There is something in that. But would not more serious-minded historians admit to-day that these were rather arguments used after the event to bolster up the position of the Reformers? But even granted that the argument was a genuine one, there still stands the problem why they wanted to destroy what centuries of men had venerated with the veneration of children for their mother.

The answer surely is that the Papacy had fallen on evil days. It no longer fulfilled in the eyes of many the functions of a loving mother. Love had gone out of the relationship between the northern kingdoms and the Papacy. The popes had been drawn into a secular struggle with the Empire; they had called upon the nations to contribute largely for this war; then at one time the Papacy had become a pawn of the French monarchy; next it had been divided—there had been contemporaneously three Popes; later the first evident rift appeared. There was the call for reform, and, as the popes were slow to move, the cry grew that perhaps the Council was above the Pope. The louder the cry, the more timorous of reforming councils did the popes become.

Next came the Renaissance and the worldly popes, themselves a scandal; and all hope of reform from that quarter seemed dead. Meanwhile, the popes were playing their game of power politics with their rival city-states of Italy. First the Papacy lost the respect of the Christian world, then love evaporated, and with love obedience.

It will be objected that, in spite of all, obedience should have survived; that may be true in theory, but it was not true in practice. Doubtless Jesus Christ, the founder of the Church, had said that he had given the keys of the Kingdom to Peter, that upon the Rock, Peter, he would build his Church, and that the gates of hell would not prevail against it. But it took St. Thomas More many a year and many a weary vigil to convince himself that the authority of the successor of St. Peter was of divine and not of human origin. Things were not as clear in those days as they have become since the definition of the doctrine of infallibility by the Council of the Vatican (1870). In the end Thomas More was ready to die for it, and he saw it with the utmost clarity; but for those who had ceased to love the Papacy as they saw it, it was an easy matter to show that it could be destroyed and no harm come to the Christian world. And that is what they proceeded to do; and that is the position which we have inherited.

But a great change has come over the world since the explosion of the sixteenth century : the Papacy is no longer a thing to be derided, nor is it merely one among a pack of petty rival city-states; it does once again stand as the spiritual power free from political affiliations, above party strife, with a recent history of charity and fearlessness. The first to give the warning against the dangerous elements in Communism, Fascism and Nazi-ism was the Pope of the time, Pius XI. May we not expect that fair-minded Christians will once again turn to the successors of Peter as once, and many times before, their ancestors had done in times of distress? May they perhaps forget the human failings of this divine institution, as Christ overlooked the weakness of Peter himself, and once again make pilgrimage to the Tomb of the Apostle and cast themselves at the feet of his successor? As Peter himself had cried to his divine Master, may they too cry to his servant and theirs, 'Save us lest we perish'. Then Jesus will surely guide his mind and ours into ways of peace.

(iii) François Rabelais

Rabelais is a typical renaissance figure, wrapped round by the Church from his earliest youth, yet inquisitive, optimistic, universal, restless under restraint, bursting with animal spirits, unaware perhaps of the part he was playing in the destruction of the slowly built-up edifice of Christendom in his admiration for all things new and his contempt for most things old.

It is thought that François Rabelais was put by his parents when still a child—somewhat as Erasmus had been—into a Franciscan friary, that of Fontenay-le-Comte. He was there in 1511; he remained there at least twelve years, and those the most impressionable in any man's life. His flight was not due to the slackness of the life in that house, rather the reverse, for it was a house of strict observance; nor did he in fact go immediately into the world—he joined a Benedictine monastery. It was only later that he went to Montpellier to study medicine, and in 1532 he was working in the *Hôtel-Dieu* (i.e. the hospital) in Lyons.

M. Etienne Gilson, in his brilliant studies, *Les idées et les lettres* (Paris, 1932), has finally disposed of the atheism myth with regard to Rabelais; he further shows that this mendicant friar's mind was impregnated with scholastic and patristic learning, and has demonstrated that those parts of Rabelais' writing which shock the modern reader by their blasphemous irreverences can be capped by similar writings of other Franciscans of the time and even earlier whose orthodoxy was unimpeachable.

For all the white-washing, a residue of revolt remains, not a revolt of heresy perhaps, nor one consciously thought out, but one of ideas. He was, after all, a contemporary of Luther, Calvin and the rest. We are concerned with his view of obedience as expounded in his two famous books, *Pantagruel* and *Gargantua*, published 1532–4. The views there expressed are startlingly 'modern'. Rabelais imagines an abbey after his own heart, and very different from the ideals of St. Benedict. The setting of the abbey of Thélème is fantastic, but the intention is serious. In chapter lvii he describes 'how the Thelemites were governed and of the manner of their living'.

'All their lives were not spent in laws, statutes or rules, but according to their own free will and pleasure. . . . In all their rule the strictest of their order, there was but one clause to be observed : DO WHAT THOU WILT.' In French the famous phrase —'*Fais ce que voudras*'.

This was the exact antithesis of the ascetical ideal; it was the overthrow of obedience. And the reason comes pat : 'Because men that are free, well-born, well-bred and conversant in honest companies have naturally an instinct and spur that prompts them to virtuous actions and withdraws them from vice, an instinct which is called honour.'

Here Rabelais has abandoned the doctrine of the Fall and Original Sin in all the descendants of Adam. He is preaching the doctrine of the fundamental goodness of human nature, so gratifying to the proud, so consoling to the indolent and the weak.

What kind of a renaissance is this? It is a new form of humanism, neither like that of ancient Greece, which was devout to the gods, nor like that of the High Middle Ages, that of Dante and St. Francis, devout to God and aware of sin, but one in which Man seems to dissociate himself from gods or God. He would be obedient no more except to his own whims and fancies. This is the natural reading of Rabelais' paradoxical book. And though it is plausibly maintained that Rabelais was often only joking, as was the way in many an obscure friary in the later Middle Ages, and that it is possible to be frivolous on the subject of vows and obedience within the four walls of a convent without harm meant, this is a very different thing; here is a book published to the world in a moment of crisis when all men are questioning these very points that Rabelais chooses to scoff at. A saint, contemporary of Rabelais, had no doubt on the point, he himself an ornament to the Christian humanism of the time. St. Francis of Sales wrote in a letter (*Lettre DCXXXVII*, vol. IV, p. 376, ed. Dom. B. Mackey, Annecy):

'Above all, beware of bad books, and for nothing in the world allow your spirit to be carried away by certain writings which weak minds admire (*cervelles foibles*) on account of a number of vain subtleties which they inhale from them (*y hument*), such as that infamous Rabelais and certain others of our age, who make a profession of calling all in doubt, of decrying everything, and of scoffing at all the maxims of antiquity.'

Suppose we admit that the friars, as seems certain from the researches of M. Gilson, joked about such matters, it only goes to prove that they could not have held them in high esteem. Besides, what may be said in jest by one may become deadly earnest for another. It seems pretty certain that some of Rabelais' jesting was in earnest.

The Rabelaisian law, then, is to do as one likes. What a liberation this! The whole of the sexual life of man is thus freed from the rule of reason and may follow its own bent, bound by no law other than itself. Here is the great discovery of Rabelais, echoed, whether knowingly or not, by Rousseau two centuries later. This is the new Gospel; we know its fruits now, as he, Rabelais, could not in his day: the breakdown of family life, the insecurity of children and wives, neurosis and race suicide for pleasure's sake. *Fais ce que voudras.* It has had its compensations, but it has also had its penalties. For man, in spite of Rabelais' optimism, is a strange unbalanced fellow whose desires are as gigantic and out of proportion as were the characters in his book.

In the history of European civilization, Rabelais stands as one of those who brought down the edifice of the moral law, leaving men autonomous in morals, free from all restraint except their own good pleasure.

(iv) JEAN JACQUES ROUSSEAU

Rousseau was for the eighteenth century what Rabelais had been for the sixteenth. They speak the same language. There is little new in Rousseau save a strange new fire and urgency. Rousseau starts where Rabelais left off.

Having overthrown the moral law and the extrinsic guide in doctrine and morals, that is to say the Pope, the Europe of the post-Reformation had the great problem of finding a working substitute. Why should men obey? what is law? how preserve liberty? If men were bound by no law but their own wills, as was the Rabelaisian teaching, how could one justify the regulated life under unenlightened despots such as flourished in the eighteenth century?

Rousseau struggled for an answer, and found one which has been taken two contrary ways ever since. Some see in him the father of the French Revolution, others the father of the Absolute State.

Rousseau said—whatever he meant by it—that men were born free, and men have taken this to mean that in the beginning man was bound by no restraint; and to make it plain that he really meant this, in one of his *Rêveries d'un promeneur solitaire* he explains that at one time he had thought he should restrain his anger as it rose, but, realizing that all his passions were good, he believed that to do so would be wrong. He really did act by the motto, *'fais ce que voudras'*.

It follows that any law imposed from without by society is a curtailment of liberty; yet he saw that a return to the primitive state was unthinkable. What therefore was to be done? The answer is the Social Contract. 'The greatest good of all is not power but liberty. The truly free man only wants what he is capable of, and does as he pleases. That is my fundamental principle' (*Emile*, Bk. II). And a little farther on, 'Let us lay down as an undeniable first principle that the first movements of (human) nature are always right'.

In the sixth Promenade of the *Rêveries* he wrote, 'I no longer have any other rule of conduct than that of following in everything my desire (*penchant*) without constraint'.

If every man is a law unto himself, how may the state operate? Who has the right to make the laws unless it be all the people? And how can they make these laws? Rousseau's answer was in fact this, that, by subjecting oneself to the General Will, every man could remain both free and bound by the law. Suppose a member of the community, having voted against the law which in fact received a majority of the votes, was unwilling to submit, Rousseau, in a famous phrase, says that he must be forced to be free.

As the idea of right has been excluded and only the idea of will remains, the sole solution is the counting of votes; and, even suppose a law was against the real good of the community, it would still have to be carried out, because it was the expression of the General Will. Indeed, Rousseau would deny that a law could be against the real good, because men being fundamentally good, they will instinctively know what is for their good.

Thus for him freedom consists in freely accepting the General Will regardless of its reasonableness—and in this he is heir of Luther who despised reason—and in the second place he considers men free even if they do not want what they have to do. And by this paradox he ushered in the dictators of the twentieth century.

So the nineteenth century began with a chorus of praise for liberty and with the decrying of obedience, with the Jesuit Order suppressed in all the Catholic countries of Europe and the orgies of the French Revolution.

A quotation from Edward Gibbon will perhaps give one a better sense of the attitude of that age to obedience than one from any other writer could; he is discussing the rise of monasticism :

'The freedom of the mind, the source of every generous and rational sentiment, was destroyed by the habits of credulity and submission; and the monk, contracting the vice of a slave, devoutly followed the faith and passions of his ecclesiastical tyrant' (*The Decline and Fall,* ed. Bury, vol. IV, p. 66).

The division between the view that the above passage represents of monasticism and that of the medieval men is astonishing. The one considers this obedient spirit as the greatest slavery, the other as the truest freedom. This contrast is an indication of how far from its earlier principles the civilization we call Christendom had travelled.

But we cannot put the blame for this blindness upon those who like Gibbon were blind. The blame lies farther back, as we have repeatedly said, upon those men who, having the rich tradition, perverted or destroyed it.

Thus it is true that behind the ill will shown to the Catholic Church lies an historical experience which cannot be lightly shaken off. This experience is perhaps the most potent force there is for the failure to reintegrate European life along Christian lines.

The Church claims to speak with the voice of God. All just men agree that they must obey God's voice when they hear it, but they are loath to accept the voice of the Church as the voice of God, not only because it is irksome to do so—and this is a potent deterrent—but because the Church throughout her history has produced appalling examples of depravity along with those wonderful examples of holiness. That is the truth, and we must not deny it for the sake of controversy.

So, when we condemn the theories of a Rabelais or a Luther or a Rousseau, we do it with the beating of our own breasts, for none of them perhaps, in spite of pride or lust, would have gone to the lengths he did but for the evil he saw in the Church which claimed to be the very Mystical Body of Christ.

We must explain to them that while Christ did promise to safeguard the truths he taught when on earth, he never promised to make those guardians impeccable or free from the common sins of men. In twelve Apostles there was one Judas.

CHAPTER XII

THE RALLY

(i) St. Thomas More

PROVIDENCE must have been very active to have provided so complete and perfect a contrast to Luther and Rabelais in the person of Sir Thomas More, knight, one-time Chancellor of England. Luther turned his back on learning, Rabelais turned his back on tradition; Thomas More was the most complete example of the learning of the Renaissance, but at the same time he stood by tradition with a tenacity which cost him his life. He believed in man as Luther did not, but he believed also in Original Sin, which Rabelais seemed conveniently to have forgotten.

More's house at Chelsea was the model of the time: that delicious garden, the monkey, that gay conversation, those learned visitors, that throng of merry children, the sweet-natured Margaret with her scholarly ways, the lute playing and the madrigals of an evening. But hidden were also the hair shirt, those nightly vigils, that Friday dedicated to the Passion, that daily remembrance of the Cross at Mass in Chelsea church.

More was as acutely aware of the need for reform as any Luther or Rabelais; but, with his legal mind attuned to fine distinctions, he could disentangle the abuse from the thing. The former he would cut out, the latter he would preserve.

The crux came with the King's Matter—the dissolving of the marriage with Catherine of Aragon—the Pope's refusal, the marriage nevertheless with Anne Boleyn. Then came Henry's answer to the Pope: he claimed to be Head of the Church himself. In so far as the law of God allowed, this was ratified by the Convocations of York and Canterbury. Only one stood firm, Thomas More's friend, John Fisher, bishop of Rochester.

The Houses of Parliament also ratified it, but without the saving clause. Thomas More held his peace on this and on the King's marriage, for he saw trouble coming, and he would not trust to his own fortitude to resist torture or death, unless God gave him the sign. He was in no way bound to speak : he was now a private citizen, having given up his high office.

But finally, when brought before the Commission headed by Audley, Lord Chancellor, on 1st July, in St. Stephen's Hall, Westminster, he knew that the hour to speak had come. Now he must defend the Universal Church against the encroachment of the state, bear witness to the faith that was in him, which was : that no other head to the Church on earth under Christ could there be than the Successor of Peter, the Pope in Rome. This was a solemn moment in the history of England; it was the great stand made by the greatest man of his age for the tradition of a thousand years of Christian life.

The outcome of the struggle of this one man and a few like him, who had the courage to stand firm against the idolaters of the state, would decide the future history of this country. In the event More held his ground, but his example was not sufficient to rally those of his way of thinking to stand firm and so preserve this ancient thing. Victory went to the State and has lasted to this day.

The mind of More upon the great question of authority in the Church is known to us by his speeches as he stood condemned to die. They have been recorded in that noble biography written by Nicholas Harpsfield, scholar of Winchester, friend of Cardinal Pole and of all the family of More, with whom he shared exile in the days of Edward VI.

After the jury had found him guilty in spite of his most prudent and convincing defence, 'And incontinent upon their verdict, the Lord Chancellor . . . beginning to proceed in judgement against him, Sir Thomas More said unto him : "My Lord, when I was towards the law, the manner in such case was to ask the prisoner, before judgement, why judgement should not be given against him." Whereupon the Lord Chancellor staying his judgement . . . demanded of him what he was able to say to the contrary; who in this sort most humbly made answer :

' "Seeing that you are determined to condemn me (God knoweth how), I will now in discharge of my conscience speak my mind plainly and freely touching my indictment and your Statute withall.

' "And forasmuch as this indictment is grounded upon an Act of Parliament directly repugnant to the laws of God and his holy Church, the supreme government of which, or of any part thereof, may no temporal Prince presume by any law to take upon him, as rightly belonging to the holy See of Rome, a spiritual pre-eminence by the mouth of our Saviour himself, personally present upon earth, only to Saint Peter and his Successors, bishops of the same See, by special prerogative granted; it is therefore in law, amongst Christian men, insufficient to charge any Christian man."

'And for proof thereof . . . he declared that this realm, being but one member and small part of the Church might not make a particular law disagreeable with the general law of Christ's universal Church, no more than the City of London, being but one poor member in respect of the whole realm, might make a law against an Act of Parliament to bind the whole realm . . . alleging that no more might this realm of England refuse obedience to the See of Rome than might the child refuse obedience to his own natural father. . . .

'Then was it by the Lord Chancellor thereunto answered, that seeing all the bishops, universities and best learned men of the realm had to this act agreed, it was much marvel that he alone against them all would so stiffly stick thereat, and so vehemently argue there against. . . .

'To this Sir Thomas replied, saying that these seven years seriously and earnestly he had beset his studies and cogitations upon this point chiefly, among others, of the Pope's authority. "Never as yet," said he, "have I chanced upon any ancient writer or doctor that so advanceth, as your Statute doth, the supremacy of any secular and temporal Prince. If there were no more but myself upon my side, and the whole Parliament upon the other, I would be sore afraid to lean to my own mind only against so many. But if the number of bishops and universities be so material as your Lordship seemeth to take it, then I see little cause, my Lord, why that thing in my conscience should make any change. For I nothing doubt but that, though not in this realm, yet in Christendom about, of these well learned bishops and virtuous men that are yet alive, they be not the fewer part that are of my mind therein. But if I should speak of those that are already dead, of whom many be now holy saints in heaven, I am very sure it is the far greater part of them that, all the while they lived, thought in this case that way that I think now; and therefore I am not bounden, my Lord, to conform my conscience to the Council of one realm against the general Council of Christendom. For of the aforesaid holy bishops I have, for every bishop of yours, above one hundred; and for one Council or Parliament of yours (God knoweth what manner of one), I have all the Councils made these thousand years. And for this one kingdom, I have all Christian realms" ' (*The Life and Death of Sir Thomas More, Knight, sometime Lord High Chancellor of England,* by Nicholas Harpsfield, D.D., pp. 193–6. Early English Text Society, London, 1932).

As St. Thomas spoke those fateful words and recalled the years he had spent examining the truth as to the divine institution of the Papacy, it is legitimate for us to wonder what were the evidences which crowded into his mind as he was delivering himself to death by being hanged, drawn and quartered. He must have had strong ground for looking Death so unflinchingly in the face.

Did his ears ring with the cry of all the Fathers of the Council at Chalcedon? As the dogmatic Letter of Pope Leo was read to them, they cried out, 'Peter has spoken by the mouth of Leo'. Did he hear the voice of the African Church? *'Roma locuta est, cause finita est,'* as St. Augustine was supposed to have said.[1] Or was it Cyprian,[2] 'He that strives against and resists the Church, he that deserts the Chair of Peter upon whom that Church was founded, is he confident that he is in that Church?' (*De Catholicae Ecclesiae unitate.*) St. Jerome's dictum may have flickered across his mind : 'I, following no leader save Christ, am associated in fellowship with your blessedness [i.e. Pope Damasus] that is the See of Peter. On that Rock I know the Church was built.'

What of the Eastern Church? We have already quoted from Chalcedon. He may have remembered how the Universal Council of Ephesus accepted the Papal Legate's words : 'No one questions, nay rather has it always been well known, that the holy and blessed Peter, the Prince and Head of the Apostles, the pillar of the faith and the foundation of the Catholic Church, received from our Lord Jesus Christ, the Saviour and Redeemer of the human race, the keys of the kingdom, and that the power to bind and loose sins are given to him; he, down to this present time and always, lives and exercises judgement in his successors.' The Fathers of the Council, when the time for condemning Nestorius came, said : 'Compelled by the sacred canons and *by the letter of* our most holy father

---

[1] What he actually said was, when he heard Pelagianism had been condemned by Rome, *'Inde etiam rescripta venerunt. Causa finita est. Utinam aliquando finiatur error'* (*Sermo,* 131, 10).

[2] Cf. St. Cyprian's *De Unitate,* chapter 4, in the light of the MSS., Maurice Bévenot, S.J., London, 1938.

and fellow-minister *Celestine*, Bishop of the Roman Church, *we come of necessity* . . . to sentence against him.'

But certainly St. Thomas More must have been aware at this moment of the passage in St. Irenæus's work against Heresies: 'But as it would be very tedious, in a book of this sort, to enumerate the successions in all the churches, we confound all those who in any way . . . hold unauthorized meetings. This we do by pointing to the apostolic tradition and the faith that is preached to men, which has come down to us through the succession of bishops; the tradition and the creed of the greatest, the most ancient church, the church known to all men, which was founded and set up at Rome by the two most glorious Apostles, Peter and Paul. For with this church, because of its position of leadership[1] and authority, must agree every church, that is, the faithful everywhere.' He, an Eastern man, was speaking thus of the Papacy from Lyons not more than a hundred years after the death of Peter. Or perhaps those lovely words of St. Ignatius of Antioch to the Church of Rome: 'That Church . . . worthy of God, worthy of honour, worthy of felicitation, worthy of praise, worthy of success, worthy of purity, and *presiding over love*.' True, only gradually the right of the successor of St. Peter had been exercised as occasion demanded and as the Church grew. But even Clement, third after Peter in the chair, had written an authoritative letter to another church, that of Corinth, and in the lifetime of St. John.[2]

Such and many others may have been the texts which Thomas More, one-time Chancellor of England and England's

---

[1] The translation of this is disputed, but whichever variant is accepted it shows that St. Irenæus believed that Rome had unique superiority.

[2] Most of these texts may be found in Bettenson's invaluable *Documents of the Christian Church*, Oxford, 1943. A masterly exposition of the Papal claims written by the great Russian theologian Vladimir Solovyev has recently been translated, *Russia and the Universal Church*, Geoffrey Bles, London, 1948. See also the Anglican, H. Scott, *The Eastern Churches and the Papacy*, 1928.

leading legal mind, must have remembered from his seven years' study of that great and vital question. Having studied and decided that Christ did create a primacy in doctrine and government in the Church, he held to it and died for it.[1]

So the English without much enthusiasm passed first into schism and then in the time of Elizabeth into heresy. First they denied the authority of the Pope, and then they began to change the doctrines and the liturgy of the Church, yet preserving much and more than most of the reformed Churches on the Continent; so much so that within that Church of England there have been men who have held all or almost all the defined doctrines of the Church of Rome. But at the same time, owing to the vagueness of the terminology of their rites and doctrinal articles, others have been equally at liberty to cast all or almost all those defined doctrines to the winds.

But the essential point is not which doctrines have been salvaged and which scrapped, but this one vital element of obedience to an authoritative and living voice. Historically the change was mixed with the King's Matter of the divorce and high politics of the succession; it was mixed with the growing nationalism of the Renaissance princes; it was mixed with the decline in prestige and spirituality of the occupants of the Chair of Peter. But to-day, when the King's Matter is of no importance, when excessive nationalism is seen for what it is, idolatry, and when the Roman Church has purged itself of evils from which it suffered, is it not time to review once more the attitude of Christian men to the Papacy?

(ii) St. Ignatius of Loyola

The Society of Jesus is perhaps the outstanding example in the history of the Church of the revival of the virtue of obedi-

[1] Sir Thomas More never wrote a treatise on the Primacy of the Papacy, though he wrote much on controversial subjects. He gave as his reason the fact that Bishop John Fisher his friend had already done so and adequately. (Cf. Bridgett's *Life of Blessed John Fisher*, pp. 138–9, London, 1890.)

ence, though, paradoxically enough, St. Ignatius wished to
write no rule and to have his followers governed by love alone.
It was through the devotion they showed to this virtue
that they performed the astonishing feat of saving half Europe
from relapse into heresy and schism. What is most curious is
that according to the original intention of the earliest members
of the Order, that little band tending the sick in the hospitals
of plague-stricken Venice and Rome, preaching penance and
reform to any who would listen, were uncertain on this very
point of obedience. It is recorded that they hovered between
the idea of becoming a religious Order with vows or whether
to remain a congregation loosely bound together with no permanent vows at all. It is true that the former view prevailed,
but not improbably owing to outside encouragement, and not
least that of the Pope himself.

We are here in this chapter only concerned with the spirit of
obedience in the Society of Jesus; but some knowledge both of
the man Ignatius Loyola and of his time is essential for a true
interpretation of his teaching; for owing to a lack of this knowledge, some superficial views have been expressed.

St. Ignatius is the greatest man of his age. God fitted him
for that rôle by making him a soldier, a Spaniard and born a
Basque, that most determined race of the Iberian peninsula.
His work required great courage, great tenacity of purpose; he
lived his young life as a soldier. His work required not only
faith but a conquering certainty, a triumphal sense of victory.
Spain, the Defender of the Faith, the conqueror of the Moors,
the discoverer of America, was at the height of its greatness as
the young Ignatius grew up in his castle home among the
Basque mountains. Ignatius breathed the air of victory.

St. Thomas More was already a man when the storm of the
Reformation broke over Europe; he could write in defence of
Tradition and offer his life, but his mode of living was already
set before the peril overtook all those of that generation.

This was not so in the case of Ignatius of Loyola, who was born in 1495, and was only twenty-two when Luther affixed the Theses upon the great door of Wittenberg cathedral. The enforced withdrawal from life, when severely wounded at the little battle of Pampluna in 1521, gave him the chance to think.

Ignatius did not begin with the idea of saving Europe from Luther, nor with reforming the Church; he began with himself and he withdrew to the famous monastery shrine of Montserrat in Cataloña. From there he came out dubbed a knight, having kept vigil all one night before the high altar, not seeking mad adventure like his contemporary, don Quixote, but seeking to serve under the banner of Jesus Christ. Even when he had put himself under the banner of Christ, his concern was not Europe but Palestine. But, once engaged in the struggle in Europe, he knew what to do.

A soldier has a soldier's ways. He knows that the price of victory is discipline. Ignatius, the soldier, chose obedience as his distinguishing mark. He chose well. He and his followers reinstated this virtue, then so much maligned. St. Ignatius put it in the forefront of his programme. Though he had been a soldier, it was not a soldier's obedience that he believed in; it was to be love through and through. Any other interpretation of St. Ignatius's mind would make nonsense of the greatness of his achievement. In one of the most moving of his *Contemplations,* the Contemplation to obtain love, he writes, 'The first thing is that love ought to be placed rather in works than in words'.

Ignatius is so enthralled with the idea of being one in will with his Leader, Christ, of being obedient to him, that his pen flows strongly, and he wrote the prayer which follows :

'Take, O Lord, and receive all my liberty, my memory, my understanding and all my will, all I have and possess you gave to me; to you, Lord, I return it; all is yours, dispose of it entirely according to your will. Give me your love and grace, because that is enough for me' (*The Spiritual Exercises of St. Ignatius*, Fr. Joseph Rickaby, S.J., pp. 208, 209).

Thus Ignatius, who knew what obedience was as a soldier, proceeded to transform it as a soldier of Christ. For him it was a weapon of battle, a means to an end, the end being victory, the triumph of Jesus Christ. Therefore, in his case, over and above the traditional teaching of obedience which he would learn from the monks of Montserrat, there was this ulterior motive of practical usefulness and efficiency; that same efficiency which was the keynote of the modern nation-states in his day. This same instrument he would use in the interests of the Church. He applied the traditional teaching on obedience to his new way of living the Active Life.

Consequently, a Jesuit is second to none in his submission to the Supreme Pontiffs and to the teaching Church; witness the famous rule for thinking with the Church, and especially rule 13, 'To make sure of being right in all things, we ought always to hold by the principle that the white that I see I would believe to be black, if the Hierarchical Church were so to rule it—believing that between Christ our Lord, the Bridegroom, and the Church, his Bride, there is the same Spirit that governs and guides us to the salvation of our souls' (*ibid.*, p. 223).

This rule is not surprisingly misunderstood. We must not suppose that therefore the Church expects unreasonable obedience even from Jesuits. The famous saying can only be taken as the expression of an intense desire to fail in no way in submissiveness to Christ's Vicar. He would not set his fallible intellect up against a God-guided Church.

St. Ignatius lived in an age when obedience without delay was imperatively needed; just as the ascetical hermits of the early Church lived in an age when the ascetical control of all the passions was needed; and in these matters the appropriate saints usually show a certain divine exaggeration. The heresy which the Spirit of God made him combat was essentially the heresy of private judgement; half Europe had fallen away from the unity of the Church. It was necessary to have a body of men who would answer the Church's commands with unhesitating compliance. Delay would have been fatal. In the wild moment of battle there is no time to distinguish, hesitate, examine, suggest alternatives. It is right to obey immediately, else all would be lost.[1]

There have been occasions in military history when it was right to disobey the commander; but in the case where the command is backed by Almighty God, hesitation would be criminal.

While it is true that, in action, unquestioning obedience may be best, the sort of obedience which is irrational is not in itself the best. The highest form of obedience exists when both the mind and the will are in accord. Obedience need not kill our rationality, it should perfect it. A difficult obedience may be meritorious, but the perfect obedience occurs in those people for whom to obey is the most reasonable thing in the world. An irrational obedience of course can be among the most futile things. But we are speaking here of submission to the Church which has a commission from Christ himself to teach, from Christ who said, 'I am the Way, the TRUTH and the Life'. Keeping this in mind, let us now read the oft-quoted Constitution of the Jesuits :

'Let us with the utmost pains strain every nerve of our strength to exhibit this virtue of obedience, firstly to the Supreme Pontiff, then to the Superiors of the Society; so that in all things to which obedience may be extended with charity we may be most ready to obey his voice, just as if it issued from

[1] The difference between obedience to the Church and that to a dictator is that the latter feels himself limited by nothing, while the Church is limited by what Christ taught. A Jesuit obeys his superior only provided the command is in accord with the teaching of Christ.

Christ our Lord . . . leaving any work, even a letter, that we
have begun and have not yet finished; by the directing to this
goal all our strength and intention in the Lord, that holy
obedience may be made perfect in us in every respect, in performance, in will, in intellect; by submitting to whatever may
be enjoined on us with great readiness, with spiritual joy and
perseverance; by persuading ourselves that all things (commanded) are just, by rejecting with a kind of blind obedience
all opposing opinion or judgement of our own; and that in all
things which are ordained by the superior where it cannot be
clearly held that any kind of sin intervenes. And let each one
persuade himself that they that live under obedience ought to
allow themselves to be borne and ruled by divine Providence
working through their Superior exactly as if they were a corpse
which suffers itself to be borne and handled in any way what-
soever; or just as an old man's stick which serves him who
holds it in his hand wherever and for whatever purpose he
wishes to use it' (*Documents of the Christian Church,* by H.
Bettenson, p. 364, O.U.P.).

Anyone who has followed the book to this point will realize
that, far from being particularly original, almost every section
of this remarkable passage can be compared with St. Benedict
or, strangest of all, with St. Francis. The corpse-like obedience
is straight out of the Franciscan canon (see p. 142); while the
earlier section is almost an echo of the following from the
Rule of St. Benedict : 'The first degree of humility is obedience
without delay. . . . Such as these, therefore, abandoning their
own affairs and forsaking their own will, dropping the work
they were engaged on and leaving it unfinished, with swift
obedience follow up with their deeds the voice of him who
commands them' (chap. 5).

St. Benedict, however, certainly does not expect a blind
obedience. He wrote : 'If it happen that something hard
or impossible be laid upon any brother, let him receive the

command of his superior with all docility and obedience. But if he see that the weight of the burden altogether exceeds the measure of his strength, let him explain the REASONS of his incapacity to his superior calmly and in due season.' From which it is patent that St. Benedict expects reasonable obedience. He sums up the situation thus : 'If, after his representations, the superior still persists in his decision and his command, let the subject know that it is expedient for him and let him obey out of love' (chap. 68). And there in the long run we reach the same goal as that of St. Ignatius, but blindly is not mentioned.

The *Rules of the Society of Jesus* begins with, 'The Summary of those constitutions which concern the spiritual formation of ours, and are to be observed by all'. The 31st constitution runs as follows :

'It chiefly conduces to advancement and is very necessary that all should give themselves to perfect Obedience, acknowledging the Superior (whoever he be) in place of Christ our Lord, and yielding him inward reverence and love.'

So far the constitution has repeated St. Paul and all tradition, as is clear from the numerous quotations above. It goes on: 'And they should not only obey him in performing exteriorly the things which he enjoins, entirely, readily, constantly, and with due humility, without excuse, though the things commanded be hard and repugnant to nature.'

Here St. Ignatius seems to be quoting St. Benedict, but does he admit of representations to the superior? In fact, Ignatius does allow reasonable loopholes :

'But also they should endeavour to be resigned interiorly, and to have true abnegation of their own will and judgement, conforming their will and judgement wholly to the Superior's will and judgement.' Ah! you will say, that is precisely what everyone has been saying. But he goes on : *'In all things where sin is not perceived.'* Yet this shows, if not a divergence, at least

an extension of obedience over the subject, namely, an attempt
to control his intellect so that he should think as his superior,
just as he must think with the Church. For a Catholic to think
with the Church is not difficult, because he believes that the
Church is guided by the Holy Spirit; but we all know that
superiors, lay and ecclesiastical, sometimes are wrong-headed,
even with the best will in the world. The good Jesuit should,
however, push such doubts aside, 'denying with a kind of blind
obedience any contrary opinion or judgement of his own.
They ought to set before their eyes God our Creator and Lord,
for whom man is obeyed, and strive to act in the spirit of love,
and not with the perturbation of fear.' That is the key : love,
and the words of St. John of the Cross come naturally to
mind :

'Where love is not, put love, and you will draw love out.' [1]

But the 'blind obedience' remains an obstacle.

Besides the Rules and Constitutions of the Society, there is a
letter written by St. Ignatius to his sons at Coimbra in Portugal,
which is virtually a commentary on his teaching upon Obedience, and as such it is usually bound in with the Rules and
Constitutions. In view of the considerable discussion on the
saint's teaching on this matter, a short consideration of this
famous letter will not be out of place.

The letter should be examined in its context : it was a call
to order directed at this Portuguese house which had got the
balance of religious life wrong. It was putting the private above
the communal, mortification above obedience. The young men
were supposed to be getting on with their studies and not competing in asceticism.

After an introductory paragraph he says that, among all the
virtues he would like his sons to have, the chief should be obedi-

[1] *Obras de San Juan de la Cruz editadas y anotadas por el*
P. SILVERIO DE SANTA TERESA, *O.C.D.*, p. 287,
Tomo IV, Burgos, 1931.

ence. 'As long as this virtue flourishes, all others doubtless will flourish.' He is quite content for other Orders to surpass his in fasting and watchings, etc., but would have the distinguishing mark of his to be obedience, 'that they regard not the individual whom they obey, but in him Christ our Lord, for whose sake they obey'. Having shown that St. Paul enjoins us even to obey secular power because his authority comes from God, he declares that all spiritual superiors are Vicars of Christ.

He considers that mere external obedience is a very poor thing and scarcely worthy of the name unless 'it pass to a further degree making the will of our superior our will. . . . Wherefore, dear Brethren, lay aside wholly, as far as you can, your own wills : hand over freely and dedicate to your Creator in his ministers the freedom he himself has bestowed upon you. Consider it no small advantage of your free will that you are able to give it back fully, through obedience, to him from whom you received it. And by so doing you not only do not lose it, but rather increase and perfect it; since by this means you direct all your wills by that most certain rule of rectitude the will of God interpreted to you by him who governs you in place of God.'

But St. Ignatius is not satisfied with that. He wants, not only the will, but the mind also. The third and highest degree of obedience is to be not only of the same will as the superior, but also of the same mind. He must 'submit his own judgement to his'. . . . 'But he who wishes to sacrifice himself wholly to God, besides his will, must also offer up his understanding (which is the third and highest degree of Obedience) . . . and submit his judgement to his superior's'; and here is the saving clause, '*as far as a devout will can bend the understanding*. For though this power of the soul is not endowed with that freedom which gives the will its strength, and is naturally drawn to assent to whatever is represented to it as true, yet nevertheless *in many things where the evidence of known truth does not force it,* it may by the strength of the will be inclined more one way than another. When this happens, whoever makes profession of Obedience ought to lean towards the judgement of the Superior.'

The above is a militant way of saying that a child or son or loving disciple tries to be of one mind with his father or master. Then follows the unimpeachable and truly Ignatian reason, 'obedience being a holocaust, in which the whole man, absolutely without reserve, is offered up to his Creator and Lord in the fire of charity, through the hands of his ministers'. St. Ignatius then explains the excellence of this virtue; he gives three reasons. The first is because the most excellent and precious part of man is offered back to God; the second because man is thus made a living holocaust to God, since he thereby keeps back nothing of his own; lastly, because it is so difficult, owing to the natural inclination of men to follow their own opinions.

Next he gives three ways that make the keeping of this virtue more easy. The first is to remember to see in one's superior, not a mere man subject to error, but Christ himself. The second is the motive of love : 'You took this yoke of Obedience upon you for love of God'. The last way is to submit the mind also, for then the will acts with more alacrity.

But again there is the safeguard, 'Nor are you hindered by this . . . from laying your view before your superior; but lest self-love and your own judgement should deceive you in this, the precaution is to be taken of keeping your mind, both before and after making the proposal, quite calm and ready, not only to take up or lay aside the matter in question, but also to approve and think better whatever seems good to the superior'. This letter was written from Rome, 26th March, 1553. In the tradition of the Society the Fathers have always been encouraged to lay their case before the superior and to consider this a duty.

The sons of St. Ignatius, by their zeal and by their obedience, saved half Europe from the divisions of the Reformation; so successful were they that they might have been entirely victorious but for the outbreak of the Thirty Years War. Also, in the New Worlds recently discovered to the south, west and east, their stupendous work is not yet fully appreciated; in China and in Japan, among the natives of Paraguay and in the broad plains of North America, on the coasts of Africa, everywhere they worked with indefatigable energy.

Whether the famous sonnet was written by St. Ignatius or St. Francis Xavier or by another will perhaps never be known, but its spirit is so linked with that of the age and that complete abandonment practised by the new order of St. Ignatius, that it makes a fitting conclusion to this section, and here it is :

'I love Thee, Lord, yet not because
I hope for heaven thereby;
Nor yet since they who love Thee not
Must burn eternally.
Thou, O my Jesus, Thou didst me
Upon the Cross embrace.
For me didst bear the nails and spear,
And manifold disgrace,
And grief and torments numberless,
And sweat of agony,
E'en death itself; and all for one
Who was Thine enemy.
Then why, O blessed Jesus Christ,
Should I not love Thee well?
Not for the sake of winning heaven
Or of escaping hell;
Not with the hope of gaining aught,
Nor seeking a reward;

But as Thyself hast lovéd me
O ever-loving Lord?
E'en so I love Thee and will love
And in Thy praise will sing,
Solely because Thou art my God
And my eternal King.'

It seems to me that the original must have been the Spanish sonnet and not the Latin lines. The Spanish is as follows:

A Cristo crucificado

'No me mueve, mi Dios, para quererte,
El cielo que me tiene prometido,
Ni me mueve el infierno tan temido
Para dejar por eso de ofenderte.

Tu me mueves, Señor; muéveme el verte
Clavado en esa cruz, y escarnecido;
Muéveme el ver tu cuerpo tan herido;
Muévenme tus afrentas, y tu muerte.

Muévesme al tu amor en tal manera,
Que aunque no hubiera cielo, yo te amara;
Y aunque no hubiera infierno, te temiera.
No me tienes que dar, porque te quiera;
Que aunque cuanto espero no esperara;
Lo mismo que te quiero te quisiera.'

In conclusion it may be said that such a strong discipline both of will and mind was ideal for the time of crisis in which the Jesuits were made and in the circumstances into which St. Ignatius, almost by accident, proceeded to thrust them. It does not seem that we have yet emerged from the strained times of strife into the calm hours of peace, and therefore there is room and to spare for such heroic soldiers of Christ to-day, as there was in the Golden Age, which witnessed the founding of one of the greatest of the Orders in the Church, the Society of Jesus.

(iii) CARDINAL NEWMAN AND ANGLICANISM

Newman's renown will continue to grow as the significance of his great choice that rainy night at Littlemore is more fully understood. In a sense Newman, when he submitted to Rome in the person of the Venerable Dominic Barberi, reversed the trend of history. He reversed the verdict of a previous generation of Englishmen who put to death Thomas More, the greatest among them, for still holding to the authority of Rome.

John Henry Newman came of good Protestant stock, not Calvinist, as used to be supposed, but healthy and joyous. The influence of his Calvinist schoolmaster need not detain us; the reading of Robertson's book on prophecy merely gave him a bias against Rome; the historical writings of the Calvinistic Milner provided a false view of the Fathers, and that took years to overcome. But his later change of front was not a revulsion from Puritanism.

The thing which changed his life was none of the above, but the realization that round him was unbelief, particularly at Oxford, the fact that even the 'Establishment' was infected with Rationalist views; that the whole position of religion was being undermined by the German school of theology which submitted all to the judgement of reason. What made Newman act was the sight of the breakdown of faith in a revelation before the onslaught of private judgement. He saw that either revelation had to be the judge of reason, or reason the judge of revelation. He chose the former, once certain that a revelation had been made.

On his return from the Italian tour his mind was made up. He had a plan. He would, by writing and conversation and sermons, attempt to turn the minds of his contemporaries back to revelation as found in the primitive Church.

In his efforts to restore what he thought to be the primitive tradition, Newman was soon accused of trying to convert the Anglicans to Romish ways. The publication of Tract XC was the signal for a violent attack upon Newman's integrity. His enemies clamoured for his removal. The aim of this little treatise for the times was to show that the 39 Articles could be held in an entirely Catholic sense. Newman wished to be Catholic but without the authority of Rome and free from what he considered the accretions of the medieval Church.

'It is often urged, and sometimes felt and granted, that there are in the Articles propositions or terms inconsistent with the Catholic faith. . . . The following tract is drawn up with the view of showing how groundless the objection is.'

In order to show this, he had to delve into the story of the early Church, and he found to his horror and to his amazement that not only were all the practices of Catholicism to be found there, but also the attitude to the Church as held by the Roman Church. There in those early days were heretics claiming to be independent Churches against the General Councils, just as the Anglican Church of his own day was claiming. What difference was there between the Anglicans and the Donatists, the Nestorians, the Monophysites and the rest. In the early Church there was authority. In the Roman Church that same authority was claimed.

In short, Newman went back to revelation to escape the maze of Liberalism, and in that revelation he found the Church speaking with an authoritative voice and a promise of permanence.

There remained the question of the Development of Doctrine, and this Newman examined in his book with that name.

In any age the revealed Truths will have to be preached in the language understood by that age, and, for the intellectuals, in the language that they are using in their philosophical thought. Thus in the Middle Ages the doctrine of the Eucharist had to be expressed in the language that the men of that time used. As it presented certain philosophical difficulties for philosophers, it was stated in the language of those men's philosophy; and that happened to be, by the agency chiefly of St. Thomas Aquinas, the philosophy of Aristotle. Consequently, the mysteriousness of the fact that the outward appearance of what was Christ's body remained like bread, yet was not really bread but Christ's Body, came to be expressed in the Latin dress of Aristotelian philosophy : matter, form, substance and accidents and the rest. We find a relic of this terminology in the canons of the Council of Trent and the famous word 'transubstantiation'. Now, in so far as this word is bound up with Aristotelian metaphysics, it is not *de fide*,[1] but in so far as it expresses, if in abstract terms, the simple fact that whatever makes a thing bread has been changed into that which makes Christ's body his Body, and yet all that shows remains the same, then that is *de fide*. It is no more than what Christ said —if his words are to be taken literally—this is my Body. Nothing will ever conclude the discussions as to whether he did mean it literally except some teaching authority, as is proved by the religious history of the last four hundred years. It may be a pity that religious truths have to be dressed in such long words, but it may be necessary all the same, men being as they are.

Reunion among Christians is perhaps the most longed-for end of all Christians to-day, whether they be Free Church, Reformed, Anglican, Orthodox or Catholics. And as we approach the end of this slight study, we are therefore inevitably led to consider this problem of life or death.

In the first place the writer can only speak for his own Communion, but perhaps this is the greatest service he could do his readers, since many may be ill informed as to the true position of Catholics in these matters.

---

[1] In so far as it fits Revelation, it will never be scrapped by the Catholic Church, though it may one day be improved upon.

There seems to be a theory among Anglicans, even the most friendly, that Catholic theology has somehow broken away from the ancient mystical tradition of the early Church, particularly of the Eastern Church; that with the decisions of the Council of Trent any convert to the post-Tridentine Papal Communion would be cut off from that ancient Eastern tradition, and that he would be bound to swallow with a faith either explicit or implicit all the theological conclusions made in the heyday of medieval theologizing, even those conclusions based on deductions from revealed truths and their further developments. But this of course is very wide of the mark. Let it be quite clear that a theological conclusion is not *de fide*. As Dr. Temple is reported to have said, the *Summa* of St. Thomas Aquinas is the most comprehensive map ever made of human existence, but St. Thomas was fallible and the Church does not accept his conclusions as *de fide*—far from it.

What is the attitude of the Catholic Church to reasoning on the faith? Put briefly it is this. The last revelation came before the death of the last apostle, and since then there has been none. A revelation is the disclosure to man by God of a truth not previously known. By his own reason man may discover many new truths, but their certainty depends upon the reliability of the reasoning which led to their being propounded. However, a distinction must be made between those conclusions which have been arrived at by combining knowledge reached through reason with knowledge provided by revelation, and on the other hand conclusions arrived at by combining two groups of revealed truths. Thus the combination of Aristotelian reasoning as such with revealed truth cannot produce any *de fide* conclusion, while the combination, for instance, of the two facts, that Christ is truly man and the fact that he is sinless, might lead to the conclusion of the perfection of his will; and that, Catholics maintain, could be the subject of a *de fide* conclusion, because the conclusion is included in the premisses, both of which are of faith, or in other words, revealed truth.

Yet Catholics admit that, so long as such a conclusion rests on the theologians' reasoning power, it cannot be of faith. This will only come about if the Church with its authority proclaims that this truth is contained implicitly in the original revelation.

It was thus that Newman understood the theory of the development of Doctrine. The Catholic Church neither denies the possibility nor the usefulness of reasoning upon the data of faith, rather she encourages it, nor does she on the other hand admit that all the reasoning so done can be of faith. For Catholics the teaching of Christ is not a dead letter, nor is it snowed under by endless uncontrollable theories. Men may work on that teaching and their conclusions may be judged by the faithful with the help of the Teaching Church. Thus there is progress, but not progress by denial of what went before; it is an organic growth, a development of what is already there, a disclosure, an unfolding.

Newman was well aware of the difficulties of Anglicans, and he wrote a large book with that title. The difficulties of Anglicans in accepting the authority of Rome are legion. Some are afraid that the spirit of Rome is too legal, that it therefore chases away the spirit of love, for, so the argument would run, these two laws, obedience and love, are incompatible.

We admit that the late medieval Church was bound hand and foot by regulations, even money-making regulations; it might even be said that the modern Catholic Church with its government in Rome has too centralized an administration. Every bishop in the world has to be appointed by the Pope; the division of dioceses is done in Rome; canonizations are performed in Rome; the ultimate authority in every Order of the Church is at Rome; any book may be prohibited by Rome; serious books on the Bible have to be passed by a Roman official; no change in the liturgy may be done without the permission of the Congregation of Rites.

One might go on for a considerable time describing the way in which the Church is governed from the centre. It may have its drawbacks, but there are also advantages. In the first place, the object of the Christian life is not discussion of how this should be done, how that, but the living of the life of Christ. The unifying of authority does save us all from wasting our time arguing over disputed points. Secondly, this method does guarantee that a solution is found and rival factions do not carry on an interminable squabble which neither aids nor edifies.

But when we search in the Christian world in the last three or four hundred years for men and women who have shown immense love, we must all admit that among the most astonishing and sublime have been many from within that very Communion which was supposed to be so chained by legalism. Thus, among the greatest mystics of all time stand out those two Spanish saints of the Reformation period, Santa Teresa and San Juan de la Cruz; but besides them there are a host of less-known ones : St. John of Avila; the author of the *Spiritual Alphabet*; Fr. Augustine Baker; the great Bérulle; Anne of Jesus; the gentle St. Francis of Sales; while among those who have not only loved Christ with a supreme love but have also shown glorious love of men stand forth likewise men from that very Church; St. Vincent de Paul, the real founder of the Red Cross, or his almost contemporary, St. Camillus of Rome; that great missionary, St. Francis Xavier, whose love for men took him thirsting across the world to the farthest East. And in our own day the Curé of Ars, Sœur Thérèse of Lisieux, and Don John Bosco.

A clear pattern laid down is not an obstacle to the religious life but a positive help. Laws, even precisely as laws, are a great saving of time and worry for the Christian. Christ did not come on earth in order to found a debating society as someone wittily remarked, but in order to lay down the new law by which we could surely and safely reach heaven.

To return to Newman. Though he shows infinite sympathy and understanding of his old friends who had remained behind in the Anglican Church, and though he examines each problem on its own merits, he realized that after all had been said the essential was not there, but in that one fundamental question, ought we to return to the Mother who gave us birth? Even supposing there was too much legalism at certain times in the Church, even supposing some Italian peasants did seem to give an exaggerated devotion to the Virgin Mary, even supposing the Catholic countries of his day were not so advanced in mechanized life as the Protestant or even atheistic countries round about, would those be a justification for refusing to be a member of that Church if it was the Church God had founded? There is the crux of the matter. The discussion is really off the point unless it keeps to this problem : did Christ mean there to be a teaching voice in the Church which would not fail and its chief mouthpiece the Pope? That is the thing every sincere Christian should study with all his deepest humility and desire for truth.

Few will deny, to-day, that at the Reformation and for centuries back the Papacy had supreme authority for the Christians of the time, except for the rise of the Conciliar movement towards the decline of the medieval Papacy. Newman went behind that period and found the same outlook, though of course less developed, in the days of the early Church.

Leaving Newman for a moment, can we not see the immense advantage that would accrue to the Christian attack if it were all co-ordinated under one head upon earth, sure of itself, its faith, its discipline, its liturgy, uncontaminated by those doubts and divisions which make the unbeliever cry out, 'If you yourselves do not know what the message is, if you yourselves refuse to teach with authority, how can you expect me to waste my time listening?' There before us is this ancient, venerable, supreme institution of European culture; there it stands, claiming to derive from the earliest ages of the Church, claiming, and with all humility, to be endowed by Christ with a power to preserve his message. For God's sake, for the very work's sake, let us examine it in the spirit of friendliness, free now from all the rancours of old quarrels, the bitterness of rivalry, and of all fear of domination. The Church of Christ is not a national thing, but a supra-national body, one body, one mind, one heart, the mind and heart and body of Christ himself. Therefore should it think with one mind and love with one heart and act with one accord, visibly and strongly. That was the vision Newman had when he led his followers into the wilderness of English life, but into the arms of that very Mother who had been the Mother of English and European Christians for so many centuries before the fatal divisions.

The Church of Rome does not deny that grace is flowing from Christ among the members of the non-Papal Communions. The Spirit of God blows where it wills; where a man sincerely seeks God, there will God be found. All in good faith will receive the help from heaven necessary for their salvation; and grace being necessary for salvation, consequently they receive grace. In a very real sense, therefore, all sincere Protestants and Church of England men and women are united to Christ and so to Roman Catholics, for the link which unites all Christians together is the link of grace.

This is all true so long as these Christians are where they stand, in good faith. This was one of Newman's most firm convictions. But it still remained true that all men should be in the One Church and receiving the sacraments from priests in union with the successor of Peter. Who is there who to-day denies that we should all be One as Christ prayed we should be in those tragic moments before the Passion began? These great meetings of Churchmen from many Communions prove this universal desire to be a fact.

Though all sincere seekers of God, whether Christian or even pagan, are by their very sincerity granted by God his grace and so are united to the Mystical Body of Christ, yet they are not in the Church of Christ—which they should be also—for that is a visible thing which has its corporate worship of God according to the instructions of the Saviour when he was upon this earth.

Thus Catholics are very far from denying grace or union with Christ to members of other religions. When they speak of there being no salvation outside the Church, they mean firstly that those who know they should belong to it, but do not, are gravely sinning against the light; and secondly, that a man who is outside the visible Church, but is unaware that he is doing wrong, is in fact within it spiritually, for God will not refuse salvation to any who, with unfeigned desire, put their hearts and minds to finding him.

Newman accepted the Church's decision that Anglican Orders were of doubtful validity and was reordained a Catholic priest; he accepted that without difficulty once he had accepted the right of Rome to be obeyed. Leo XIII, many years after, pushed to it by the Abbé Portal, did not come to the adverse decision without sadness. Rome admits the validity of Orthodox Church Orders; but Rome declared Anglican orders invalid. Such things are a matter of fact, and must be decided on historical evidence, and are not a matter of feeling that grace has passed through sacraments administered. Grace, and very much grace, might and surely does pass at these moments without that proving that it is by virtue of a sacrament.

The Catholic Church makes great claims : it speaks with the voice of God; it will last for ever; it cannot err in the person of the Pope when speaking on faith or morals in virtue of his office as Head of the Church, successor of St. Peter and to the universal Church; nor will the whole Body err, whether in Council, or severally, if they all teach the same doctrine as part of the teaching of Christ; unless a man is united to that Church, either visibly or unknowingly because he wills what God wills in so far as in him lies, he cannot reach heaven. The priests of the Catholic Church have a right to forgive sins, to offer sacrifice for the people, to preach, and no others have that right, though they may have that power. All that is terrifying in its exclusiveness. Is this zealotry? Is it fanaticism? Has any group of men the right to claim exclusive powers as between God and men?

It is all a matter of *fact*. The Church does not claim it, it is Christ who gave it. He certainly founded ONE Church, which either exists or it does not; if it does, then that Church must act with the authority of Christ. Pride does not consist in claiming high things, but in claiming things which are higher than warranted by the truth. Did Christ found a Church with the power to teach? If he did, then it must teach. 'Go ye and teach all nations.'

God has revealed himself to those outside the Church—Job received a revelation. Good men in all ages have been guided by God yet, we cannot be certain that they have followed His advice. But God only once became Man, only once died on the Cross by which we are all saved, only once founded a Church, his Body, which would teach with his voice and therefore unerringly, as does the Papacy. It is therefore THE Way. These things are not a matter of what we would prefer, but of what is an historical fact. The outward modes may change, the fact must remain the same.

CHAPTER XIII

THE RECENT POPES

ALL the teaching of these recent popes on social matters is contained in principle in the writings of St. Thomas Aquinas. But the new applications of those principles made by the popes, from Leo XIII to the present day, are so novel and so relevant to us that it was thought advisable to wait until this chapter before dealing with such problems as democracy and liberty and economics and liberty. Those are our big problems. They overshadow all the rest—the problem of government and the problem of economic human rights.

When dealing with the teaching of Martin Luther, we observed that he threw overboard the power of reason and the Natural Law. He handed over to the state absolute power, submitting religion to the secular arm precisely as Marsilio of Padua had advised two hundred years before. The secular princes did not need to be told twice, they leapt at the suggestion, not only those who turned Protestant but the Catholics also. Indeed, the secular princes were exerting their power and attempting to subordinate the Church to their own ends long before the advent of the Reformers. Philip of France, in his dealings with Boniface VIII, is but the outstanding example of this Erastian spirit.

In Catholic countries, notably France and Spain, the spirit of absolutism is clearly visible; it is reflected in the manners and writings of the day. Thus at Versailles when the king, 'le Roi Soleil', Louis XIV, went to the royal chapel, the courtiers did not face the altar during Mass, but the king, who was in a gallery at the back. The clergy, in spite of misgivings, at the 'assemblée du clergé' in 1682 and at the bidding of Bossuet who drew them up, passed Four Articles. The first claimed that secular princes were independent of the Pope in secular affairs and the Pope had no power to depose them. The second claimed that the authority of the Councils was above that of the popes. The third declared that the Gallican Church was independent of the Pope in its organization and elections. The fourth was that the Papal teaching depended for its authoritativeness on confirmation by a General Council. Bossuet only did this thing in order to avoid worse evils, and, according to a conversation with Fénelon, he believed 'in the indefectible orthodoxy of the Holy See' (Pastor, *Lives of the Popes*, vol. XXXII, p. 294). The fact that France was delighted when the Pope condemned these articles in April of the same year (*ibid.*, p. 298) does not disprove the point that even Catholic governments were going along the road of absolutism.

The literature of the Golden Age in Spain is another interesting guide to the atmosphere of the time regarding the authority of kings.

Busto Tabera, the hero of the famous play, *The Star of Seville*, written by the greatest dramatist of the age, Lope de Vega, in or about 1616, is called before the king. He falls on his knees, and when told to rise makes the following typical speech :

'I am well where I am, for if the king is to be treated like a saint at an altar, I have chosen a suitable posture' (Act 1, sc. iv). Then, later in the play, when the king orders Sancho to kill his friend Busto, Sancho says, when torn between love of friend and duty to his king, although he thinks the king's command is wrong, 'There is no law that can oblige me to do it— but yes; for although the king may be acting unjustly I must obey his law, and God will chastise him after' (Act 2, sc. xiii). Or remember the beautiful play by the same author, *Peribáñez y el Comendador de Ocaña*, and how Casilda, the farmer's wife, goes to Toledo for the feast day of Our Lady, and how she meets the king. 'What? Are kings made of flesh and blood?'

It was this attitude to kings which was shattered at the French Revolution, and to that extent the Revolution was a good thing. But unfortunately the revolutionaries did not substitute the right attitude towards authority in place of the wrong one which they had discarded. The kings had claimed to speak with the voice of God; this had been so obviously hypocritical that the people, led by the fiery eloquence of Jean Jacques Rousseau, had abandoned the attempt to find the voice of God in governments and were content to find their own. Authority no longer came from God, it came from the People.

Article III of the Declaration of the Rights of Man, passed by the National Assembly in August 1789, reads: 'The source of all sovereignty resides essentially in the nation.'

According to the Catholic tradition, law had been the expression of the Mind of God; now it was to be the 'expression of the will of the community.' So reads Article VI.

This is not to say that the entire work of the Revolution was bad, because this is far from the case. The National Assembly did recognize the existence of the Supreme Being even in this Declaration. It declared: 'In the presence of the Supreme Being, and with the hope of his blessing and favour, the following sacred rights . . .'

But nowhere does it state that its rights or its laws are derived from him. It can only say that these rights and laws are derived from the Will of the People. What they will is right.

Pius IX lived in a different world from that of Leo XIII his successor. Though Leo does not contradict him or his Syllabus, the outlook is new. Pius, who had experienced the discomforts of a democratic revolution in his Papal states, was in no mood to see the good in the new thought of his day. Leo, who had spent from 1846 to 1878 in the backwater of Perugia as its bishop, receiving distinguished visitors on their ways to and from Rome, listening to their talk of the vast awakening, north of the Alps, and the almost equally vast slumber south of them, had pondered for those thirty years upon the crisis in Christendom, the fateful collapse of the restoration of Monarchy, the rise of Liberalism, the spread of the Industrial Revolution. When called to the Chair of Peter his message was ready.

In the political field he had three major contributions to make to the discussion of the day; the first was to lay down once again the true nature of liberty; the second was to show whence came the ultimate source of all authority; the third was to lay bare the fallacies of Liberalism.

In the economic field his contribution was to establish the right of a man to property and to a wage and to combine with other men; all these are based on the right to liberty of each human person.

In an age which had spent itself philosophically, the return of Leo to St. Thomas was perhaps one of the greatest events in the nineteenth century. On the subject of liberty, as for all the rest, he sought for his inspiration in the massive thought of the greatest of the medievals. The act of free-will is not adrift from reason, but an operation of the thinking mind; liberty is a quality of the will by which it can choose. Now it cannot choose unless it chooses something, therefore it must have an object. This object is put before it by the mind as good to choose.

If the object is all possible good, an infinite good, the will is sure to take it, because it has no reason not to and every reason for accepting it. But should the object be only partially good, then there are some reasons in favour of taking it and some against. It is perfectly obvious from this description that the will is naturally moved by reason, and rightly so. If it is moved by anything else, that is a kind of slavery—for instance, if it is forced by fear or by some passion.

Pope Leo therefore starts his analysis by making the freedom of the will a reasonable act. It comes under truth and is not independent of it. He restores the primacy of truth. But, if that is so, then in the matter of laws and of governments, a government is not just only because the majority have given their willing assent, nor is a law just because ordained by the will of the people; but only on condition that the government acts according to right reason, and that the laws are also in accord with the truth, have they the right to be obeyed.

Law is the expression of what it is reasonable to do. The Natural Law is that part of the reasonable plan of God for his universe which we, with our small human minds, can discover, in so far as it concerns us as human beings. One precept of the Natural Law is that men naturally live in society. Now this is contrary to the revolutionary interpretation of Rousseau, which was that men are born free and enter into society of their own free-will, but need not, should they not wish. If Rousseau is right, then all authority in the state resides in the multitude; if the Church is right, then the ultimate authority is God. In Rousseau's view all laws cannot be other than the will of the people; in the case where God is considered as the ultimate source of authority, all laws must be in accordance with his Divine Laws.

The nineteenth century saw the attempt of Europeans to live according to the Liberal sentiments of the French Revolution. Most present-day thinkers would agree with us that they were not eminently successful, though the reason they might give for the failure would not be the same. But one self-evident difficulty for pure democracy is that the will, not guided by any law outside itself, is a blind thing dependent on the whims of the mob. Leo wrote, 'Therefore the true liberty of human society does not consist in every man doing as he pleases, for this would simply end in turmoil and confusion, and bring on the overthrow of the State; but rather in this, that by means of the laws of the State a man may the more easily live his life in accordance with the commands of the eternal law. Likewise, the liberty of those who are in authority does not consist in the power to lay unreasonable and capricious commands upon their subjects, which would equally be criminal and would lead to the ruin of the commonwealth' ('Libertas Praestantissimum,' *The Pope and the People,* p. 76).

Those two outcomes we have seen in our own lifetime : they are the failure to govern as shown in French political life between the wars, and the tyranny of Hitler, which was really a reaction against liberal democracy during the same period. But what of England?

Leo and his successors have never denied the good in democracy; it has always been one of the principles of Catholic teaching that the people wherever possible should have a share in the government. They did in the Middle Ages in the city-states and in the guilds. These things were self-governing. It was only with the rise of the more efficient and more powerful nation-states that the tendency towards autocracy became marked. In England some of the elements of the medieval liberties survived through the age of absolutism; the chief of these is the Houses of Parliament. These Houses represented the people of England, originally according to class, now according to locality only.

There are two conflicting theories about the attitude of the Members of Parliament. One school of thought believes that they are merely mouthpieces of their constituencies, that they go to Westminster with a 'ticket', a mandate, that they have to vote according to instructions. This is the way of European democracies. The members are voting machines for the party behind them.

The other theory is that the people of England choose men and women for their ability to act with judgement; on each point that comes up each Member of Parliament makes up his mind on the evidence. This is the Catholic view.

There remains a practical point, much insisted upon by the great Edmund Burke, which is that unless the parties in parliament are big and carry the power of a majority of votes, then government will be wrangling among party factions, each out for its own ends and not for the good of the country. Consequently, says Burke, it is necessary for every man in parliament to stand by the party on major issues, except in those things where his conscience is at variance with it.

The word 'conscience' in this connection is so typically English that it is the key to the understanding of the English spirit in relation to politics. Always every major issue is presented to the people as a moral issue; the reason is that the English are thoroughly Christian in spirit, even if their reasons for being so are now of the haziest variety. Politics are part of religion, a matter of right or wrong. This is of the utmost importance, for it means that in the main the issues are not decided simply according to a majority vote but according to an ethical code. So long as that remains, English politics can work. But when there are signs that politics are being governed, not by morality, but by intrigue or covetousness—and there are signs even now —then the traditional way of Christian democracy in England will have ended, and, after a period of corruption and chaos, we may revert to the unintelligent, unliberal, unchristian way of a dictator. *Quod absit.*

Thus Leo, in his great defence of true liberalism, of preserving liberty within the confines of right reason and the Natural Law, is fighting the battle of the English way, based as it is on a Christian tradition more than a thousand years old.

But there are indications that the old Catholic foundation of English society is being removed piece by piece. The Catholic attitude to marriage is that it is indissoluble; laws have been passed granting divorce in certain cases—they are tending to multiply. The Church teaches that the civic rights of the parents may not be lightly overridden; they have such a right over the children's education. The English laws on education are tending to force children into the state schools, where only a mongrel religion—if any—can be taught.

On the other hand, in economic matters the laws are approaching rather than withdrawing from traditional ways. Social justice is in the forefront of the policies of both the major parties, Labour and Conservative. The conditions of the workers, their pay, the hours they work, the control of big business and the banks, have now all received close scrutiny, and laws have been passed whose aim—whether in fact satisfactory is another matter—is social justice.

This, however, is a digression, for, before passing on to the economic side of the papal teaching, we still have to consider the thorny question of the 'modern liberties', namely, the right to say and write whatever one likes, the right to teach children anything, the right of liberty of conscience. The difficulty of discussing these famous liberties is that everyone gets very excited and most people are firmly convinced that they already know what the Church's teaching on the matter is and they know it is 'die-hard' and fanatical, reactionary and fascist—whatever that now means—whereas the Church's attitude is probably, as we hope to show, quite different and almost what every decent Englishman thinks naturally. The only difference will be where each of us draws the line.

If we believe in God we presumably believe he had a plan as to what was intended to happen, how we should behave. Therefore in so far as we do not behave as he had planned, we in a sense wreck that part of the arrangements. Whether a man does it knowingly or not makes a difference to his guilt, but he wrecks the plan whether he knows he is doing so or whether he does not. On these lines Catholics would hold that it is unreasonable to give equal opportunity to the man who is wrecking the plan, whether knowingly or not, as to those who are co-operating with the plan as far as they are able.

Do we know what the plan is? There's the rub. If we do not, is there any solution at all? It can only be the solution of the majority, the decision of the greater number, the decision of brute force.

Catholics, however, believe that in one small vital section of human knowledge there is a certainty which has come to us by a direct revelation from God. Non-Catholics seem to think, sometimes, that Catholics have their whole life mapped out for them, that they are not allowed to think; that their minds are bound in chains, even in historical and in scientific matters. In fact, there has been no revelation about science, and we are as free to follow the truth as anyone; in history we do, it is true, hold that at a certain time a man appeared who claimed to be God and that he revealed facts about God and our destiny. They are facts which the human mind unaided could not have discovered and are not contrary to reason. Truths discovered by reason will never clash with these truths once revealed. The liberty to search for truth remains with a Christian as much as, if not more than, with a pagan, for a Christian has not only all the data the pagan has, but a few more pieces of information as well.

Catholics, then, are convinced that they have a few very vital truths which will save all mankind. Therefore they claim the right to propagate these truths everywhere and particularly to their own children, who are their own first and the state's very much last.

Would a Catholic state allow opinions contrary to its own teaching to be propagated? That is the crux.

Spain is interesting; it allowed Jews and Arabs to live within its borders. The great university city of Toledo is a glorious example in the Middle Ages of the tolerance by the Church of non-Christian elements within its gates. There, Jew and Arab taught alongside Catholic professors. It was only after the conquest of Granada by the autocratic rulers, Isabella and Ferdinand, that the Jews and the Arabs began to be persecuted. Spain had been reconquered from the Moor, but the Moor was by no means dead, the Mediterranean was alive with Moorish pirates, the north coast of Africa was a nest of malcontents ready to renew the struggle. The Spaniards were afraid for their lives; they cannot be exonerated, they may be excused.

In the past, Catholics have not always tolerated the spread of contrary opinions—the Albigensians and Waldensians are well-known and sad examples. The Inquisition, in so far as it attempted to twist men's consciences by force, was wrong. Yet the Church would always claim the right to shield her immature members, as a parent would its child, from being contaminated by error. The best method is persuasion, for the Church is not afraid of truth but only of error decked out as truth. And the more culture spreads and men are capable of real judgement, the more the Church will only counter error with preaching truth. Force is a lamentable admission of failure; it never converted anyone. Alcuin wrote of the forcible conversion of the Saxons by Charlemagne, 'You can thrust baptism on men but not faith'.[1]

The Church does not acknowledge that the parent or the state has an absolute right to teach children falsehoods. But, to avoid worse evils, it allows this to happen in certain circumstances.

Liberty of conscience is also one of the rights that the Church does also uphold. The reader then may ask, what of the passage in Leo's encyclical, 'Libertas Praestantissimum,' which reads as follows : 'Liberty of conscience . . . if by this is meant that everyone may, as he chooses, worship God or not, is sufficiently refuted by the arguments already adduced' (*ibid.*, p. 89)? Does this imply that a man has not got a right to choose

---

[1] *M.L.* 100, col. 194; ep. xxvi, to Arno of Aquila.

his own religion or none? It would seem so if we compare this passage with one in an earlier letter, 'Immortale Dei,' where Leo condemns those who hold that 'everyone is to be free to follow whatever religion he prefers' (*ibid.*, p. 57). But Leo is in both these passages condemning, not the following of one's conscience, but the refusal to follow any conscience, he is condemning the man, who, refusing to admit that he has to choose, does as he *feels*. The Church always forbids any forcible conversion. Man is bound to follow his own conscience, even if it is in error. But it is, nevertheless, error.

There remains yet another formidable problem: what should the state do or not do in regard to error? Should it give equal rights to truth and falsehood, good and evil? All states answer this in the negative in things which they themselves think important. None would allow the propagation of ideas which would in fact destroy the state; we in England allow anarchists and communists and various revolutionary forces to operate in the open, not, however, for their own sake, but mostly because we feel safer when we know where they are and that they are not forming secret societies. Leo speaks much on the same lines: 'While not conceding any *right* to anything save what is true and honest, [the Church] does not forbid public authority to tolerate what is at variance with truth and justice, for the sake of avoiding greater evil, or of obtaining or preserving some greater good' (*ibid.*, p. 89).

Turning to economic matters, the same principle of liberty prevails. Underlying the papal approach to property, wages, trade unions, state interference, trade associations and the like, is the idea that a man is essentially free, that this gift is the greatest gift God has ever given to any creature, is part and parcel of his soul. He is free because he is a spiritual being who can think and choose. Therefore let men think and choose and lead the full life. This, Leo says, is only possible if a man has property, for this gives him independence and a chance to act upon his own initiative, to use his brains on something which is his own, instead of being a cog in the wheel of the industrial machine.

The whole purpose of the Church's teaching on social matters has been to preserve the true liberty of each individual person. For Christians the central point of this earthly creation is not a group, this race or that in history, but each individual soul, for each has an eternal destiny, distinct though interwoven with the destiny of his fellows.

Thus the teaching of the Church on the state is concerned with two main points: on the one hand the popes wish to safeguard the individual from too powerful a state or government, and on the other they encourage the state to act to save citizens from becoming slaves of one another. In other words, Liberty is the aim of the Catholic social teaching. During most of the nineteenth century the states of Western Europe took too little interest in the welfare of the downtrodden, due to the state being impregnated with the theories of *laissez-faire*. With the utmost difficulty trade unions made their way; laws regulating wages for men—we do not speak of women or children—were unheard of in the nineteenth century in England; laws for conditions of labour and so forth, except for women and children, were also not known in this country. The process was slow, and the Church encouraged the governments of the world to control the liberty of some in order that others might achieve some measure of freedom.

To-day the situation is reversed. The state, having tasted power, grows in appetite with each meal, and the danger seems to be more an encroachment by governments on the liberties of individuals than a safeguarding by those very governments of the liberties of their citizens. But the state is not the only offender. The trade unions, which were encouraged in the nineteenth century in order to foster the liberation of the workers from the thraldom of the capitalist, have tended to go beyond their province, and instead of confining themselves to the purposes for which they were created, have entered into the political arena as almost equal partners with the government in power. In France this situation has gone farther than in Great Britain, but even in the latter there are signs of attempted dictation to the government by the trade unions.

It was with this situation that Pius XI had to deal during all his pontificate, and the great anti-totalitarian encyclicals followed one after the other—that against the Fascism of Mussolini in 1931, that against the totalitarianism of Communism in 1937, and the great condemnation of Hitler and his regime, the Nazi menace, in 1937.

All these great documents and many other utterances made at various times were part of a stupendous effort to save that elementary human right of Freedom from the modern believers in the servile state. Cardinal Faulhaber of Munich, Bishop Von Galen of Munster, Cardinal Count Preysing of Berlin, Cardinal Hlond of Poland, Archbishop Stepinac of Yugoslavia, Cardinal Seredi of Hungary and countless others, kept up the struggle fearlessly until it seemed that they were almost the only valiant men that remained who could, or dared, raise their voices in protest. And, as I write, it goes on : first Budapest, then Prague.

With this fear of the omnipotent state in mind, Pius XI enunciated the principle that a bigger organization should not undertake that which could be done sufficiently well by a smaller. Again, the aim is to protect the individuals from exploitation by the great machine, and to give more and more men liberty of action.

Most of these matters, either of political or economic or international concern, are matters of justice; but the popes repeatedly, especially the present one, Pius XII, in his encyclical letter, 'Darkness over the Earth', press the point that justice will not be done unless charity also is present. Unless we love our neighbour we will not, in fact, be just. This is true in the international and in the individual sphere. The rights of the backward races, for example, will only be recognized if we see the backward peoples as our brothers in Christ. This appalling race snobbery is thoroughly unchristian but very natural in a pagan world which can only judge by intelligence or riches or power. In a Christian world men are judged primarily by none of these things, but by the fact that they share one supreme equality before God, namely, that they have all been redeemed by him and are therefore loved by him. All men are loved by God, we are all brethren with Christ in the new dispensation of the Christian redemption, and being brethren should love one another.

This is fundamental in a discussion of world affairs. For there is in fact no other basis for justice between all men. Thus we return once again, and this time upon an immensely important plane, a world plane, to the idea of Christian love. Without it the world itself may founder. With it the world could certainly be saved.

CHAPTER XIV

SŒUR THÉRÈSE OF LISIEUX

WE began with the love of God for men, Jesus dying on a cross; we may fittingly end by a study of the Carmelite nun, Thérèse Martin, Saint Thérèse of Lisieux, whose one aim was to love.

The outline of Sœur Thérèse's life is too well known and too ordinary to require anything but a cursory recital here. Thérèse Martin was born in 1873 in the town of Alençon, where both her pious parents carried on businesses; her father was a jeweller and her mother a manufacturer of lace, 'point d'Alençon'. Thérèse was the youngest of nine. Two brothers had died in infancy and the remainder, all sisters, became nuns. She herself (in 1889) entered the Carmel, where all save one of her sisters had preceded her. She died in 1897 at the age of twenty-four. Nothing very remarkable, one might say. The only exciting event had been a pilgrimage to Rome, when she had dared to speak to Leo XIII about her vocation. For the rest it was stereotyped, 'petit bourgeois'. Her toys and her clothes may still be seen at Les Buissonnets, the villa at Lisieux, where the family went after the mother's death. Yet Thérèse Martin was canonized twenty-eight years after her own death. The only example comparable with this was the canonization of St. Francis within twenty-five years of his.

Though the externals of Sœur Thérèse's life were ordinary, her internal life was exceptional. She is an outstanding spiritual influence of the twentieth century. In a nutshell, the reason is that her sanctity was concentrated in love and nothing else. In spirituality she emphasized the primacy of love. There is a letter to Marie Guérin, her cousin, in which she wrote, 'You ask me for a means of reaching perfection. I only know one : love.' (Dated, 1894.)

Providentially, she was made to write an account of her own soul's life, *L'Histoire d'une Ame*. Here is recorded the process of her designing the Little Way to God and her own growth in holiness.

Even in the days of her childhood she longed to be a saint. 'My God, I choose everything, I will not be a saint by halves, I am not afraid of suffering for thee, I only fear one thing, and that is to do my own will. Accept the offering of my will, for I choose all that thou willest' (p. 25).

Her first taste of that love, which surpasses all understanding, was at her first Communion, and the description she gives in her 'Life' deserves to rank for its simplicity and depth with those of the great St. Teresa and St. John of the Cross :

'But I would not and I could not tell you all. Some things lose their fragrance when exposed to the air, and so too, one's inmost thoughts cannot be translated into earthly words without instantly losing their deep and heavenly meaning. How sweet was the first embrace of Jesus ! It was indeed an embrace of love. I felt that I was loved, and I said : "I love thee, and I give myself to thee for ever." Jesus asked nothing of me, and claimed no sacrifice; for a long time he and little Thérèse had known and understood one another. That day our meeting was more than simple recognition, it was perfect union. We were no longer two. Thérèse had disappeared like a drop of water lost in the immensity of the ocean; Jesus alone remained—he was the Master, the King ! Had not Thérèse asked him to take away her liberty which frightened her ? She felt herself so weak and frail that she wished to be for ever united to the Divine Strength' (p. 59).

It may seem to some that this is irrelevant to the purpose of this book, these effusions of a girl in a convent. But it is not so, for until we all learn to love God as she loved her God, we cannot right the world in which we live so precariously. Here is the authentic note of the saint, that directness, that simplicity, that unswerving purpose of putting God first. She once told a friend, 'Yes, from the age of three I have never refused our good God anything' (p. 229).

At times she wrote almost extravagantly. 'To give pleasure to God, I would consent to be plunged into hell, but in order that in that place of blasphemies he should be loved.' According to Mère Agnès de Jésus, she added in the margin on reflection, 'I know quite well that such a thing could not give him glory; but when one loves, one experiences the need to say a thousand follies' (*Diocesan Enquiry*, 2348, Mère Agnès).

One day a picture of the crucifixion partly slipped out of her prayer book as she came back from Mass; she saw one of the transfixed hands of Jesus. 'From that day the cry of my dying Saviour, "I thirst!" sounded incessantly in my heart, and kindled therein a burning zeal hitherto unknown to me' (p. 73).

The problem now was how to show this love; she was too weak to undertake any extraordinary mortification; she was an enclosed nun, so that the mission-field seemed to be closed to her; she was a woman, and the priesthood was also impossible; martyrdom was far off.

Her answer was in her Little Way, and, simply expressed, it is enfolded in the sentence, 'I have never given God anything except love'. As St. Benedict had extended love over the commands of the Rule, so now she, Sœur Thérèse, was to extend the mantle of love over every action of the day. 'How shall I show my love, since love proves itself by deeds? . . . I will let no tiny sacrifice pass, no look, no word. I wish to profit by the smallest actions, and to do them for Love' (p. 185). She saw God as her loving Father; he had a tender care of her during every movement; not an instant passed but it was by his will. She was his child, she preached the doctrine of

spiritual childhood, 'To remain a little child : that is, to recognize one's nothingness, and like a little child to wait upon the
good God for everything' (*Novissima verba*, August 6th, 1897).

In this devotion to the Fatherhood of God and spiritual
childhood she was developing, whether knowingly or not it is
difficult to say, the spirituality of St. Francis of Sales, with
whom she had great kinship of spirit. In his book on the Love
of God, he described at length how the will of God extends
over all his creation and how this divine will is known to us
in his holy inspirations, in the teaching of the Church and
simply in the happenings of every day—that providential arrangement of things by which all happenings save sin are from
his wisdom and his will. Sœur Thérèse grasped this point with
the simple directness of a child, and therein found the solution
to her problem of how in her littleness to show her love every
second of her life. She could do it by doing all and accepting
all as from the loving will of her God, her dinine lover. 'I long
to do God's will perfectly, I have no other desire.' That was
her cry, and the above was her answer.

Obedience to the Church and to the Rule are thus only part
of her all-embracing campaign to turn all into the gold of love.
In the final transport of the autobiography she cried, 'I am a
child of Holy Church, and the Church is a Queen, because she
is now espoused to the Divine King of Kings' (p. 185). Truly,
she was its child. The Church had preserved, for her, confidence
in the Word of God; the Church had defined the true nature
of Christ, so that from her earliest infancy she could call to
him as her God and trust his every word, trust that he could
and would help her in her hourly trials; the Church had
guarded through the ages her belief in the reality of the
Eucharist, so that when she first went up to the altar to receive
the host, she knew that she was receiving God made Man; the
Church too, in the person of her priests, had confirmed her in
her dark and difficult journey to her simple way of love. In this

she was like all mystics who travel in utter darkness and need the confident hand of their Mother the Church. She gives them an assurance that this their way is safe. The Church had taught her of heaven; it was the first word she had ever learned how to write. There was no irksomeness in her relationship with the Church, it was as it should be for us all : we travel to God alone, our minds to God's mind, our wills to his will, our being to him. But the Church is there as a guide and a help, showing us the danger-points, confirming our inspirations, loading us with the grace of God for strength on the journey. Sœur Thérèse had little time to accomplish the task that God in his Wisdom had designed for her, she had no time to spend proving every step of the way. God provided her a spiritual mother, the Church. Her teaching on obedience is as sure as all else. 'O my God! from how much disquiet do we free our-selves by the vow of obedience ! Happy is the simple religious. Her one guide being the will of her superiors, she is ever sure of following the right path, and has no fear of being mis-taken, even when it seems that her superiors are making a mistake. But if she ceases to consult the unerring compass, then at once her soul goes astray in barren wastes, where the waters of grace quickly fail' (p. 145).

She obeyed, not only the superior, but also her sisters. Once when sitting down from complete exhaustion while the others were singing a hymn, one of the sisters told her to rise. She did so immediately; and on being reproved by Sister Geneviève for doing so, she replied, 'I have acquired the habit of obeying everyone as though it was God who was showing me his will' (*Apostolic Enquiry,* 1029, Sr. Geneviève).

She died with words of love on her lips, and she sums up her own life in these words :

'My God, thou knowest that I have ever desired to love only thee. . . . Love attracts love' (pp. 174–5).

EPILOGUE

'The great task before the world to-day is the salving of
Europe, materially, politically and spiritually.' These are words
of General Smuts from a speech he made at Cambridge on
the occasion of his being made Chancellor of the university,
9th June, 1948. Rarely did a man speak more truly. Europe
is the heart and the soul of civilization; Europe has been most
deeply impregnated with the teaching of Jesus Christ; Europe
is the most highly skilled in the arts and sciences; Europe is the
mother of many nations. If Europe does not live, the world
will be long in reviving.

General Smuts made it plain in his speech that Europe
might succumb from lack of faith in her destiny. That again
is the true diagnosis. When a people or a group of peoples loses
its confidence in the way of life that it has led for generations,
then the devil which it cast out at the beginning may return,
and with it seven devils worse than the first. This is the danger
to-day from the pagan, materialist philosophy of Communism.

What is the answer? Faith! Yes, but faith in what? We
cannot manufacture faith in order to bolster up a regime.
Faith depends upon reasonable grounds. It is the very casting
aside of reasonable grounds which has been the destruction of
faith in Europe. Positively the Reformers abandoned faith as
a *rational* thing. Negatively the Church has had to suffer a vast
attack upon her traditional grounds for believing in the revelation of Christ. To-day there is a great cloud of scepticism over
Europe, a sense of vague uncertainty : what is truth?

If the diagnosis is correct, that Europeans have lost their
faith, the remedy has to be discovered. The remedy is either
the lost revelation reaffirmed, or a new revelation. And before

seeking a new Word from God, should we not, we lost sheep of Christ, look back to him, in order to see whether perhaps it was not he who abandoned us but we who abandoned him? After all, is that revelation of the first century bogus? Was it all a dream? or perhaps did not God speak to men clearly and unmistakably? If we examine the road by which we diverged from Christ, might we not find that the reasons which led us to take each turning as it came were wrong-headed reasons?

Quite simply the process, therefore, was as follows. Men of Western Europe first cut themselves adrift from the Papacy, which claimed to be the living voice of Christ. But these men wanted to remain true to Christ and his revelation. Then, in a later generation, men of our world abandoned Christ and wished to remain true to reason, accepting Christ in so far as his teaching agreed with what their reason told them. Finally, their descendants, finding that each man's reason led him to different conclusions from his fellows, finding themselves in a morass of conflicting views, abandoned reason and hung on to their own desires; whatever each wants, that is good for him.

This has led to disaster, for where there is no unity of thought, there is chaos, war and revolution.

It is the initial bifurcation that was made for the wrong reason. Should Western man have abandoned the institution we call the Papacy? There lay spiritual authority, the clear voice, certitude in matters beyond human reason, in matters revealed. It was this centre of unity, whether we believe it of divine origin or not at this point in discussion, which welded Europe together in its youth, gave it unity of doctrine and singleness of purpose. It taught, and it teaches, that men are made for heaven and teaches how to get there.

Catholics are bound to defend the teaching of Christ to the death if men threaten to kill them for holding to it; but Catholics are not bound to defend the actions of other Catholics, not even the popes themselves. Christ did not come to save the just but sinners. The Church is not holy in the sense that all her members are saints, but in the sense that her teaching is holy, that she bears the instruments of holiness with her throughout the centuries, and that some show holiness in their lives in a way so sublime that Christ shines through them.

Therefore, we are the first to condemn the behaviour of those popes who brought discredit upon the Church— Alexander VI being the chief specimen; we condemn that traffic in indulgences, those slack and dissolute monks and friars wherever they are found; we would condemn our own lives for being unworthy of the mercies of Christ; we recognize that the Reformers had ample justification for their criticisms of the state of the Church. But there were two kinds of re- formers : those who left the Church in disgust and those who tried within the Church to put it right—the Luthers and the St. Thomas Mores.

Obedience, where obedience is due. For, according to the interpretation put upon the facts of history, as given in this book, the civilization into which most of us have been born, began with a Christian society of men and women obeying Christ in person, it spread by that obedience being given to his chosen disciples, and that, not only because they repre- sented him but because he lived on in them. This same Chris- tian society created a world of its own, largely based on this supreme idea of obedience. It believed itself to be something more than a merely human institution; it considered and con- siders itself to be the very life of Christ continuing in the world —'Now not I live but Christ who liveth in me', as St. Paul said. Christians in the Ages of Faith and Catholics to-day believed and believe that the Kingdom of Christ, or the life of Christ, is not some vague aspiration, some distant entity, which might materialize no one knew when, but an ever- present visible reality : the Church with its centre in Rome, speaking with the authority of Christ. Let us turn, then, once again to the successor of Peter and to the Church which has an unbroken history and no uncertain voice, hearken to the words of the Master, and thus find the law of Christ. This will give us true liberty, so that with love we may be obedient and fulfil the holy Will of God.

INDEX

229 ff.; and liberty, 229 ff.; and
'modern liberties', 233; and
Perugia, 228 ff.; and Pius IX,
228; and St. Thérèse, 240; and
St. Thomas, 155, 229; and
toleration, 234 ff.
Lerins, 106
Liberal Christians, 16
Liberty: St. Augustine and, 72,
73 ff.; St. Benedict and, 95 ff.;
and Christ, 53; Church and,
166, 233 ff.; of conscience,
18 ff., 235; end of, 168; 'libertas
erroris', 68; St. Francis and,
136 ff., 146; and the Gospels,
15, 42; Greeks and, 23 ff.; and
law, 20, 94 ff., 150, 155, 192,
195, 228 ff.; Leo XIII and,
229 ff.; modern liberties, 233 ff.;
St. Paul and, 51 ff.; personal,
22; spread of, 97 ff.; St. Thomas
and, 148, 152 ff.; from this
world, 64, 136
Lindisfarne, 101
Lingard, 116
Liturgy, 132 ff.
Lope de Vega, 227
Lorain, M. P., 124
Louis of Bavaria, and Marsilio,
173
Louis the Pious, 114
Love: in act, 93; Aristotle and,
28; St. Augustine and, 76 ff.;
St. Benedict and, 92 ff.; and
desire, 43; two elements in, 62;
Eros and Agape, 77, 78; St.
Francis and, 137 ff., 145–146;
and friendship, 156 ff.; in Gospels, 40 ff.; of God, 9, 15, 47,
157; St. Ignatius and, 206; the
Jews and, 29; and law, 20; and
obedience, 42, 62, 93, 144,
158 ff., 160, 189; of Papacy,
98 ff., 115, 124, 140, 189 ff.; St.
Paul and, 52 ff.; St. Peter and,
53; Pius XII and, 238–239; and
prayer, 47, 160; reason and,
156; supernatural, 156; St.
Thérèse and, 240 ff.; St.
Thomas and, 155; types of, 156;
union with God, 156, 161 ff.
Luther, Martin, 20, 177; and
authority, 188; break with
Rome, 183 ff.; and Councils,
185; and Fathers, 185; and

humanism, 187; and St. Ignatius, 206, 226; and indulgence,
184; and law, 186; Leipzig, 185;
and master race, 188; and
nature, 187; and Nominalism,
186; and reason, 187; and
Sacred Scripture, 185; and
works, 187

M

Mabillon, 106, 107, 124
McCann, Abbot Justin, 85 n., 116
Machiavelli, 34, 177, 179
Mâcon, 117, 120
Macrina, sister of St. Basil, 62
Manicheans, 73, 75
Mann, M., 110 n.
Marcus Aurelius, 25
Maritain, J., and Luther, 187
Marriot, W. K., 180
Marsilio of Padua: and Aristotle,
172; Defensor Pacis, 171; doc-
trine of, 171 ff.; life of, 171,
173 ff.; and Louis of Bavaria,
173; and Papacy, 172; and state
of Italy, 173; and William of
Ockham, 174, 178, 226
Martin, St., Pope, 165
Martin, St., of Tours, 106
Mary, Christ's Mother, 40
Mieszko, 125
Milan, 86
Miltiz, Charles von, 185
Monophysites, 217
Monte Cassino, 80, 97; and St.
Thomas, 147; destruction of,
100; restoration of, 130
Montpelier, Rabelais at, 192
Montserrat, 206, 207
More, St. Thomas: compared to
Luther, 198; the humanist, 198;
and Rabelais, 198; and the
Reformation, 205, 216; speech
in Westminster Hall, 200 ff.;
study of Papal claims, 190–191,
199
Moslems, mysticism of, 162
Mussolini, condemned by Pius XI,
238
Mystical Body: and the Church,
54; and liturgy, 133; and love,
156, 157; and obedience, 85, 96,
248; and voice of Christ, 46,
223, 248